Forbes

GREATEST BUSINESS STORIES OF ALL TIME

by
DANIEL GROSS
and

The Editors of *Forbes* magazine

A Byron Preiss Visual Publications Book

John Wiley & Sons, Inc.
NEW YORK • CHICHESTER • BRISBANE • TORONTO • SINGAPORE • WEINHEIM

This text is printed on acid-free paper.

Copyright © 1996 by Byron Preiss Visual Publications, Inc., and Forbes Inc.
Published by John Wiley & Sons, Inc.

Forbes is a registered trademark of Forbes Inc. Its use is pursuant to a license agreement
with Forbes Inc.

Interior design: Michael Mendelson.

Special thanks to Julie Fenster for her immeasurable work on the material.

PICTURE CREDITS: Page 4: Independence National Historical Park, Philadelphia, PA;
pages 22, 58, 74, 122, 158: Archive Photos, New York, NY; page 40: Rockefeller Archive
Center, North Tarrytown, NY; page 90: Merrill Lynch, New York, NY; page 106: David
Sarnoff Research Center, Princeton, NJ; pages 142, 232, 266, 284, 314: AP/Wide World
Photos, Inc., New York, NY; pages 176, 212: Bettmann, New York, NY; page 194: Xerox
Corporation, Rochester, NY; page 246: Intel Corporation, Santa Clara, CA; page 298:
Harley-Davidson Motor Company Archives, Milwaukee, WI. All rights reserved.

Library of Congress Cataloging-in-Publication Data:

Gross, Daniel, 1967–
    Forbes' greatest business stories of all time / Daniel Gross and the editors of Forbes
magazine.
    p.   3m.
    Includes index.
    ISBN 0-471-14314-6 (cloth : alk. paper). — ISBN 0-471-19653-3 (pbk. : alk. paper)
    1. Success in business—United States—Case studies.   I. Forbes.
    II. Title
    HF5386.G779   1996   96-34245
    338.7'0973—dc20   CIP

Printed in the United States of America

10 9 8 7 6 5 4 3 2 1

CONTENTS

ACKNOWLEDGMENTS

This book was a collaborative effort in the true sense of the word. While my name appears as the author, several other people at a variety of institutions assisted in the completion of this project: Michael Sagalyn of Byron Preiss Visual Publications enlisted me to join this project; Julie Fenster played a key role in the development of several chapters, especially Robert Morris and Wal-Mart; and Janet Coleman at Wiley also reviewed and edited the book.

Laura Schoeffel at Byron Preiss Visual Publications spent more time on this project than any other person aside from me. Working under challenging circumstances, Laura showed a great degree of patience, good humor, fine judgment, and intellectual engagement.

My thanks also to Kathy Huck, Amy Chisam, Dinah Dunn, and Katherine Miller at Byron Preiss. Brian Connolly, John Boris, Josh Israel, and Betsy Duquette were diligent and careful fact-checkers. Marianne Cohen and Craig Schneider were equally meticulous copyeditors.

Paul Mitchinson and Jon Rosenberg, friends and former colleagues at Harvard University's history department, provided valuable research assistance, and Blake McKelvey graciously sent me his personal manuscript of his biography of Joseph Wilson.

I would also like to thank my family for their support, especially my brothers, Leon and Michael Gross, and my sister-in-law, Vicki Gross. I would never have become a writer were it not for my parents. Barry and Sandra Gross, a professor of English and a professional editor, respectively, not only taught me how to read and write; they have provided support—financial and otherwise—on every decision I have ever made, and remain an inspiration to me.

The person to whom this book is dedicated, my wife, Candice Savin, came into my life at about the same time as this book project, and she has brought me infinitely more joy than any volume ever could. Her patience, compassion, and love—and the thrill of our marriage—made time fly and troubles seem as nothing.

Daniel Gross

New York, August 1996

FOREWORD

This is a book of heroes. Make no mistake about it. The people whose stories are collected here earned that status as surely as any soldier or athlete or explorer or statesman you can name. By making and selling, by organizing and financing, by discerning and serving the needs and desires of others, they have done more to affect who we are and what we are today than all but a handful of history makers.

In doing so, most of them got rich; some, very rich. Indeed, names such as Morgan, Rockefeller, and now Gates are virtual synonyms for vast wealth. But for all the success told of here, these are far from tales of greed and avarice.

Wal-Mart gave rural Americans, people of modest means, more choice and quality for less cost. Its founder, Sam Walton, became the richest man in the world—his fortune was worth close to $28 billion when he died in 1992—by stretching other people's scarce and hard-earned dollars further. He improved on the margin the quality of life for millions of people. That is his real legacy, and it points to the ethical heart of business: service to others. Without it, no enterprise and no entrepreneur can succeed.

"Success is coming to be spelt service" is how my grandfather, B. C. Forbes, put it in the introduction to his 1917 book, *Men Who Are Making America*. In many ways, this current volume is descended from that extraordinary collection of biographical sketches that made his reputation. Its success enabled him to start *Forbes* magazine.

Personality stories are common coin today in business journalism, as they are everywhere else. But in the early decades of the twentieth century, prior to my grandfather's efforts, business reporting consisted of not much more than dry statistics. There was little attention regularly paid by the press to the people behind the figures. In a very real way, B. C. Forbes pioneered a new genre of journalism. In fact, he was widely regarded as "the humanizer of business."

A poor Scottish immigrant who made good himself, my grandfather believed passionately in America as the land of opportunity and in the possibilities for individuals to succeed here. He saw his profiles of the great business leaders of his day as being, first and foremost, educational and inspirational for common souls like himself. They were real-life Horatio Alger stories. Today you would probably find them in the self-help section of the bookstore.

They were lessons in basic virtues, such as integrity, self-denial, hard work, self-reliance, ambition, courage, and, perhaps above all, what his era called stick-to-itiveness. With these qualities, B. C. was convinced, anyone could better himself. He was also very aware of what he called the "rarer and higher qualities" that marked the subjects of his profiles—and those collected here.

Not many are endowed with the talents to become a Henry Ford or a John Johnson or a Mary Kay Ash. Still, we can strive, and there is little doubt that we will be more successful for the effort than we would have been otherwise. That was the essence of B. C. Forbes's message eighty years ago and of ours today.

I can think of no better way to conclude this foreword than by quoting from him: "How can I attain success? That is what every rational human being wants to know."
Read on!

Timothy C. Forbes
July 28, 1996

Forbes®

GREATEST BUSINESS STORIES OF ALL TIME

Robert Morris, the first U.S. Superintendent of Finance.

ROBERT MORRIS: AMERICA'S FIRST FINANCIER

As the richest person in America during the Revolutionary War, Robert Morris was commonly known by the single name that encompassed his profession, his accomplishment, and his genius: he was referred to simply as "the Financier."

In the 1770s, when the United States was in its first throes of independence, Morris served as a statesman in the company of Adams, Franklin, and Jefferson. But by 1781, with the nation on the verge of forfeiting that independence to bankruptcy, he was the only choice for the newly created government post of Superintendent of Finance, a position equivalent in the desperate days of 1781-82 to the head of the emerging executive branch. Before resigning in 1784, Morris had formulated a workable plan to restore the solvency of the United States.

Though hindered from instituting his strategy completely, Morris at least staved off panic and managed to maintain the army—an estimable accomplishment. He also replaced the uncomfortable standoff between government and commerce that remained from the colonial era, establishing a closer yet freer relationship between government and business. "To do any good, [we] must infuse into traders of America a spirit of enterprise and direct their attention to such objects as will most benefit the publick," Morris insisted. ". . . Their own interest and the publick good goes hand in hand and they need no other prompter or tutor."

Robert Morris was the country's first real businessman, and in many ways his life is a model for the millions of people who have found success in the American economy he helped to create. While Morris inherited very little money, he built his fortune slowly on reputation, connections, and attention to detail. From his base in Philadelphia, he formed myriad partnerships, eventually charting ships and investments all over the world. Most other early Americans were farmers, who regarded self-sufficiency as a virtue on a personal or a national scale. But in the Financier's world, interdependency meant opportunity, and if it was managed properly it was a virtue for an individual or, more important, for a developing economy.

Reversals and debacles took away all of Morris's money by the end of his life. Still, even a debtor's prison could not tarnish his optimism. Down to his very last days, he looked forward to starting yet another new business.

FRIENDS AND FORTUNES

Born in England in 1734, Robert Morris moved to Maryland twelve years later with his father, a merchant of the same name. The elder Morris led a lively social life, starting several common-law families even as he maintained his small stake in the shipping business. Under the circumstances it was expedient to follow the custom of the day by arranging an apprenticeship for his son, so he found a promising place for Robert with a shipping company in Philadelphia: Willing and Company. If young Robert was too old to rate as an outright prodigy, he was nonetheless remarkable for a fifteen-year-old; left in charge of the business in Mr. Willing's absence, he managed to corner the mid-Atlantic market in flour.

Having inherited his father's genial personality, Morris became one of the most popular young men in Philadelphia. Even the boss's rather dour son, Thomas Willing, liked Robert Morris. Willing eventually offered a full partnership to the twenty-year-old former apprentice. They had their warehouse on Water Street (then known as King Street) in Philadelphia, and the sidewalk out front would be piled with cargo throughout every spring and fall when the ships docked from the sea. At the time, the city claimed hundreds of ocean-going ships, with dozens of firms behind them, but within ten years Willing & Morris was the most successful of them all, with outright ownership of six vessels.

Willing & Morris made good profits, sending cargo back and forth to the West Indies and, as a natural sideline, speculating in the bulk commodities they traded: tobacco, flour, sugar, and indigo. Paper money, issued by individual colonies as bills-of-credit, found favor with some investors as an avenue of speculation, and Morris was able to make important connections with French investors, by obtaining "paper" for them. For his own accounts, which were meticulously kept, he found that he could make as much money in three months by sending a ship to the islands as he could make in a year and a half by speculating in paper.

Morris was no gambler, though; his relaxed ease in social situations contrasted with his slavish attention to the smallest details in business. Punctuality, he liked to say, "was the best part of a man's trading capital." He schemed, he hedged, he drew tight contracts, but mostly he chose his investments very carefully. Once he admonished an overzealous junior partner: "It is absolutely necessary that you shou'd curb that very keen eager desire of missing *nothing*."

Unlike the elder Robert Morris, he married just once, and happily. Even marriage contributed to his business career; his bride, Mary White, came from an important family. Through the years, their various homes in Philadelphia or out in the country were lushly furnished and, in addition to the family's six children, were typically filled with many friends. Morris never drew lines around the different aspects of his life. Even in the anxious days at the outbreak of the Revolutionary War, he wrote to the future Virginia governor Benjamin Harrison about a grand time he'd recently enjoyed: "You see I continue my old practice of mixing business and pleasure, and ever found them useful to each other."

Few people had spare cash in colonial America, and banks did not exist. The stock market did not exist, either. Investment at the time was a highly personal endeavor, not an institutional one; when a promise from a merchant was considered an unimpeachable bond, Willing & Morris were especially known for the integrity of their dealings. Yet written contracts were vital in more complex dealings between individuals, a fact well known to Great Britain when, in 1765, it effectively taxed all investments in the colonies by charging for a stamp to be placed on every legal document, newspaper, and book. Being particularly sensitive to anything that affected commerce, Morris was at the forefront of the colonists' successful effort to force the repeal of the Stamp Act. As was the case with many who joined him, this was a first step away from loyalty to Great Britain.

THE PRICE TAG OF FREEDOM

Morris was to be a central figure to the great events of the American Revolution. A delegate to the Continental Congress, a signer of the Declaration of Independence, a member of Benjamin Franklin's elite Council of Safety (which operated in support of independence in the city of Philadelphia), he was a passionate patriot. However, nothing— absolutely nothing—intervened between Robert Morris and his business interests. His attitude did not reflect merely the myopic view of a self-made man; it was the philosophy of an eminently practical one. To Morris, and to many others, commerce swirled as naturally through lives as it swirled through government—one could not have business without public administration. Robert Morris's vast wealth grew when he became actively engaged with plans regarding the new nation's future, rendering him even more indispensable to the floundering nation.

Americans were independent and in general self-sufficient. And they did not want taxation—with or without representation. The nation was administered by the Continental Congress, a unique body in the annals of governance in that it was authorized to print money, take on debt, raise an army, and make vast purchases—all of which it did—but did not have the power to levy a tax to pay for any of that. The war effort, the only real function of the federal government in the first years of the country, went ahead on the basis of various means of financing, only some of which were valid. Unfortunately, the most effective of them in the short run was also the flimsiest overall.

On a formal basis, rich colonists loaned the government money at a healthy return of 4 (later 6) percent. Private loans were an important source of financing early in the war. Later the Continental Congress demanded, or requisitioned, payments from the individual states that resulted in more frustration than cash for the new nation. Through 1778, individuals in France, prodded unceasingly by Benjamin Franklin and others, loaned the United States money; soon after 1778, the French government itself became officially allied with the United States and made grants and loans. In the most popular means of raising revenue, the government simply confiscated the property of Tories or those thought to be sympathetic with the British. However satisfying such confiscations may have been, they were negligible as a source of revenue in the long run.

The new government funded itself mainly through bills of credit, paper money backed by nothing except the future ability of the United States to redeem it in "hard" currency. This financial tactic was supposed to be a temporary measure, but the bills continued to proliferate as they were the only easy solution to the problem of inflation that they then exacerbated. Soon, they were truly not worth the paper they were printed on, and production ceased.

So the United States went to war without any money. In fact, the new nation, though rich in principles, faced the might of the British army in the spring of 1775 with but a few crates of gunpowder and no guns, uniforms, ships, or supplies. Any other country in that situation, even a brand-new one, would have levied a tax, but America, as Morris once observed, was not like any other country. Benjamin Franklin explained the difference as it concerned the American Revolution: "the contest being upon the very question of taxation, the laying of imposts, unless from the last necessity, would have been madness."

Still, the war cost the United States about $16 million annually. Over the first five years of it, 1775 to 1780, the Continental Congress took in, in one way or another but not through taxes, about $45 million and in April 1781 the national debt amounted to a breathtaking $24 million. Yet there was virtually nothing tangible to show for it. The nation abounded in foodstuff, but its army was in rags. Procurement, the priority of supplying an army in the field, was so despicable that in the winter of 1780 one governor actually sent General Washington a load of blankets and included a bill for the lot.

George Washington and the other generals watched their men languish, truly hungry, nearly naked, and sorely ill-equipped to care for themselves, let alone to wage battle. Great Britain watched, too, and waited for the would-be nation to cave in on its own worthless money. Even in France, enthusiasm for the United States waned with the approach, which was seemingly inevitable, of fiscal ruin. The French ambassador received direct orders: Offer the Continental Congress great affection, but no money.

With no system of public debt, the United States was lucky to have survived as long as it did. General Washington, who was not one to say anything he didn't mean, threatened to disband the army altogether unless the otherwise prosperous new nation found a way to supply it regularly and fairly, starting immediately. So it was that in the winter of 1780–81 the only matter before the Continental Congress was the imminent collapse of the government's financial structure.

The Articles of Confederation, which were finally ratified by all states, went into force on March 1, 1781. Although the Articles granted each state a veto power, the document called for the creation of a general treasury, "which shall be supplied by the several States, in proportion to the value of all land within each State," and gave Congress the exclusive right of striking coin, regulating trade, and borrowing.

With the new infrastructure in place, the Congress now needed a chief financial officer, a person with experience in mercantile affairs who could clamp down on costs, re-establish the nation's credit, and place the new nation's finances on a sound footing. A few members, including Samuel Adams, would have voted against the concentration of executive powers in a single person acting as the Superintendent of Finance (the nation didn't even have a president, yet, after all), but once the post was created, the vote was unanimous. The person to fill it was Robert Morris, the merchant prince of Philadelphia. After ruminating about the scope of the problem, Morris accepted the job with two provisos: that he could choose his own staff and that, while he was in office, he could maintain his full array of business interests.

The announcement of Morris's appointment, on February 20, 1781, revived the hope of many Americans. The quartermaster in Philadelphia wanted to waste no time in sending word of the breakthrough to General

Washington, who was then stationed with his men along the Hudson River, but the army could not afford to hire an express rider. When Washington finally heard that the Financier was in charge, he was as relieved as the lowliest private. The army was trying to save the new nation, and finally, someone was on hand to save the army.

GENERAL WASHINGTON AND CITIZEN MORRIS

In the summer of 1781 he worked hard to repeal America's embargo law, which banned the import or export of goods with any part of the British Empire. The law may have sent strong signals in diplomacy, but it had less practical impact than the British blockade of American trade. Nonetheless, it offended the sensibility Morris had maintained throughout his career as a merchant: "Commerce should be perfectly free," he wrote (and repeated often), "and property sacredly secured to the owner."

Once sworn in as the Superintendent of Finance, Morris knew exactly what to do, but even he did not know what to do first. His own priority was the establishment of a national bank, and after just three days he sent the Congress his detailed description of it. His bank would be both the "pillar," he called it, of a system of public debt and the first step in truly uniting the various states. His plan for the "Bank of North America" was typical of Morris: a vision of how a partnership of private business interests should support the public good. It would be privately managed, with its assets at the disposal of the government, and owned by the individuals who bought shares in it.

Capitalized at $400,000 (1,000 shares at $400), the new bank was meant to grow within four years to control $4 million. Even more importantly, it was supposed to serve as the symbol of a stable, safe American money policy. The bank's own printed paper notes were not empty promises; they would be readily redeemed for coin during regular hours.

By the time the bank was opened, though, fewer people than ever could scrape together as much as $400 in cash. Not one initial subscriber could be found in all of South Carolina, according to the governor.

The Bank of North America was an ambitious start. As the only national bank at the time, it was the kind of far-reaching and reassuring solution that was expected of the Financier in his new job. It had to wait, though, because even more urgently, Morris had to feed the army, and his first months were spent marshaling resources as heroically as Washington marshaled troops. With no time to re-establish the credit of the nation, Morris often used his own money to purchase supplies for Washington and his men. While he was at it, he could not resist engaging in profit-making speculations on the government's behalf, a practice he later claimed to be inappropriate, except in such dire times as those of the war. He bought groceries for the troops, found sound sources for bulk supplies, and coerced governors into sending cattle. To accomplish all that needed to be done, he called in favors from his long, long list of friends and acquaintances. On one occasion, he personally paid the troops one month's salary, a necessary inducement for them to march with Washington toward Yorktown.

Morris's efficiency, his attention to detail, and his very promptness in all of his dealings kept the army supplied during its turning-point siege of Yorktown, while his professionalism renewed morale through the ranks. In effect, he was a white-collar soldier who received much credit at the time for turning the tide of the war in America's favor.

"The variety of business I am obliged to do in detail so engrosses my time that I cannot pay attention to those general arrangements which are the proper objects of my appointment," Morris wrote, although before the end of his first year he had made substantial progress. He completely reorganized the Treasury Department and acted to establish the U.S. mint. On the basis of Morris's very acceptance of the job of Superintendent, the French renewed their payments. Upon the arrival of hard currency from France, the Bank of North America finally solidified, opening its doors on Chestnut Street in Philadelphia in January

1782, less than one year after Morris proposed it. With no working U.S. monetary unit, the bank used the Mexican dollar to keep its accounts. The institution was not immediately the great success that Morris hoped for, but it survived, making a noticeable contribution to the war supply and providing for some time the only solid evidence of stability in the American economy.

During 1781, the Financier's first year in his post, he gave the single greatest gift that he possibly could make to secure the fate of the United States: "My personal credit, which thank Heaven I have preserved throughout all the tempests of the War, has been substituted for that which the country had lost. I am now striving to transfer that credit to the public," he wrote. In backing the on-going obligations of the United States with his own gold, he was a one-man treasury for a country without one. He issued and personally signed paper money, known as "Morris notes," that were fully redeemable for gold. Morris offered his own name and reputation as the bridge leading from ruin to order for the fledgling republic.

Circulation of solidly backed paper money was not merely a temporary means of restoring fluidity to the American economy. Morris notes were intended to be the means of collecting the seemingly inevitable federal taxes that Morris insisted were necessary. If the states would agree to implement this system, the nation had a chance to create the ebb and flow of controlled public debt. As the leading proponent of the new taxes, though, Robert Morris edged outside of purely financial matters. He was the government's first powerful executive, and he began to interpret federal powers on his own practical, not philosophical, terms. He seemed poised to use his position to knit the states together into something more than a loose confederation. He was, in short, a Federalist. But to be a Federalist at that early point in the history of the government was to be a captain without a ship. Morris tried hard to build one around him.

After the British surrender at Yorktown in October 1781, Superintendent Morris set out to establish not just one tax but a direct system of predictable, reliable taxes: a land tax, a poll tax, and an import tax. At the same time, he cited a complementary problem in national debt management: expenditures within both civil and military offices of the government were entirely unmonitored. As the nation's best deal maker, he understood the power of a long-term agreement, and he introduced and enforced "contracting" as a means of securing lower prices and making accurate projections of future outlays. In sweeping some of the inefficiency out of the procurement process, Morris made a major advance toward establishing firmer credit for the nation.

Ultimately, though, he failed to convince a majority of state representatives that taxation was necessary to the conduct of the war. The politicians were more concerned with containing one another than with containing Great Britain. Without incoming taxes, Morris tried to depend on the revenues promised in requisition payments, but almost none were forthcoming. (Requisition payments were instituted on the presumption that since the states held the power to tax they could pass revenue onto the national government.) No state wanted to pay if its neighbors wouldn't, so none did.

Early in 1783, when it was expecting $2 million, the Treasury received exactly one payment: $5,500 from the State of New Jersey. Meanwhile, the national debt was well over $16 million, not even including outstanding paper notes. Morris had counted on the war to bring the states into true union. In fact, as the prospect of peace approached in 1782–83, the possibility of eliciting an agreement on taxation only receded. In effect, the states had won their own war, emerging with independence and without having had to pay for it in ceded powers or in money.

Morris was a cool player, even in the worst of times, but in his later years in office, he grew desperate to achieve what he had set out to do: "draw forth and direct the combined efforts of united America." Trying to spark concessions, he predicted that after a peace treaty was signed a civil war would break out between the squabbling states, or that the nation's disgruntled soldiers would dissolve into an uncontrollable rabble and punish the countryside that had unnecessarily punished them throughout the conduct of the war. Predictably, one of the states found a way to stall negotiations. In this case, it was Rhode Island's representative who explained that his state could not act on any matter such as taxation until issues related to Western lands had been settled.

Such blather exasperated the Financier. He hated what the job of Superintendent had become; that is, holding the nation's finances together not by introducing order but by struggling to control the reins of its chaos. In January of 1783 he threatened to resign if the internal situation did not change, and he consented to remain only after receiving the assurance that the Congress would finally and seriously address the matter of taxation. It did not.

Morris had one last card to play against the intransigent states, aware as he was of two assumptions that swirled through state capitals all that summer. The first was that the soldiers in the army would revolt if they were discharged without being paid, and the second was that Robert Morris was the only man who either could pay them or make arrangements to do so. He tried to use the situation to force the states to cooperate, but they held out mere promises, and in the end it was Morris who capitulated. He felt compelled to set aside the power struggle and act, both for the public good and because he believed it would be dishonorable not to pay the men something for victory. So he borrowed $350,000 from a broker and averted the crisis by dispersing at least partial wages through the ranks (after Morris left office, no one ever bothered to repay the $350,000).

In September 1783, the Treaty of Peace with Britain was finally ratified. A year later, the Financier could see that he had done everything he could, and he could do no more. He resigned in November 1784, and no keen effort was made to stop him. Robert Morris had not accomplished his plan of establishing an unimpeachable financial structure for the "young and rising Nation," as he called it. Yet he had saved that nation.

THE NATION SURVIVES, BUT THE FINANCIER IS RUINED

After the war was over, Morris's future appeared enviable. He still had a large fortune and a strong influence over the future of the nation. The need to resolve questions over the assumption of state debts and the payment of national debts were among the many factors leading to the Constitutional Convention of 1787, which Morris attended. Indeed, the Constitution, as ratified by delegates meeting in Philadelphia in 1787, realized many of the central powers for which Morris had campaigned inside and outside of office. On that occasion, it was he who had the honor of nominating George Washington as the first president. Robert Morris was subsequently elected a senator for Pennsylvania. Throughout the years of the first presidency, when the national capital was Philadelphia, Washington and his family stayed in Morris's house.

Washington naturally offered his old friend the cabinet post of Secretary of the Treasury, but Morris declined. He was anxious to return to business and recommended Alexander Hamilton, a younger man who matched Morris in Federalist sensibilities, if not in personality. They were not friends, but Hamilton carried through major aspects of the Morris plan, without its familial, almost sentimental, insistence that business and government could be partners in financial activities. Hamilton was also able to establish a system of public debt, attached to a central bank and mint, leaving commerce entirely independent.

Robert Morris's downfall in business was as breathtaking as his rise had been forty years earlier. If his ideas regarding government seemed to make more progress after he left his highest office, it is tragically but equally true that he fared much better in business before he left his post. In the 1790s he caught the so-called "land fever" and bought enormous tracts in Virginia and western New York State, in addition to smaller parcels all over the country. He owned over 8 million acres, and was, in a matter of a few years, the nation's largest landowner. His friend George Washington tried to dissuade him from committing his fortune to a type of investment so foreign to him, but the rising values were too much of a temptation. Land was also irresistible to Morris because it offered him the chance he craved to create private businesses that would help the nation and the people in it. In developing his tracts, he took inordinate care in laying out neat communities, even in frontier areas; moreover, his agents sold parcels at fair prices only to prospective homeowners, discouraging the blight caused by careless speculators.

One hundred years after Morris's agents began to sell land in the pastoral Genesee River Valley in New York, a grand celebration was held in his honor, and one of the speakers concluded his description of the development of the area by saying that "Nearly every home in the western part of the beautiful valley . . . is connected with the name of Robert Morris, and though all others may neglect his memory, and even forget the name of the great financier of the revolution, his fame will live on in this historic region as long as the people love the land on which their children were born and in which their fathers sleep." The original land office was turned into a museum, dedicated in his memory.

The fact that land is so timeless may be compelling, but it ruined Morris. In running ships to the Caribbean, three months was a complete transaction, cash to cash. As the nation's great landowner, Morris soon found that he had no cash. When debts mounted, he had no liquid funds with which to pay them. Land prices did not have to fall much to start him on an irrevocable downward spiral. Of all the embarrassments he faced, the most ironic was that the Bank of North America, his own creation, brought one of the first suits against him. "Disappointments have put it out of my power to pay punctually" was all that he could say in response.

In the land purchases, Morris seemed almost maniacal, continuing to buy even when he was being hounded by creditors, even when he could not sell the land he already had. He forgot his own advice, tendered years before to his junior partner: "It is absolutely necessary that you shou'd curb that very keen eager desire of missing *nothing*."

ROBERT MORRIS'S BROKER

I sent for Mr. Haym Salomon several times this Day to assist me in raising money," Robert Morris noted in his diary for August 29, 1782. It was a typical entry in the years when hard cash was scarce in the new United States and when Haym Salomon was always at the ready if Morris needed him. Like Morris, Haym Salomon was foreign-born, a Pole with Jewish and Portugese ancestors. Like Morris, he built his own fortune in Philadelphia. As a leading broker in "paper" money before the Revolutionary War, Haym Salomon became the official broker for Morris's Office of Finance, seeking out customers for the notes issued by his boss.

In the worst times, though, not even Salomon the broker could induce anyone to invest fresh capital in the fight for independence. And at such times, he had only one customer left. Asserting his fervent patriotism, even at the expense of his business sense, he made outright loans of $211,000 to the young government and purchased bills totaling $353,000, most notably during the desperate effort to meet the army payroll at the war's end. When the country turned to Robert Morris, Morris turned to people like Haym Salomon, and Salomon could not have given more: when he died in 1785, he was broken in health and completely penniless. His fortune was never repaid, but even so, it had not gone to waste. It helped to start a nation.

Robert Morris, the richest man in the colonies, was among the poorest in the United States. On February 14, 1798, he was arrested for nonpayment of debts and held in custody until he could be placed in debtor's prison the next day. That night, he was alone with nothing left of his empire, except, at sixty-three, just what he had started with. He sat in a little room, holding his father's gold watch, and he wondered if he would be allowed to keep it.

Debtor's prison was a sort of rudimentary apartment complex, where the typical prisoner stayed for a few weeks while friends and relatives raised the funds to settle the debt. Robert Morris was not like any of his fellow inmates, but perhaps he was like William Dorrit, the Dickens character who also fell from the upper class into debtor's prison: "Crushed at first by his imprisonment, he had soon found a dull relief in it."

Morris would remain in the prison for three years, tending a garden, writing to his family, and receiving visitors, including George Washington, who spent part of an afternoon with his old friend and adviser. Alexander Hamilton visited too. Outside the walls of the prison, Morris was neither forgotten nor reviled for his predicament. President-elect Thomas Jefferson made it clear that he would appoint him Secretary of the Navy, if he could extricate himself. It was not to be. Morris's family and friends couldn't possibly raise the $3 million he owed. But eventually a new bankruptcy law was passed, inducing creditors to settle with debtors. After Morris left prison, he lived very modestly, awaiting one rumored government appointment after another. None came to pass, and he decided to become, in effect, an antiques dealer, using his honed eye to make purchases at auction for resale in a shop. He died in 1806 before he actually entered the business, but he died hopeful, as ever, about his prospects. His epitaph notes simply that he was Financier of the United States during the Revolution.

Franklin is remembered as the young nation's great diplomat, and Jefferson its philosopher, while Morris was its financier. The business of finance is hard to understand, except for those working intimately within it. Even while Morris was fulfilling the duties of the Superintendent, some observers speculated that he wasn't rich at all, but was just a clever schemer who made himself seem well-to-do. Others accused him of using the post only to expand his enormous fortune, a rumor that especially offended Morris when it took hold in the ranks of the army.

As a statesman *and* an unabashed businessman, Robert Morris was a rare combination in the colonies and in the nation that emerged from them.

In public service for so many years, Morris met the critical juncture of 1781–82 and used the tools of finance to give his struggling nation something more precious than money: he gave it the time that it needed. For that he ought to be remembered.

Cyrus Hall McCormick transformed modern agriculture with the reaper.

CYRUS McCORMICK'S REAPER AND THE INDUSTRIALIZATION OF FARMING

I n the summer of 1831 an audience of several dozen gentleman farmers, hired laborers, and slaves gathered in a wheat field on John Steele's farm in Rockbridge County, Virginia, to watch a horse-drawn wood-and-iron device mow down the golden crop in waves. The impresario behind this show was twenty-two-year-old Cyrus McCormick. Born in 1809, the same year as Abraham Lincoln, McCormick proved an emancipator of a different sort. The reaper, invented by his father, liberated hundreds of thousands of Americans from agrarian drudgery. The process of industrialization, which turned the nation's economy into the world's most productive force, could not have been complete without the mechanization of farming. And as the historian William Hutchinson noted, "Of all the inventions during the first half of the nineteenth century which revolutionized agriculture, the reaper was probably the most important."

The McCormicks weren't the only ones to devise a reaper. Many other companies and individuals had developed similar technology. But, as the historian Herbert Casson wrote, Cyrus "invented the business of making Reapers and selling them to the farmers of America and foreign countries." His genius was to gain and protect patents for the technology, and then turn his invention—one that skeptical farmers were prone to brand a "humbug"—into a commercial necessity. By traveling throughout farm country in the 1840s and staging theatrical demonstrations, McCormick established the reaper as a commercially viable product. He also pioneered tactics that businessmen have used ever since: free trials, money-back guarantees, installment buying, and a fixed price for his machines. McCormick eventually moved his young enterprise from rural Virginia to Chicago, where he built a factory that grew into an industrial powerhouse and the company we know today as International Harvester.

A YOUNG MAN RECEIVES A GIFT OF TECHNOLOGY FROM HIS FATHER

Cyrus McCormick was the oldest of eight children born to Polly and Robert McCormick, a descendant of Scotch-Irish Calvinist immigrants who had arrived in the colonies in 1734. A prosperous farmer, Robert McCormick owned several hundred acres on a sprawling estate that included a grist and saw mill at Walnut Grove, Virginia. Walnut Grove lay in the fertile Virginia Valley between the Blue Ridge and Allegheny Mountains, a region untouched by the industrial revolution that was then gathering steam in England and the Northeastern United States. In rural areas, farmers harvested wheat in much the same way as their predecessors had done in the fourth century, that is, on foot, felling the shafts with a sickle and tying the cut grain in bundles.

Although he lacked formal schooling, Robert McCormick was a polymath and a gifted mechanic. "My father was both mechanical and inventive, and could and did at that time use the tools of his shops in making any piece of machinery he wanted," Cyrus McCormick later wrote. In the early nineteenth century Robert McCormick experimented with a variety of mechanical devices to make farming easier and less labor intensive. He developed a plow for hillside fields, a machine for breaking down hemp, and, most notably, a horse-drawn device for reaping wheat. In a remarkably productive period from 1830 to 1831, he obtained several patents, even one for "an improvement in teaching the art of performing on the violin."

But Robert McCormick's inventive talents did not extend to financial matters and, as Cyrus noted, "most of his inventions dropped into disuse after the lapse of some years." Fortunately, Cyrus McCormick supplemented his father's technical genius with a penchant for and interest in making money. He later recalled a time when he was out horseback riding while still a teenager: "My reflections were upon the thought of the possibility of realizing a million . . . at the same time feeling that the thought was enormous, and that it seemed like a dream or like dwelling in the clouds, so remote, so unattainable, so exalting, but so visionary." The dream became more attainable when Cyrus was given the means through which he would realize a million dollars and more. As the eldest son Cyrus stood to inherit the bulk of his father's estate. In 1830, when Cyrus turned twenty-one, Robert McCormick essentially deeded the reaper to him and with it future ownership of the tool and the technology behind it.

GAINING PUBLICITY THROUGH PUBLIC DEMONSTRATIONS

In 1831, when an estimated 70 percent of America's workforce, including 1.18 million slaves, tilled the soil, six people took an entire day to harvest two acres of wheat. McCormick's reaper could bring in ten acres in that time with two people. The need was clear, and the product existed to fill the need. The challenge was to find a way to bring that product to its market in an era that lacked any form of mass medium through which to reach potential customers.

Dramatic public demonstrations were the only truly convincing marketing techniques. And the spectacle Cyrus McCormick staged on John Steele's farm in 1831 was but the first of the reaper's many public trials. The following year he put on a second production in the nearby town of Lexington. This time, the reaper fared poorly on the hilly land. But an audience member, William Taylor, offered to let McCormick try the machine in his adjacent, more level fields. After the reaper churned through six acres, McCormick dragged the device into the Lexington courthouse square, where a local teacher is said to have pronounced, "This machine is worth a hundred thousand dollars."

Still, the McCormicks didn't rush to make the reaper widely available. The family believed that another of Robert's devices, the hemp break, had more immediate commercial potential. Cyrus assumed the role of chief promoter of this machine as well. But while he traveled to Kentucky to peddle and demonstrate the hemp break, the reaper was never far from his mind. He wrote home to propose building a few reaping machines in Kentucky. Robert McCormick proved reluctant to press ahead. "I think the building of a grain machine in that country might be attended with difficulty," he responded, summoning Cyrus home, "as it will require a good deal of new modeling which when done at home is free from the watchful and jealous eye of strangers."

Many farmers, having seen demonstrations or read articles about machines being developed in England and in the United States, were building their own reaping devices. Truth be told, no one person can really lay claim to having invented the first reaper. As Cyrus McCormick Jr. later said, "In the case of a simple farm tool of this kind, it might have been as well to have used the word 'constructed' instead of 'invented.'" In fact, the Ohio-based inventor Obed Hussey demonstrated and patented his own reaper in 1833. It is likely that, after learning of Hussey's machine, Cyrus McCormick applied for a patent on the machine he and his father had built in 1831. For a $30 fee, the twenty-five-year-old in 1834 received a fourteen-year patent, signed by President Andrew Jackson.

At that time, a patent was more than a legal necessity. As a seal of approval and originality, it represented a potent marketing tool. In 1834 Cyrus McCormick wrote a letter to the editor of *Mechanics' Magazine* charging that his competitor's design "is a part of the principle of my machine, and was invented by me, and operated on wheat and oats in July, 1831. . . . I would warn all persons against the use of the aforesaid principle, as I regard and treat the use of it, in any way, as an infringement of my right."

Writing letters to tiny newspapers was not, however, an efficient mode of spreading the word. In order to make the dispersed farming public aware of his father's invention, McCormick still had to show it to skeptical farmers. This challenge was especially difficult because McCormick had no reaper to sell. Like a producer unwilling to open his show until every last kink has been worked out, Cyrus was reluctant to press ahead. "Since the first experiment was made of the performance of my machine, I have, for the mutual interests of the public and myself, been laboring to bring it to as much perfection as the principle admitted of, before offering it to the public," he wrote in 1834.

The reaper's further development was inhibited by the family's involvement with other commercial ventures. In 1836, Robert and Cyrus McCormick set up an iron mining and smelting operation they called Cotopaxi. But the new business quickly faltered when iron prices collapsed, leaving the McCormicks to face a crowd of angry debtors. ". . . I have since felt [this] to be one of the best lessons of my business experience," Cyrus wrote in 1874. "If I had succeeded in the iron enterprise I would perhaps never have had sufficient determination and perseverance in the pursuit of my reaper enterprise to have brought it to the present stage of success."

As they gradually freed themselves from their Cotopaxi obligations, Robert and Cyrus McCormick, joined by his younger brothers Leander and William, began to refocus their creative and commercial efforts on the reaper. In the summer of 1839, Cyrus re-instituted his public demonstrations, and again the machine received rave notices. ". . . To say that we were pleased with its operation would but poorly express the gratification we experienced," exulted the Staunton (Virginia) *Spectator*. "It is certainly an admirable invention." In an effort to magnify the effect of such impartial opinions, Cyrus McCormick used the reviews as advertisements, buying space and running them in other newspapers.

Nonetheless, the reaper was slow to catch on. In 1840, when it still took thirty-seven hours of backbreaking labor to harvest an acre of wheat by hand, Cyrus McCormick sold two homemade machines for about $110 each, but they both broke down. After correcting the flaws in the Walnut Grove shop, the family sold seven reapers in 1841. Cyrus recalled that "they all gave satisfaction, allowance being made for defects which I had afterward to correct." Unlike his father, Cyrus McCormick showed an ability to focus completely on a single product. "His whole soul was wrapped up in his Reaper," one neighbor said.

AN ITINERANT SALESMAN SIGNS UP FAR-FLUNG LICENSEES

Attention to detail was crucial because the McCormick reaper faced competition; Obed Hussey's machines had garnered favorable reviews as well. And as farmers proved willing to have the competitors plow their fields in demonstrations, the inventors squared off in public. Planters in

Virginia staged a competition between the two rivals in 1843. As a board of judges watched, the McCormick machine mowed down seventeen acres, while Hussey's smaller reaper completed just two.

By the harvest of 1844, Cyrus and his family members had sold fifty machines for about $100 each from their base in Walnut Grove. Forty-two were sold in Virginia. Since no farmer would purchase such an expensive product without first seeing it perform, the reaper's market was by definition local. And even if a farmer in central Pennsylvania wanted to acquire a McCormick reaper, he would have had great difficulty taking delivery. Since no railroad or major waterway served Walnut Grove, shipping the reapers was prohibitively expensive.

McCormick reasoned that this dilemma could be solved if reapers were manufactured closer to their far-flung customers. In October 1843 he placed an advertisement in the Richmond *Semi-Weekly Whig*: "As it is not at all probable that I can always manufacture the reaper to supply the wants of the country, I propose to form partnerships for their manufacture and also to sell patent rights." Several entrepreneurs jumped at the offer, but virtually all of them were in neighboring Virginia counties. The total production of reapers rose to seventy-five in 1844, with fifty made by the McCormicks at Walnut Grove and twenty-five by licensees.

After arranging to have a few machines sent by freight to distant cities like Cincinnati and St. Louis, McCormick lugged a reaper over the back roads west of the Alleghenies, where the land was more level, grain cultivation more prevalent, and labor more scarce than in Virginia. He demonstrated the reaper at agricultural fairs, on private farms, and in cities to manufacturers who might be interested in buying licenses.

Among the first licensees to sign on was Backus, Fitch & Company, of Brockport, in upstate New York, in 1845. On a lengthy swing through what was then called the West, he enlisted licensees in Missouri, Ohio, and Illinois. While each deal was different, most licensees paid McCormick $20 for each reaper they made and sold. Others paid what was in effect a franchising fee in exchange for exclusive rights to a particular area. In an effort to expand the reach of the reaper, Cyrus enlisted a cousin, J. B. McCormick, as a traveling agent responsible for Tennessee and Missouri.

Despite its obvious labor-saving benefits, the reaper remained a hard sell, largely due to its $100 price. In his pitches, Cyrus McCormick appealed to farmers on economic grounds, arguing that the machine could pay for itself with saved labor.

While Cyrus took the reaper on the road, his brothers and father worked to improve its performance. The main deficiency was that the reaper still required a person to walk alongside and rake the felled wheat off the platform. But in 1845 the McCormicks added a special seat on which the raker could sit. "I can now warrant the raking of the wheat from the machine to be accomplished with ease and completeness by a man comfortably seated upon it," he wrote in the Mount Morris (New York) *Spectator*. This design, which became known as "Old Reliable," would prove the Model T of reapers—and the company's main product for nearly two decades.

As demand grew steadily, McCormick encountered a quality control problem. His licensees were irksome and unreliable. Some simply couldn't produce machines quickly enough to meet the market's demand. Others balked at adding improvements such as the raker seat. "You will be surprised when you read that not the first motion was made by Backus, Fitch and Co. to build a machine!" McCormick wrote home during one of his perpetual tours. "Without anything like a reasonable excuse . . . B.F. and Co. just neglected the business."

Meanwhile, increased demand overwhelmed the small Walnut Grove facility where the McCormicks drew on their own stock of timber, purchased finished steel from a local man, and employed a few laborers. But while they built seventy-five reapers in 1846, the output was nowhere near sufficient to fill all the orders that came in. With eager customers ranging from upstate New York to the far side of the Mississippi River, making reapers was no longer a cottage industry. The family realized that its business would suffer if it didn't relocate its manufacturing headquarters closer to the new customers in the burgeoning West. As William McCormick wrote in 1857: "Much as I love old Virginia, we should have starved in our business had we remained there." This bold move played a pivotal role in the firm's ensuing success.

PULLING UP STAKES AND BUILDING A FACTORY IN CHICAGO

While Cyrus was away on business, Robert McCormick died on July 4, 1846. His death was traumatic, but it served as the impetus for his sons to leave Virginia and explore the new Western markets. By virtue of its victory in the Mexican-American War, the United States would gain vast tracts of land in the West. As the government opened up new areas to homesteading, immigrants and Easterners flooded into the great plains and prairies. Many of them sowed the freshly plowed fields with sturdy grain seeds.

Cyrus McCormick ultimately chose to relocate to Chicago in 1847, where he struck a manufacturing partnership with a prior licensee called Gray and Warner. The frontier town, then a far cry from Carl Sandburg's "city of big shoulders" had just 17,000 souls and few paved streets. But the growing city stood at the center of the nation's shifting center of gravity. Moreover, Chicago's location on the shores of Lake Michigan afforded the company crucial access to rivers and canals. The new partnership built nearly 500 reapers for the 1848 harvest.

McCormick and Gray feuded over nuts-and-bolts financial details. To avoid litigation Gray sold his stake to William Ogden and William Jones, wealthy Chicago investors who were content to take a passive role in the business. The following year, for reasons that are still unclear, Ogden and Jones agreed to sell out to McCormick for $65,000, making Cyrus McCormick the sole proprietor. That year—1849—the company's 123 employees made 1,500 reapers.

Freed from his partners, McCormick engineered a rapid expansion of the plant on the banks of the Chicago River. By the time he was finished in the early 1850s, the factory covered 7,600 square feet on two stories. River frontage allowed workers to load the completed machines, weighing about a half ton each, directly onto barges and boats. After 1851, when the last of the early licensing agreements expired, all machines were made in the Chicago plant under the supervision of Leander McCormick, who had moved West to work with his brother. Stung by their early reliance on outside suppliers, the McCormicks sought to make their factory self-sufficient. For a time they continued to purchase sickles from a company in Massachusetts, and guard fingers, which held the grain in place to be cut, from a New Jersey firm. Soon, however, they dismissed all outside vendors and built an iron foundry to forge their own components.

As output rose dramatically, McCormick developed a rudimentary distribution system. The methods he devised to market the larger products resulted in several business innovations: The company hired sales agents who had responsibility for entire states or groups of states. In one of the first examples of such a system, agents set up shop, received sample machines, and took commissions on sales. In another innovation, farmers were allowed to buy the reaper on the installment plan, with payments stretched between harvests. "It is better that I should wait for the money than that you should wait for the machine that you need," McCormick said. Finally, in an early example of the customer service that would come to characterize American business, he offered free trials and money-back guarantees.

Efficiently produced and widely distributed, the reaper came to be hailed as a revolutionary device. In August 1854 the *Pennsylvania Farm Journal* noted: "The age of scythe and cradles may now be said to have passed very much away, and to be among the things that were." Just as the Ford Model T became an icon of American technological prowess in the early decades of the twentieth century, the McCormick reaper symbolized the country's agricultural mechanization and self-determination. McCormick took his machine to the first world's fair in London, in

1851, where the reaper was displayed in the famed Crystal Palace and churned through fields in exhibitions. Besting Hussey's machine and the local competition in field trials, the reaper won a gold medal. "The Reaping machine is worth the whole cost of the exposition," the *London Times* reported.

Having at last reached a wide consumer market with their reaper, the McCormicks' production quadrupled between 1851 and 1859, from 1,004 to 4,119 reapers. Meanwhile, economies of scale combined with savings on materials reduced the manufacturing cost per machine, from $56.92 in 1853 to $46.58 in 1859. Since McCormick kept the price relatively stable, the reaper soon became affordable for most potential customers. By 1860, Western farmers brought in about 70 percent of the nation's wheat harvest with the reaper. With the help of this machine, U.S. wheat production soared from 100 million bushels in 1849 to 173 million bushels in 1859. True to its promise, the reaper allowed fewer farmers to do more work, and in 1860, 59 percent of the active workforce labored in agriculture, down from 70 percent in 1830.

With the boom in the wheat market, McCormick's company had become a major enterprise, and by 1860 Cyrus was the millionaire he had dreamed of becoming. He started to play an active role in the Democratic Party and in the affairs of the Presbyterian Church. And it was at church one Sunday that he met Nancy Fowler, the daughter of a storekeeper from upstate New York, who was visiting friends in Chicago. McCormick proposed to her by mail, and the two were married on January 26, 1858. Over the next seventeen years they had five children. Cyrus Jr., the eldest, born in 1859, would later fill his namesake's position at the firm.

THE REAPER CREATES AN INDUSTRIAL POWERHOUSE

By providing an effective way to harvest wheat rapidly, the reaper had already helped affect the flow of economic history. But in the 1860s it would influence the outcome of the most pivotal event in the nation's history. Although devised by a slave owner from Virginia, the reaper proved to be a key asset for the Union cause in the Civil War. When the war started in 1861, there were enough harvesting machines in the Northern wheat fields to do the work of a million slaves. "The reaper is to the North what slavery is to the South," War Secretary Edwin Stanton wrote to McCormick. "By taking the place of regiments of young men in the western harvest fields, it released them to do battle for the Union at the front and at the same time keeps up the supply of bread for the nation and the Nation's armies."

Even as the guns sounded at Fort Sumter, McCormick and his agents were peddling a new, improved reaper. The self-rake machine featured a mechanism that automatically swept the grain off the platform onto the ground in neat piles, thus eliminating the need for a raker to ride on board. By 1864, two-thirds of the reapers made by McCormick had this feature.

As the war continued to devastate the nation, McCormick realized there would be little domestic business. So, in 1862, he went to England and spent the next two years abroad with his family, taking the self-raking mower on a grand tour of Europe. The machine won prizes in Germany and performed well in tests in Belgium, Russia, and Italy. In the winter of 1863-64, McCormick wrote home to a colleague: "I've been *working hard* & hope to accomplish something but time is required to effect the general & extensive introduction of a new implement in Europe." In spite of the successful trials and positive publicity it generated, the reaper didn't find a market on the Continent because local manufacturers were scarce and transoceanic transport was difficult to arrange. And in many areas of Europe, landowners weren't interested in investing in machinery that would ease the labors of their tenants.

When the Civil War ended, the company resumed its U.S. growth and continued to build more efficient machines—until disaster struck. The Great Fire of Chicago on October 8 and 9, 1871, laid waste to 3.5 square miles of the city and left nearly 100,000 people homeless. Among the $188 million worth of property destroyed was McCormick's factory, in which he had invested some $2 million over the years and which had produced a staggering 10,000 reapers during the previous year. "I at once determined to proceed with the work of rebuilding," McCormick wrote. Abandoning the old factory site, he purchased 160 acres along a branch of the Chicago River and spent $619,000, to build a massive factory with a main plant measuring 200 by 360 feet (ten times the size of the 1848 original), a 440,000-square-foot warehouse, and a foundry and blacksmith shop along 1,300 feet of river frontage. It opened in February 1873 and quickly began to produce reapers. In 1875, the rebuilt company had sold 13,031 machines.

STAYING AHEAD OF COMPETITION BY ACQUIRING NEW TECHNOLOGY

In the post-Civil War years, McCormick & Co. took a different approach to toward developing new products. With the clout of a big industrial plant, an internationally recognized brand name, and a dominant domestic sales network, McCormick no longer had to develop his own technology. Rather, the company was content to let hungry entrepreneurs develop new inventions and prove their field-worthiness. After watching successful, small-scale debuts, the company would then acquire the patents and incorporate them into their new products. As William Hutchinson wrote of the firm in the 1870s: "Invention became the tool, and the inventor the employee of the manufacturer."

In 1860, for example, Charles and William Marsh developed the harvester, which conveyed the grain from the reaper's platform into a bin for binding. Farmers could bind the grain while riding the machine, thus doing as much in a day as three or four binders could before. In 1873, McCormick bought the Marsh patents. To observers, the new wrinkle represented yet another step forward in the march of human progress. "Of the ten or twelve sweating drudges who toiled in the harvest-field, all were now to be set free—the sickles, the cradlers, rakers, binders—every one except the driver, and he (or she) was to have the glory of riding on the triumphal chariot of a machine that did all the work itself," wrote the historian Herbert Casson.

That triumphal chariot rode proudly through the fields of the Northern and Western United States for decades. And in the late 1870s, in large part due to improved transoceanic shipping and greater production capacity, the world market that Cyrus McCormick had been seeking finally materialized after nearly two decades. Between 1875 and 1885, the McCormick company pushed into Canada, Australia, New Zealand, and Argentina. In July 1878 alone, the firm sent 550 machines to New Zealand. "By 1880 the sun never set upon McCormick machines," Hutchinson wrote.

In his seventies, McCormick continued to accompany his machines on their world tours. In an age before television and video, seeing still preceded believing. "Dear Papa, who has fought so many battles of the reapers, looks at the coming struggle, and quite naturally is eager to be in the midst of it," wrote Nancy McCormick to one of her sons in 1878. "He feels that this may be his last great international fight, and he wants a fair field and no favor. I sometimes think that success will depend on his presence." That year, when the U.S. grain crop totaled 429 million bushels, McCormick traveled to France, where he received the rank of Officer of the Legion of Honor and an award from the French Academy of Sciences for having "done more than any other living man for the cause of agriculture in the world."

Still, the firm remained very much a family business. In 1879, when it produced nearly 20,000 machines and earned $722,000, the partnership was transformed into McCormick Harvesting Machine Company, with Cyrus controlling three-fourths and Leander owning the remaining quarter. Upon his graduation from Princeton, Cyrus Jr. was inducted into the family business. Much like his father, Cyrus Jr. was enterprising and ambitious. He set about modernizing and expanding the factory in the early 1880s, adding electric lights and boosting production: in 1884,

THE FORMATION OF INTERNATIONAL HARVESTER

Upon Cyrus McCormick's death, his twenty-five-year-old son, Cyrus Jr., took over the business. By 1902 the Chicago plant—the company's sole manufacturing facility—accounted for 35 percent of the country's farm machinery. McCormick still faced competition from other implement makers and from the growing challenge of new companies making farm machines powered by gas and steam.

Concerned about potentially destructive competition, Cyrus McCormick Jr. did what so many other businessmen of the era did: he paid a call on the offices of J. P. Morgan in New York. With Morgan partner George Perkins, the McCormick executives concocted a plan to merge their company with three other leading companies. The plan was for the newly formed company to purchase the assets of the other companies for $60 million. Augmented by $50 million in accounts and receivables and $10 million from Morgan, the International Harvester Company was capitalized at $120 million. Morgan himself suggested adding the name International to the company. At its creation, the trust, with Cyrus McCormick Jr. as its president, held 85 percent of the country's farm machinery market.

Like most other large enterprises, International Harvester came under antitrust scrutiny in the 1900s and 1910s. But the government didn't break up the company. For despite its size the company faced robust competition, first, from veteran implement makers like John Deere and, later, from automobile companies like Ford, whose gas-powered tractors quickly gained market share in the 1910s.

1,400 workers built 55,000 implements, compared with 20,000 in 1880, and they made virtually every part of the machinery at the Chicago factory. Cyrus McCormick Sr. remained involved well into his seventies. "If I had given up business, I would have been dead long ago," he said in 1884. Indeed, he worked up until his death, just a few weeks later.

Cyrus McCormick left behind an American landscape visibly altered by his invention. Wheat sprung from the soil in Eastern mountain valleys, the great plains of the Midwest, and newly settled parts of California. With the help of tools like the reaper, U.S. wheat production had increased from four bushels per capita in 1847 to ten at the time of Cyrus McCormick's death. The effect on the American workforce was nearly as dramatic. When McCormick first demonstrated the reaper, almost three-fourths of the population worked on farms. But over the next several decades, freed or displaced American farm workers moved to the cities and took up work in the growing fields of industry and infrastructure.

Of course, the industrialization of agriculture was not complete in 1884; not until the 1950s did the number of tractors in America's fields first surpass the number of horses. But the long-term trends McCormick helped set into motion in the mid-nineteenth century continued to alter the American economy. In 1961, when the vast, technologically obsolete McCormick Works in Chicago were finally leveled, fewer than 9 percent of all Americans worked in agriculture. And they grew enough food to feed the nation's population several times over. While the reaper was not single-handedly responsible for urbanization and the industrialization of agriculture, the history of these trends couldn't be written without mention of Cyrus McCormick and his reaper.

John D. Rockefeller, founder of Standard Oil, in 1884.

JOHN D. ROCKEFELLER AND THE MODERN CORPORATION

ad the *Forbes* 400 existed at the turn of the twentieth century, John Davison Rockefeller would have reigned at the top of the list. Living for nearly a century, and surviving decades of competition in the Darwinian oil industry he helped to create, Rockefeller amassed a fortune of $900 million in 1913 and provided the basis for one of America's greatest philanthropic foundations.

In its infancy, oil was a chaotic, haphazard business. Wildcatters could drill a crude oil well or build a refinery with a small capital outlay. Rockefeller was among the first to set up refineries in Cleveland, which lay at the terminus of the railroad lines leading out of the Oil Regions of Pennsylvania. U.S. oil production soared from 2,000 barrels during 1859 to 450,000 a year later, and by 1862, it had gushed to three million barrels. With each successive year, Rockefeller's fortune grew. In the mid-1860s, when the end of the Civil War signalled a period of unprecedented economic expansion, Rockefeller brought in new interests, recapitalized his firm, and began to buy out the competition. By 1870, when he formed the Standard Oil Company of Ohio, Rockefeller owned all of the refineries in his home base. He would ultimately own nearly all of the nation's oil industry.

Rockefeller recognized that refining oil would not insure his firm's survival, as refining capacity was outpacing demand for its product. In an effort to control the oil's means of transportation to market, Standard established terminal warehouses, pipeline networks, and even barrel factories. Most significantly, Rockefeller muscled rebates from the railroads, whereby he would receive enormous price reductions for a guaranteed cargo. For a time he even forced the railroads to pay him rebates on oil shipped by his competitors.

Many of Rockefeller's practices were subsequently—and infamously—deemed illegal under antitrust legislation. And the integrated system of production and distribution he established was not entirely unprecedented. His most lasting contribution lay in the systems of professional management he developed that integrated the many aspects of his business. In the words of the great business historian Alfred D. Chandler, "An understanding of the history of the Standard Oil Company is essential to the understanding of the rise of the large corporation in the American economy."

A BOOKKEEPER BECOMES A FORCE IN THE EARLY OIL REFINING INDUSTRY

John D. Rockefeller was born in 1839 on a small farm in upstate New York during the presidency of Martin Van Buren. In 1853, his father, William Avery Rockefeller, an occasional farmer, small-time entrepreneur, and scam artist, moved from upstate New York to Cleveland with his deeply pious wife and five children. Growing up in the booming industrial city on the shores of Lake Erie, John took less after his father than his somber mother, from whom he learned the value of thrift. "How well I remembered then, as I remember now, the words of my dear mother," he recalled much later in life. " 'Willful waste makes woeful want!' "

Rockefeller put this adage to practice when, upon completing secondary school and a few business courses at Folsom's Commercial College, he found work as a $4-a-week bookkeeper for a Cleveland dry goods merchant. As he detailed the company's operations in a ledger book, he first grasped the intricacies of commercial enterprise. "John D. seemed to have no inner life unconnected with numbers," as his sympathetic biographer David Freeman Hawke wrote. This job, Rockefeller later said, "formed a large part of the foundation of my business career." Obsessed with attaining professional and financial independence, John scrimped and borrowed for three years, until he had enough—$1,800—to set up shop in 1859 as a dry-goods trader with Maurice Clark, a British immigrant. The business thrived, especially after the outbreak of the Civil War in 1861, when the army bought huge quantities of grain, pork, and other staples.

Meanwhile, a few hundred miles to the East, adventurers were beginning to deal in a far more precious commodity: oil. In the 1850s, kerosene extracted from coal and shale began to replace whale oil as a safer and more reliable source of energy. Researchers soon realized they could refine kerosene from the vast fields of petroleum lying just under the surface of Midwestern valleys and mountains. The U.S. oil industry boomed after August 27, 1859 when "Colonel" Edwin Drake plunged his salt-mining rig into an Allegheny Mountain valley near the tiny lumber town of Titusville, Pennsylvania. Prospectors thronged into what became known as the "Oil Regions," as the industry flourished, and public demand for the new fuel grew rapidly. They poured the crude oil into barrels, trundled them onto barges, and floated them down creeks and rivers to railroad junctions heading east and west. Many of the barrels wound up on the rails of the Atlantic & Great Western Railroad, and the western terminus of that line, Cleveland, emerged as a small refining center. The chemistry behind refining—heating crude oil with steam power to distill gasoline and kerosene—was relatively cheap and simple. By 1863, the 20 small factories huddled along the banks of the Cayuhoga River produced about 100,000 barrels of refined oil each month.

Rockefeller watched as Cleveland-area businessmen made quick fortunes in oil refining, and he too was caught up in the heady excitement. In 1863, he and Clark invested $4,000 with an acquaintance, Samuel Andrews, to build and operate a refinery. Although it bore a noble name, the Excelsior Works, the enterprise was really a humble collection of wooden sheds. While Andrews devised ways to improve the efficiency of the refining process, Rockefeller handled other aspects of the business, insisting in particular that all profits should go right back into the company. "I wanted to go in the army and do my part," Rockefeller later said, explaining why he didn't fight in the Civil War. "But it was simply out of the question. There was no one to take my place. We were in a new business, and if I had not stayed it must have stopped."

At a time when Charles Darwin's theories on evolution were first gaining wide currency, the oil industry seemed to hew to the scientist's new creed. The only businesses able to survive the competition were those able to adapt to rapidly shifting circumstances. Because of the unexpected rise in production, the price of crude fluctuated wildly— plunging from $10 a barrel to fifty cents a barrel between January and June of 1861. In 1864, the price per barrel ranged between $4 and

$12.13. The price swings were further aggravated by transportation problems: a few railroads held a stranglehold on the delivery of oil. As profit margins shrank amidst heightened competition, many speculative operators perished.

A SMALL PROPRIETORSHIP DEVELOPS INTO A PRIMITIVE COMPANY

Unable to control the price of vital raw materials, Rockefeller focused his attention on the costs of the industrial commodities that he could control. Barrels, which cost about $2.50 apiece, were one of the Excelsior's main expenses. In 1864 Rockefeller used some of his reinvested capital to set up a barrel-making operation on the refinery's property, reducing the per-barrel cost to about 96 cents. Determining that the best way to boost his profits was to raise production, he borrowed money to open a second refinery, the Standard Works. But he ran into conflict with his partners who were unwilling to go further into debt to finance expansion. In February, 1865, he bought them out for $72,500. He later reflected, "I look back on that day in 1865 and it seems to me one of the most important in my life. It was the day that determined my career." Weeks after the transaction, Rockefeller dissolved the dry-goods company and focused all his energies on oil.

The company's early success was due to Rockefeller's extraordinary drive and legendary attention to detail. "I shall never forget how hungry I was in those days," he later recalled. "I stayed out of doors day and night; I ran up and down the tops of freight cars when necessary." By 1865, the Excelsior Works had become one of the largest Cleveland refineries, producing about 505 barrels each day. From the outset, the U.S. oil industry sent much of its refined output to Europe, where oil products were in high demand as illuminants and lubricants. In 1866 alone, exports boomed from 600,000 barrels to 1.5 million. In a far-sighted move, Rockefeller enlisted his younger brother, William, to open a New York office where he would promote kerosene exports. With this action, Standard became one of the first refiners to expand its scope of operations. And as William made contact with foreign buyers, the company established an independent distribution channel for its products.

In a second step toward the division of executive labor, Rockefeller brought in Henry Flagler as a partner in 1867. Flagler, who had built a small fortune as a liquor and grain wholesaler, used his expertise in transport to negotiate and cut deals with the railroad operators. Insuring an affordable and reliable means for delivering the product assumed greater importance as output for Standard Works increased to 1,500 barrels a day by 1869. And here the economies of scale began to kick in. "While unit costs for a refinery with a 500 barrel daily throughput was around six cents a gallon, those in the refinery with a 1,500 barrel throughput dropped to three cents a gallon and probably less," wrote Alfred Chandler, quoting the oil historians Harold F. Williamson & Arnold Daum. Greater production enhanced Standard's leverage with producers and suppliers. "Paint. Glue. We bought ours far lower than anyone else could, since ours was a steady demand for the largest quantities . . . ," Rockefeller later said. In a further effort to insulate his enterprise from the predations of suppliers and vendors, he acquired his own fleet of wagons, storage depots near railroads, and warehouses in New York Harbor.

In the post-Civil War years, oversupply and overcapacity wreaked havoc in the refining industry. As prices for refined kerosene fell more than 50 percent between 1865 and 1870, most refiners' per-gallon margins shrank from 19.5 cents in 1865 to 7.9 cents in 1869. Standard also suffered, with its profit margins shrinking from 43 cents per gallon in 1865 to 17 cents in 1870. Rockefeller's margins were higher than the industry average because of Flagler's shrewd negotiations with the railroads. In 1870, he cut a deal with the Lake Shore Railroad, a subsidiary of the New York Central: Standard would guarantee to ship sixty carloads of refined oil a day over Lake Shore's tracks from Cleveland to New York, if the railroad would grant Standard a rate of $1.30 a barrel—35 percent off the published rate of $2 a barrel. Rebates like this one were a common practice between railroads and their major customers, and while it provided large firms with unfair advantages over rivals, it was perfectly legal.

CONSOLIDATING THE CLEVELAND REFINING COMPLEX

The railroad deals confirmed what Rockefeller had long suspected: size begets advantage. Surveying the refining business in 1870, the 31-year-old began to think about expanding further. Despite the oil industry's chaos, Rockefeller had a clear vision of where it was going, and the key role his company could play in it. Following his instincts, he and his associates set out to combine all of Cleveland's refineries into a single firm in order to gain still greater leverage over railroads and crude oil producers. And since corporations could borrow and issue stock much more easily than could partnerships, Rockefeller merged the two partnerships that ran the Excelsior Works and Standard Works refineries into The Standard Oil Company. Capitalized at $1 million, Standard Oil would eventually grow into a multibillion-dollar enterprise. "None of us ever dreamed of the magnitude of what proved to be the later expansion," he recalled.

Once Standard Oil was established, Rockefeller approached weaker competitors with a simple proposition: join us or face the ravages of heightened competition. "We will undertake to save you from the wrecks of the refining business and give you a return on the capital which you have in the plant and land; or, if you prefer we will take the business off your hands," he said simply. When making his pitch, Rockefeller was the picture of somber propriety. Having inherited a deep religious faith from his mother, he was a regular at the Euclid Avenue Baptist Church in Cleveland, and served as the Sunday School's superintendent. Devoid of bluster or emotional display, Rockefeller measured his words carefully, and appraised adversaries with piercing blue eyes. But those who resisted his initial overtures would receive a concise, matter-of-fact follow-up. "You can never make any more money, in my judgment. You can't compete with Standard," he told one reluctant refiner. "We have all the large refineries now. If you refuse to sell, it will end in your being crushed."

Given their shrinking profit margins and difficulties in dealing with the railroads, many refiners found Rockefeller's offer impossible to refuse. Among the biggest and first to enlist in his campaign was Clark, Payne & Company, the largest local rival. After this merger, smaller firms quickly fell into line. Within two years Rockefeller had bought twenty-three companies, eighteen of which were refineries, with all but one of them located in Cleveland.

By the end of 1872, Standard had boosted its capacity sixfold and was refining 10,000 barrels a day. With 80 percent of Cleveland's refining industry under its roof, the company already stood as the nation's largest refining complex, and some businessmen thought Rockefeller had grown too big too quickly. "It has no future," said Robert Hanna, a Cleveland refiner. "The organization will fall by its own weight." But in this age, heft was a prerequisite for survival, and Standard fed on its competitors like a bear bulking up for winter.

Rockefeller began to seek points of leverage against potential prey. In 1872, he joined the South Improvement Company, a shell corporation erected by refiners to formalize rebate agreements between railroads and oil firms. Under the compact, members of the company would receive 40 percent to 50 percent rebates for crude oil and 25 percent to 50 percent for refined oil from a group of railroads in exchange for supplying a guaranteed cargo. The Pennsylvania Railroad would receive 45 percent of the members' cargo, with the New York Central and Erie railroads, each receiving 27.5 percent. In addition, Standard—and Standard alone—would receive a percentage of the full cargo fare paid by rival refiners. The scheme, which appeared corrupt even by the loose mores of the day, quickly collapsed after enraged crude oil producers led protests in the Oil Regions. Undaunted, Rockefeller sought a different means of organization. In August 1872, he gathered members of the oil industry to form the National Refiners' Association (naming himself president) to negotiate terms with producers on behalf of all refineries. When it, too, fell apart (due to a depression that began in 1873), he characteristically rationalized his anti-competitive efforts as an attempt to bring order to a chaotic sector of the economy. "Among so many men untrained in business there were many who could not be relied upon to aid in solving a problem so difficult as the reformation which my associates and I sought to bring about in this industry," he said later.

SEEKING STABILITY THROUGH HORIZONTAL AND VERTICAL INTEGRATION

Despite the lack of a refiners' association, Standard's size alone left it in a position to swallow up its weaker competitors. As the oil fields in Pennsylvania boomed, U.S. production rose from 5.3 million barrels in 1871 to 9.85 million two years later. But after the onset of a five-year-long depression in 1873, crude oil prices started tumbling, dropping from $4.40 a barrel in 1871 to $1.15 in 1874.

Having consolidated the Cleveland-area refineries into one large industrial enterprise, Rockefeller moved simultaneously in two directions: horizontally and vertically. Operating out of five rooms in an office building in downtown Cleveland, he and his partners acquired refineries in other parts of the country. Chief among these were Jacob Jay Vandergrift's Imperial Refining Company, based in the Oil Regions, and Charles Pratt & Company, which had refineries in New York, Philadelphia, and Pittsburgh.

Standard also bought interests in a new mode of transporting crude oil: pipelines. The first of these, a modest 5-mile affair, had been built in 1865. Control of these pipelines could enable Standard Oil to circumvent the railroads. In the 1870s, Rockefeller began snapping up pipeline companies, soon owning most of them. In 1873, after he outbid Com-

modore William Vanderbilt for control of a pipeline concern, Vanderbilt remarked: "That Rockefeller. He will be the richest man in the
country!"

As Rockefeller added satellite refineries and pipelines, creating a
nationwide factory, he encountered a new management problem. In the
nineteenth century, corporations were generally prohibited from owning
or controlling companies in states other than their home state. So in
theory, the original Standard Oil Company couldn't operate outside of
Ohio. Rockefeller had skirted this legal unpleasantry through a subtle
sleight of hand. He would instruct any out-of-state company he acquired to turn over its stock to a Standard officer as a trustee, and
continue to operate as an ostensibly independent concern. In the
1870s, for example, when Standard bought Jabez Bostwick & Company, Rockefeller allowed Bostwick to run the business under his own
name—but only on paper.

As Rockefeller built his empire, the division of executive labor,
begun in the 1860s, became even more important. The historian Allan
Nevins noted: "Never had any corporation faced a situation comparable
in magnitude and confused variety with that of the Standard in the fall
of 1877." To compound the problem, there was no established management model to help Rockefeller. The concept of corporate business management didn't exist in the 1870s. Rockefeller's task was made even
more difficult because the men he had to work with were strong-willed
entrepreneurs who were accustomed to ruling their own outfits. But he
offered a financial incentive to cooperate. Whenever possible, he brought
the management of companies he acquired into the Standard fold. He
also paid for acquisitions in Standard stock, which was not publicly
traded, giving the sellers immediate stakes in the success of the larger
venture. "His greatest contribution, beyond the concept of the Standard
Oil combination itself, was the persuasion of strong men to join the
alliance and to work together effectively in its management," wrote the
Standard historians Ralph and Muriel Hidy.

While the home office in Cleveland set overall policy, the heads of the previously independent companies remained semi-autonomous. Jacob Jay Vandergrift, who joined the firm as a director when Standard acquired his refining concern, was in charge of the pipelines; Jabez Bostwick handled the purchasing of crude oil in the Oil Regions; Flagler continued to work out favorable deals with the perpetually hostile railroads; and longtime Standard lawyer Samuel Dodd came on as chief counsel. With these arrangements, Standard began to take on the appearance of what we would recognize today as a modern corporation. While Rockefeller remained the ultimate authority, he had laid the groundwork for a division of professional management. In 1879, according to one subordinate, Rockefeller described his governing philosophy of delegating responsibilities as: "It is this; nobody does anything if he can get anybody else to do it."

Rockefeller and his colleagues realized that they could not keep on top of every aspect of the company's holdings, since they had grown so large and complex. To supervise its operations, Standard Oil began to develop committees, which met at the company's New York offices. Since data was required to monitor the performance of units, the New York-based directors decreed that managers responsible for different business units should file quarterly reports to the board. In an effort to be close to its new headquarters, Rockefeller moved his wife, Laura, and their four children to New York, where they took up residence in a four-story brownstone on 54th Street, just off 5th Avenue. (The family also kept a large estate in Westchester County called Pocantico Hills, complete with its own 12-hole golf course.)

ROCKEFELLER FORMS A TRUST TO MANAGE AN UNWIELDY ENTERPRISE

By 1877, the historian Albert Carr noted, "no one could ship oil in quantity anywhere in America without the approval of Standard Oil." Such power brought the company a great deal of unwanted attention, from competitors, politicians, and various legal authorities. In 1879, for example, the New York State Assemblyman Alonzo Hepburn opened a public investigation into Standard's relationships with the railroads. But Rockefeller and his officials generally got off lightly—in part because they engaged in the then-common practice of bribing key state legislators—and Rockefeller continued to increase his sphere of influence.

By the 1880s, international demand for petroleum and its byproducts boomed as industrial machines and combustion engines required ever-increasing quantities of fuel. This led to a race to slake the world's thirst for oil. Despite its dominant position in the American market, Standard now faced external competitive problems. Massive oil reserves had just been discovered in the Russian Caucasus, and they became active wells. A railroad from the Baku oil fields to the Black Sea was slated for completion in 1883. Such competition meant that American oil firms faced pressure to reduce their prices, pressure that even the mighty Standard Oil could not ignore.

Standard's managers found a solution: The formation of a trust would streamline the growing company by enabling it to control costs, increase profits and improve management. In 1881, Samuel Dodd drew up the agreement in which shareholders in the dozens of companies controlled by Standard would trade their shares in the companies for shares in the newly created trust. Rockefeller owned about 28 percent of this new stock. In exchange, control of the enterprises would revert to a group of nine trustees, including the Rockefeller brothers, Flagler, Bostwick, and a few other key executives. An arrangement of this magnitude was unprecedented in American business. When it became effective on January 2, 1882, the trust already controlled 80 percent of the nation's refining business, 90 percent of the nation's pipelines, and held dominant positions in related areas such as tank cars, petroleum byproducts, and barrel making.

But the trust posed new management challenges. Initially, the trustees allowed the managers of subsidiaries to run the units, while reserving the right to approve any appropriation over $5,000. The trustees' Executive Committee—whoever happened to be at 26 Broadway in New York—met every day at lunch. "Our general rule was to take no important action till all of us were convinced of its wisdom," said Rockefeller. Consensus was necessary, for the Trust was now an assemblage of interrelated and interdependent companies. The smooth functioning of the whole was predicated on the reliable performance of every constituent unit. Thus, while granting the subsidiaries a degree of autonomy, the central administration imposed substantial requirements on them. Each Standard unit was expected to show a profit on its own, for example. And George Vilas, a salaried trustee, began to visit different units and impose uniform financial reporting requirements on them.

With this new division of executive labor, the trust began to work through committees consisting primarily of senior executives from its large constituent units, aided by a permanent staff at the New York office. Separate committees dealt with transportation, exports, manufacturing, cases and cans, cooperage, lubricating oil, domestic marketing, and production. The trust's executives expanded the industrial powerhouse in new directions. They spearheaded a drive into marketing, establishing a network of retail stations that would insure a steady flow of quality-controlled refined product to the public. This drive boosted the number of company-owned kerosene and gas stations from 130 in 1882 to 3,500 in 1906. The process of vertical integration was complete when Standard finally began drawing crude oil from the ground. In 1881, after prospectors hit major veins in the flats near Lima, Ohio, the company began to snap up oil fields near its historic base. By 1891, Standard drew 25 percent of all the American crude that was taken from the ground, and by 1895, crude extraction accounted for 14 percent of the company's earnings.

Standard Oil Company now embodied the principle of a twentieth century factory—it facilitated a continuous flow of raw materials through various links in a production chain until it emerged as a finished consumer product. Rockefeller could control every movement of a drop of oil, from the time it was pumped to the earth's surface in Pennsylvania to the time a California farmer purchased a gallon of kerosene at a local Standard station.

In the 1890s, Rockefeller, though only in his fifties, essentially removed himself from the daily affairs of the Standard Oil Company, in large part on the orders of his doctor, who warned of an impending physical breakdown if he continued to work. In the ultimate expression of the new distinction between management and ownership that Rockefeller had pioneered, he and his entire generation of associates gradually left the business in the hands of a younger group of salaried executives with proven managerial mettle.

Rockefeller devoted much of the rest of his life to charity. He endowed the University of Chicago in 1892, and set up a foundation that dispensed millions to educational and health efforts around the world. These activities did little to assuage a public resentful of his wealth, power, and control over a commodity as vital as oil. Crusading journalists and the popular press viewed him as predatory and hopelessly corrupt. In 1888, the New York *World* dubbed Rockefeller "the father of trusts, the king of monopolists, the czar of the oil business." The muckraking journalist Ida Tarbell, wrote, "There was something altogether indescribably repulsive about him," after seeing him in church.

A LONG RETIREMENT DISTURBED BY ANTI-TRUST PROSECUTIONS

Following the example of the immensely successful Standard trust, large firms in other industries imitated Standard's mode of organization. Soon

RE-ENGINEERING REFINING

Soon after the formation of the Standard Oil trust in 1882, the committees set about rationalizing and consolidating Standard's far-flung and occasionally disparate parts in search of greater economies of scale and operating efficiencies. Cutting costs was the only way to maintain profit margins in an era when the supply of oil was rising rapidly. An obvious place to start was Standard's large number of refineries acquired over the years. Between 1882 and 1885, the trust slashed its roster of refineries from fifty-three to twenty-two, mothballing obsolete facilities while enhancing the productive capacity of those that remained. And by 1885, three Standard refineries, in Bayonne (New Jersey), Philadelphia, and Cleveland—the three largest in the world—produced nearly 40 percent of Standard's total output of 17.7 million barrels. That year, total U.S. production stood at 21.5 million barrels.

This consolidation further boosted Standard's advantage over the few remaining independents. By the mid-1880s the most efficient independent refiners had cut average costs to 1.5 cents per gallon. Meanwhile, Standard's average per gallon cost dropped from .543 cents in 1882 to .452 cents in 1885. In the same period, its profit margin nearly doubled, rising from .53 cents per gallon in 1882 to one cent per gallon in 1885.

only a small cluster of enterprises held a strangle-hold over crucial industries like tobacco, steel, and telephones. In response to such unfair monopolies, President Theodore Roosevelt's administration launched a series of attacks on Standard and other large corporate combinations. As the most visible and powerful of the trusts, Standard garnered special attention. In June 1906, Herbert Hadley, Attorney General of Missouri, announced that he intended to prosecute the trust based on a Bureau of Corporations report that described in detail Standard's immense size and power, including the complex network of 88,000 miles of pipe line and the 68.2 million barrels of crude that entered its refineries annually.

In the new era of reform-minded government, Standard couldn't make the troubles disappear through graft, and the legal battles began to take their toll. In the summer of 1907 a Federal court ruled against Standard's Indiana unit for its longstanding practice of taking rebates from railroads, and assessed a $29 million penalty. Although Standard's legal team successfully appealed that ruling and won a new trial ordered by the appeals court, in May 1908, Frank Kellogg, a special prosecutor appointed by Roosevelt, called for the break up of Standard of New Jersey, as the trust's corporate parent was known. While Standard's lawyers challenged the case all the way to the Supreme Court, the high court, led by Chief Justice White, ruled against the trust on May 15, 1911. In a 20,000-word opinion, the Supreme Court found that Standard was an "unreasonable" trust and ordered it to divest its thirty-eight subsidiaries by transferring back to stockholders of the original companies all the stock they had exchanged for shares in the trust.

Ironically, the trustbusting had the effect of further enriching Rockefeller, who owned 244,500 of the 983,383 trust shares. As an original shareholder in many of the companies that had banded together to form Standard, Rockefeller suddenly found himself in possession of a diversified portfolio of stocks in various oil-related businesses. Weaned from their parent, many of the liberated Standard units continued to thrive. The shares of many former trust components found public markets, and investors clamored for stock in the well-managed companies. The rising tide lifted Rockefeller, too. Allan Nevins, the indefatigable biographer, estimated Rockefeller's fortune at $900 million in 1913.

Rockefeller outlived the trust, as he did nearly all his contemporaries and competitors. No longer able to participate in the management of the nation's largest industrial enterprise, he spent much of his final two decades at Pocantico Hills and at The Casements, his home in Ormond, Florida, playing golf and tending to his gardens. He died in 1937 at the age of 97.

John Pierpont Morgan, Wall Street banker.

J.P. MORGAN SAVES THE COUNTRY

I n the fall of 1907 the future of America's financial system hung in the balance. A period of solid growth following the bitter recession of 1903 had degenerated into prolonged, feverish speculation. As the economy began to slow, over-extended companies had difficulty raising funds. In October, a New York financier failed in a reckless bid to take over United Copper Company, which caused a major trust company and two brokerage houses to collapse. This precipitated runs on New York's trusts and banks, as anxious depositors queued up on the streets of lower Manhattan to salvage their savings. With money and credit suddenly scarce, high-flying financiers were ruined, and even the largest and most significant institutions—including the New York Stock Exchange—had difficulty obtaining the funds that fueled their daily operations. Since there was no government body that could combat financial crisis, public authorities watched helplessly from the sidelines.

Onto this stage strode the only person capable of saving the show: John Pierpont Morgan. As the nation's leading corporate statesman, its most powerful financier, and the force behind U.S. Steel and General Electric, Morgan emerged from semi-retirement and worked to restore order to a system paralyzed by crisis. In late October and early November 1907, the seventy-year-old Wall Street veteran assembled a group of prominent bankers in his private library to act as an informal rescue committee. Time and again, he raised huge sums of money in a matter of hours to provide life-support to institutions like the New York Stock Exchange and the New York City government. And before it was all over, Morgan persuaded leaders of the trusts to create a salvage fund to bolster their troubled colleagues.

Morgan's leadership in this time of crisis marked the great last act in a career that stretched from the Civil War to the presidency of Woodrow Wilson. "It was Morgan's supreme moment, the final measure of power and its ecstasy," wrote his biographer Lewis Corey. His actions helped convince the financial world of the critical need for a central government agency—the Federal Reserve System—that would act as he had to provide stability for the modern banking system and financial markets.

A CRISIS OF CONFIDENCE BREWS IN THE FALL OF 1907

J.P. Morgan was born in 1837, a descendant of Welsh ancestors who had come to the Massachusetts Bay Colony in 1636. His father, Junius Spencer Morgan, was a prominent international banker, and he made sure his son had a first-rate education and a smooth entree into the financial world. J.P. began his career in 1856, and in the next four decades he leveraged his banking expertise into control of large segments of the boom-and-bust railroad industry. So pervasive were his holdings that in 1895, as the *New York Tribune* noted, "There are only a few Wall Street interests of moment which J.P. Morgan & Co. have not some connections with." But Morgan's leadership was even more impressive than his holdings. By the turn of the century, J.P. Morgan had demonstrated again and again that he could impose order on chaotic situations and change entire industries through sheer strength of character.

In the fall of 1907, Morgan headed for Richmond, Virginia, to attend the three-week-long Triennial Episcopal Convention. He settled into a mansion he had paid $5,000 to lease for three weeks. Despite the opulent surroundings, he did not rest easy. He repeatedly received disturbing telegrams from New York that warned of impending fiscal disaster. "If one came during a meal, he tore it open, read it; then putting the palms of both hands on the table, a habit of his, he looked straight ahead with fixed eyes and deep thought for a few minutes," Bishop William Lawrence, another convention attendee, recalled.

Morgan blamed the sour business climate partly on President Theodore Roosevelt, the great trust buster. In the preceding years, Roosevelt's Administration had been overtly hostile to many of the large corporations dominated by Morgan and his allies. The president was the nation's chief opponent of industrial consolidation, while the banker was its greatest practitioner. In August 1907, the president used the bully pulpit to rail against "malefactors of great wealth." For Morgan's part, the staunchly Republican financier resented what he saw as the president's class warfare. "I'd even vote the Democratic ticket to get that fellow out of the White House," Morgan once said. "If he had his way we'd all do business with glass pockets."

At Roosevelt's urging, the government had investigated the business practices of John D. Rockefeller's massive Standard Oil Company. A court fined Standard Oil $29 million after finding it had illegally extracted rebates from railroads. The verdict, combined with the prospect of increased regulation by an emboldened Interstate Commerce Commission, depressed the market-leading railroad stocks. Mounting evidence of a widespread credit crunch further stressed the market. As the overheated economy began to cool, even blue-chip companies began to find money scarce in the capital markets. *Dun's Review* noted that 8,090 companies with total liabilities of over $116 million had failed in the first nine months of 1907, with the September figures showing the highest level of bankruptcy since the near-depression of 1903.

But every conflagration needs a spark, and the Wall Street speculator F. Augustus Heinze provided one. Heinze was president of the Mercantile National Bank and had interests in several other companies. In October he tried to corner shares of the United Copper Company using funds from Mercantile. On Monday, October 14, the price of United Copper soared from $39⅞ to $60 in a fifteen-minute trading frenzy. But when Heinze's takeover attempt failed on Tuesday, October 15, the company's shares plummeted thirty-five points from its high of 60. The next day it fell even farther to ten. United Copper's shocking plunge helped depress stocks to a four-year low. But the failed takeover bid created a more immediate problem: Mercantile National Bank was forced to shut down. The two brokerage firms that handled Heinze's accounts and abetted his failed takeover, Gross & Kleeberg and Otto C. Heinze & Company, also closed their doors.

The declining stock prices spelled trouble for many other financial institutions, especially the trusts. While commercial banks usually kept 25 percent of deposit liabilities in reserve funds, the trusts adhered to no such standards. Moreover, in an effort to attract deposits, the trusts often paid out dangerously high interest rates. And since they loaned out money against the value of securities on deposit, the sharply declining stock prices meant they had less and less collateral to back the loans. Aware that trust companies were woefully short of cash, depositors became concerned about the safety of their funds. Although Morgan was worried about the rumors of troubled trusts, he remained in Richmond. His stature was such that a hasty return to New York might spark a greater panic. "We felt it would be a mistake for him to show any anxiety over the situation and that he should come home at the time he had originally appointed," recalled his aide George Perkins.

SATURDAY, OCTOBER 19: MORGAN TAKES ACTION

The confusion in New York stemmed in part from the fact that there was no agency—corporate or government—to provide a set of safeguards for the financial markets. Ever since Andrew Jackson closed the Bank of the United States in the 1830s, the country had lacked a central bank to regulate the money supply and watch over the banks' affairs. During periodic bank crises, notably in 1873 and in the 1890s, there had been calls for greater federal involvement. But in each instance voices quieted when the banks and other financial institutions recovered. While each state maintained a set of laws that governed banking, no government agency—federal, state, or local—was empowered to conduct a bailout should several institutions fail at once. And no government official had the moral authority or fiscal muscle to muster support from captains of financial industry.

By the weekend, the situation became so severe that Morgan needed to act. The crisis he faced was twofold. As *The Wall Street Journal* put it on Monday, October 21, when stocks fell to their lowest levels since 1903, "It may be said that in addition to more money we need more confidence." So, Morgan changed his mind: "They are in trouble in New York: they do not know what to do, and I don't know what to do, but I am going back," he told Bishop Lawrence. He had long been a corporate arbiter who once ironed out bitter disagreements by collecting rival railroad executives aboard his 165-foot yacht, the *Corsair*, and keeping them captive until they reached an agreement. At root, he was a relentless seeker of order; a banker, not a speculator. So Morgan rushed back to Manhattan to take center stage in a drama that would unfold in several acts.

Upon his arrival from Virginia, he immediately summoned James Stillman of National City Bank and George F. Baker of First National Bank to a room in his library that was draped in red brocade from Rome's Chigi Palace. Later, the troika would be joined by the Morgan partner George Perkins and two young financial experts, Benjamin Strong and Thomas Lamont of Bankers Trust. In addition, John D. Rockefeller, the railroad executive Edward Harriman, and the financier Jacob Schiff immediately put themselves at Morgan's disposal. Morgan was not only the star of this hastily produced drama; he was the director. As George B. Cortelyou, the Secretary of the U.S. Treasury, later said: "By the consensus of opinion, he was regarded as the leading spirit, I think, among the businessmen who joined themselves together to try to meet the emergency. . . . He was generally looked to for guidance and leadership."

After all, Morgan had played similar roles at least twice before, stepping in when government failed to act when in fiscal distress. In 1877 Congress adjourned without appropriating money to pay soldiers. Morgan offered to front the $550,000-a-month payroll and set up a disbursement system. Morgan came to the government's rescue again in 1895 when the U.S. gold reserves fell dangerously low. At the time, he traveled to Washington in a private railroad car and announced: "I have come down to see the President, and I am going to stay here until I see him." The banker met with President Grover Cleveland the next day. Soon after, Morgan arranged to secure $50 million in gold from Europe in a private-bond sale, thus saving the Treasury from insolvency. In the fall of 1907, it was clear that Morgan had to step in again. Highlighting the federal government's fecklessness, as the fiscal crisis came to a head Congress stood in recess, and President Roosevelt was off hunting bear and deer in the wilds of Louisiana. Meanwhile, "bears" were roaming freely and safely on Wall Street.

MONDAY, OCTOBER 21: RUNS ON TRUSTS CAUSE CHAOS

Unlike the two crises Morgan had resolved previously, the current situation defied a simple solution. Charles T. Barney, a prominent financier who ran the formidable Knickerbocker Trust Company, had been involved with Heinze and the failed Mercantile National Bank. Concerned that the Knickerbocker would follow the Mercantile into insolvency, frantic depositors, armed with empty bags and valises, lined up at the Knickerbocker's lavish main office on Fifth Avenue and 34th Street on Monday morning in an attempt to retrieve some of the $60 million on deposit. "The greater part of the crowd apparently was made up of men of small capital, clerks and representatives of firms in the district," the New York Times noted.

As they waited, Morgan, whose own firm also had money deposited at Knickerbocker, was deciding whether these depositors would be made whole. In the latter years of his career, the powerful banker had often been referred to joshingly as Jupiter. But now he truly wielded the power of life or death over troubled trust companies like Knickerbocker. In a marathon session, Morgan heard urgent pleas from Knickerbocker officials. Although Barney knew Morgan personally, and Morgan was in fact a Knickerbocker shareholder, the ad hoc rescue committee, in one of its first moves, deemed the Knickerbocker beyond salvage. "I can't go on being everybody's goat," Morgan said. "I've got to stop somewhere." So at 12:30 P.M. on Tuesday, after giving out $8 million to depositors, the Knickerbocker folded.

WEDNESDAY, OCTOBER 23: MORGAN STOPS THE BLEEDING

As he left the office that afternoon, Morgan tried to offer some reassurance to the jittery public. "We are doing everything we can, as fast as we can, but nothing has yet crystallized," he said. Nonetheless on Wednesday, October 23, the Trust Company of America, which held a large chunk of the Knickerbocker's stock, was hit by a similar run. Just after 9 A.M., a crowd of more than a thousand depositors fidgeted outside the bank's Wall Street area offices. The financial district's sidewalks and streets became clogged with people. Early that morning, the Trust's president, Oakleigh Thorne, tried to calm the throng: "We have plenty of cash on hand and are facing the situation calmly." But the public wasn't reassured, especially when high-profile individuals began to panic. Thomas McAvoy, the leader of Tammany Hall, performed a highly public flip-flop. A few days earlier he had deposited several thousand dollars in the Trust Company. At 11 A.M. he assured friends that he had "every faith in the institution." But, as the New York Times reported, "Later, however, Mr. McAvoy changed his mind and got into line."

Around noon Oakleigh Thorne waded through the crowds to Morgan's office at 23 Wall Street, begging for a $2.5-million cash injection to stay afloat. Morgan was faced with a dilemma. He disliked the trusts, believing them to be inherently unstable. When talking about trust company relief, he said: "Why should I get into this? My affairs are all in order." But his grudging sense of public-mindedness ultimately won out. He realized that continuing failures like Knickerbocker would not only wipe out large and small depositors, but would trigger runs on banks and generally sap confidence and funds from the healthy few that remained on firm footing.

Morgan ordered Thorne to round up collateral. As Strong recalled: "Mr. Morgan had a pad in front of him making figures as we went along, and when he was satisfied that collateral had been delivered adequate for an advance, he would ask Mr. Stillman to telephone over to the

National City Bank to send over currency for the amount determined upon." After reviewing the situation, he ultimately found the Trust Company of America worthy of salvation. "This, then, is the place to stop this trouble," Morgan declared. By 3 P.M., he had sent over enough cash to keep the Trust open. Later in the day, a porter came from Morgan's office holding a large box, followed by men with suitcases containing cash and securities. The rescue effort continued through the night as anxious depositors huddled in line. Under Morgan's direction, a group of banks agreed to establish a $10-million fund to bolster the ailing Trust. The Trust Company of America remained solvent, but suffered a $47.5-million drain in deposits.

The improvised approach stopped the bleeding but didn't provide a long-term solution to trust companies' woes. To make matters worse, the trust company presidents proved unwilling to help one another. So Morgan and his associates quickly deemed it necessary to erect a salvage fund to deal with the ongoing crisis.

With Washington finally awakened to the severity of the problems, Treasury Secretary George Cortelyou came to New York on Tuesday night at Morgan's request. At 12:30 A.M. Morgan paid him a courtesy call, which proved effective. The next day Cortelyou offered government assistance—but only to a limited degree. "The government can offer relief only through the national banks and private financial interests when they are united," he said. On Wednesday, Cortelyou agreed to deposit $25 million of government cash into selected New York City banks, which could use the capital to bolster the troubled trust companies and banks.

THURSDAY, OCTOBER 24: A CREDIT CRUNCH THREATENS THE NYSE

Despite the large injection of public funds, there were fresh runs on banks on Thursday. The Hamilton Bank of New York and two Brooklyn banks closed temporarily. Though the banks were solvent, people believed their deposits safer under a mattress at home than in a vault. The banks and trust companies didn't have on hand the cash they needed to back all deposits, so they began to call existing loans and stopped making new ones, thereby exacerbating the crisis.

The next near-casualty of the credit crunch was the New York Stock Exchange. The exchange's brokers and dealers needed to borrow money on a daily basis to conduct business. The call rate—the rate at which institutions and individuals lend each other money due without notice—usually stood at about 6 percent. And even though desperate borrowers were offering 100 percent, there were no lenders.

Just before noon, NYSE president Ransom H. Thomas crossed the street to 23 Wall Street and told Morgan he didn't have the funds to stay open until the regular closing time of 3 P.M. The Stock Exchange would have to shut down. Morgan realized the impact this would have on the public. *"It must not close one minute before that hour today!"* he declared. The financier quickly summoned the heads of the city's major banks and told them they had to come up with $25 million within ten minutes. A little after two, when it was announced that just under $25 million had been raised, cheers arose from the floor of the Stock Exchange. "The action of J.P. Morgan & Co. in offering $25 million on the stock exchange at 10 percent was one development during the day which indicated that the strongest financial interests in the Street are watching the situation closely and stand ready to render what assistance is necessary to legitimate banking institutions," *The Wall Street Journal* editorialized.

OCTOBER 25–27:
A WEEKEND EFFORT TO BOOST PUBLIC CONFIDENCE

Throughout the week, Morgan shuttled between his Wall Street office and his library, remaining on call 24 hours a day. "He did not seem to see the throngs in the street, so intent was his mind on the thing that he was doing," the banker Herbert Satterlee wrote. "He simply barged along, as if he had been the only man going down the Nassau Street hill past the Subtreasury. He was the embodiment of power and purpose."

As the leader of the rescue effort, Morgan's every move was watched, his every utterance written down. He had generally found the notion of public relations completely alien. "Pierpontifex Maximus," as a churchman accurately dubbed him, carried 200 pounds on his beefy six-foot frame. Balding, sporting a bushy walrus mustache, a famously large nose, the man had become a ripe target for cartoonists. Comments like "I owe the public nothing" did not make him a more sympathetic figure.

Under the circumstances, however, Morgan was forced to assume a more public role. On Thursday afternoon, October 24, he attempted to reassure the public. "If people will keep their money in the banks, everything will be all right," he said. Over the weekend, clergymen were asked to pound this message into their congregations. On Saturday, Rabbi Joseph Silverman of Temple Emanu-El on Fifth Avenue called for optimism, urging people to brush aside greed and not hoard their funds. On Sunday, Archbishop Farley held a special mass for businessmen at St. Raphael's Catholic Church. "I have confidence in the solvency of the banks," he proclaimed. But on Sunday night, some 118 people waited with umbrellas in the rain outside the Lincoln Trust Company, at Fifth Avenue near 25th Street, anxious to withdraw their money.

OCTOBER 28–29:
MORGAN AVERTS A NEW YORK CITY BANKRUPTCY

On Monday, October 28, a new crisis arose. New York City found itself in need of $30 million to pay salaries of teachers and other employees, and to meet general obligations. The city regularly issued revenue bonds to pay its bills. But given the circumstances in the marketplace and the general shortage of cash, the city couldn't borrow. Rather than turn to the state or the federal government, it turned to the *de facto* authority: Morgan. Mayor George B. McClellan and other officials visited the library and told him the city faced the prospect of default.

If the nation's largest city were to go bankrupt, it would have sent a horribly negative message to the markets and the nation. Morgan responded immediately. On Tuesday, October 29, he organized a syndicate of banks to buy for cash $30 million of the city's 6 percent revenue bonds, with an option to purchase an additional $20 million. Then Morgan had the banks hand their bonds over to a clearing house that issued $30–million worth of certificates backed by the bonds. Those certificates were immediately added to the accounts maintained by the city at National City and First National banks. With these funds, New York met its most pressing financial needs.

NOVEMBER 1-4: MORGAN ORGANIZES A TRUST BAILOUT FUND

By Wednesday and Thursday, the panic seemed to have subsided. And although the second weekend presented another problem for Morgan, it also provided an opportunity. Despite the aid given to the Trust Company of America and a few other smaller trusts, many of the poorly capitalized institutions still teetered on the edge. Morgan and his colleagues decided that the solvent trust companies should create a fund to help save ailing trusts. Over the weekend, trust company presidents gathered in the library's West Room while bankers and other Morgan advisers held all-night sessions in the lavishly appointed East Room. "A more incongruous meeting place for anxious bankers could hardly be imagined," the Morgan partner Thomas Lamont wrote. In this climactic finale, Morgan bludgeoned the trust company presidents into subscribing to a $25-million loan for the trusts. At 4:45 A.M. on Monday,

AN OPPORTUNITY AMID CRISIS

During the panic Morgan refused to take a commission on the New York City loan, and did not generally profit from the crisis. But being Morgan, he did not miss a good opportunity that came his way during the second weekend. Moore & Schley, a brokerage house, was virtually insolvent. Among its most worthy assets were 157,000 shares that represented a controlling interest in the Tennessee Coal, Iron & Railroad Company (TCI), one of the few remaining competitors of Morgan's mammoth U.S. Steel.

If Moore & Schley were to dump the stock *en masse* to raise cash, the move would have triggered a fresh banking crisis. So Morgan came up with a plan under which the U.S. Steel Corporation would acquire the shares at a heavy discount with its own highly rated gold-backed bonds.

Since such a transaction would plainly violate antitrust laws, Morgan quickly dispatched two of his lieutenants to seek Roosevelt's approval. On the night of Sunday, November 3, the industrialist Henry Frick and U.S. Steel's Elbert H. Gary went to Washington. Faced with the prospect of fresh financial trauma, the president agreed to endorse the transaction. On Monday, the White House gave its word that it would take no action against the acquisition. "The action was emphatically for the general good," the great trustbuster later said. The financial analyst John Moody later calculated the TCI shares, which Morgan acquired for a total of $50 million, to be worth about $1 billion. However, this favorable outcome didn't change Morgan's general opinion of Roosevelt. When the president went on one of his legendary safaris to Africa in 1909, the banker said: "I hope the first lion he meets does his duty."

November 4, the exhausted bankers caved in and signed on the dotted line. "There's the place, King," Morgan said to Edward King, nominal head of the trust presidents. "And here's the pen."

In those tense final hours, Morgan also engaged in maneuvers that would bring direct benefits to a firm he helped control. When orchestrating a bailout of Moore & Schley, a troubled brokerage house, Morgan arranged for U.S. Steel to buy one of Moore & Schley's main assets: a large block of shares in the Tennessee Coal & Iron Company.

WEDNESDAY, NOVEMBER 6: THE CRISIS SUBSIDES

On Wednesday, the market registered its first gain, effectively ending the panic. The same day, the federal government agreed to issue new debt in the form of low-interest bonds and to spread the proceeds throughout banks. Lines at trust companies started to move more quickly. Gold, which had been ordered from Europe at the height of the crisis, began to arrive. Seven–million dollars' worth had already docked, and the *Lusitania* had just arrived with $10 million more.

The drama ended, and rave reviews began to roll in. "MORGAN CLEARS UP THE WHOLE TRUST SITUATION," one headline blared. *The Wall Street Journal* fairly gushed: "Nothing in Wall Street history has been more important or dramatic than the day and night conference in Mr. Morgan's library of the leading financiers of Wall Street. . . . He has been distinctly the man of the hour, the undisputed leader who has stood between the business of the country and disaster."

AN ERA ENDS AS MORGAN RETIRES

Morgan retired after the panic, but his example proved an impetus to broader action. Politicians and bankers alike realized the government needed to take a stronger role in keeping the financial system together. "Something has got to be done," said Senator Nelson W. Aldrich. "We may not always have Pierpont Morgan with us to meet a banking crisis."

The end result was the Aldrich-Vreeland Currency Act, passed by Congress in May 1908. The measure was intended to guard against future money shortages by letting national banks issue notes secured by non-federal bonds at the direction of the treasury secretary. The legislation also created a National Monetary Commission, with Aldrich at its head, to make further recommendations on federal monetary policy to Congress. This process ultimately culminated in the Federal Reserve Act in 1913, which created the twelve-unit Federal Reserve System under the leadership of the Federal Reserve Board. By monitoring the nation's monetary supply and insuring the availability of capital to banks, the Federal Reserve now affords the security that in 1907 only Morgan could provide.

While J.P. Morgan & Company executives had extensive influence over the legislative process, Morgan didn't live to see the passage of the Federal Reserve Act. In the middle of February 1913, Morgan took sick in Egypt, traveled to Rome, and checked into the Grand Hotel, where he died on March 31, at the age of seventy-five. Morgan left an estate valued at $68.3 million, 44 percent of which represented his interest in the House of Morgan. The rest consisted of holdings in an astonishing number of corporations, including the National Bank of Commerce, several railroad systems, and industrial conglomerates like International Mercantile Marine Company, which built the *Titanic*. His son, John Pierpont Morgan Jr., took over the family firm, and remained chairman of J.P. Morgan & Company until his death in 1943. But he was hardly the leader his father had been. As *The Wall Street Journal* wrote on April 1, 1913: "There will be no successor to Morgan."

Henry Ford atop his creation, the Model-T, in 1896.

HENRY FORD AND THE MODEL T

On May 26, 1927, Henry Ford watched the fifteen millionth Model T Ford roll off the assembly line at his factory in Highland Park, Michigan. Since his "universal car" was the industrial success story of its age, the ceremony should have been a happy occasion. Yet Ford was probably wistful that day, too, knowing as he did that the long production life of the Model T was about to come to an end. He climbed into the car, a shiny black coupe, with his son, Edsel, the president of the Ford Motor Company. Together, they drove to the Dearborn Engineering Laboratory, fourteen miles away, and parked the T next to two other historic vehicles: the first automobile that Henry Ford built in 1896, and the 1908 prototype for the Model T. Henry himself took each vehicle for a short spin: the nation's richest man driving the humble car that had made him the embodiment of the American dream.

Henry Ford invented neither the automobile nor the assembly line, but recast each to dominate a new era. Indeed, no other individual in this century so completely transformed the nation's way of life. By improving the assembly line so that the Model T could be produced ever more inexpensively, Ford placed the power of the internal combustion engine within reach of the average citizen. He transformed the automobile itself from a luxury to a necessity.

The advent of the Model T seemed to renew a sense of independence among Americans who had lost their pioneer spirit to industrialization. Yet the methods that Henry Ford devised for producing his car so efficiently advanced that very industrialization. Like its inventor, the Model T represented both high ideals and hard practicalities.

A TINKERER IN AN EMERGING INDUSTRY

By rights, Henry Ford probably should have been a farmer. He was born in 1863 in Dearborn, Michigan, on the farm operated by his father, an Irishman, and his mother, who was from Dutch stock. Even as a boy, young Henry had an aptitude for inventing and used it to make machines that reduced the drudgery of his farm chores. At the age of thirteen, he saw a coal-fired steam engine lumbering along a long rural road, a sight that galvanized his fascination with machines. At sixteen, against the wishes of his father, he left the farm for Detroit, where he found work as a mechanic's apprentice. Over the next dozen years, he advanced steadily, and became chief engineer at the Edison Illuminating Company. At twenty-four, Ford married Clara Bryant, a friend of his sister's; he called her "The Believer," because she encouraged his plans to build a horseless carriage from their earliest days together. For as Henry Ford oversaw the steam engines and turbines that produced electricity for Detroit Edison, inventors in the U.S. and Europe were adapting such engines to small passenger vehicles. On January 29, 1886, Karl Benz received a patent for a crude gas-fueled car, which he demonstrated later that year on the streets of Mannhelm, Germany. And in 1893, Charles and Frank Duryea, of Springfield, Massachusetts, built the first gas-operated vehicle in the U.S.

In the 1890s, any mechanic with tools, a workbench, and a healthy imagination was a potential titan in the infant industry. Even while continuing his career at Edison, Ford devoted himself to making a working automobile. In 1891, he presented Clara with a design for an internal combustion engine, drawn on the back of a piece of sheet music. Bringing the design to reality was another matter, but on Christmas Eve 1893 he made a successful test of one of his engines, in the kitchen sink.

The engine was merely the heart of the new machine that Ford hoped to build. On weekends and most nights, he could be found in a shed in the back of the family home, building the rest of the car. So great was his obsession that the neighbors called him Crazy Henry. However, at 2:00 A.M. on June 4, 1896, Crazy Henry punched a large hole in the wall of his shed, and emerged at the wheel of an automobile— *his* automobile. In the weeks that followed, Ford was often seen driving around the streets of Detroit.

Later that year, Ford attended a national meeting of Edison employees. Thomas A. Edison had been Ford's idol for years. But at the meeting, it was Edison who asked to meet the young inventor, after word got around that the obscure engineer from Detroit had actually built an automobile. "Young man, you have the right idea," Edison said. "Keep right at it." Ironically, he was most adamant that Ford not waste his time trying to make a car run viably on electricity.

Back in Detroit, Ford showed that he was no mere hobbyist: he sold his prototype for $200. For three years, he watched the new field of automaking develop, and he progressed along with it. In 1899, thirty American manufacturers—most of them based in New England—produced about 2,500 cars. Still, most Americans in the market for automobiles became accustomed to buying imported ones. In 1898, though, the domestic bicycle industry faced an unusual slump and many manufacturers decided to turn to automaking to keep the factories busy.

Offered a senior position and part ownership of a new company, the Detroit Automobile Co., Ford, thirty-six years-old, quit the Edison Illuminating Company. Across town, the firm that would become Oldsmobile was launched at the same time. The Detroit Automobile Co. failed, without producing any cars, and Henry Ford was ousted by angry investors. (The firm survived, emerging from reorganization as the Cadillac Motor Car Company.)

BUILDING A MOTORCAR FOR THE GREAT MULTITUDE

Ford continued to pursue his dream. Early automobile promotion took place largely on the racetrack, where manufacturers sought to prove roadworthiness by putting their cars on public view and pressing them to their very limits. In 1901, Henry Ford poured his expertise into a pair of big race cars, one of which he entered in a ten-mile match race against a car built by Alexander Winton, a leading automaker from Ohio. The race took place in Grosse Pointe, Michigan, and Ford's car won. Because of the victory, the coal merchant Alexander Malcomson agreed to back Ford in a new business venture. In 1903, they formed the Ford Motor Company, in association with about a dozen other investors. Capitalized at $100,000, the company actually started with cash on hand of about $28,000. Some investors contributed other types of capital; for example, the Dodge brothers, John and Horace, agreed to supply engines.

The company purchased most of the major components for its new models, a common practice of the day. Teams of mechanics built cars individually at workstations, gathering parts as needed until a car was complete. In 1903, Ford's 125 workers made 1,700 cars in three different models. The cars were comparatively expensive, and their high profit-margins pleased the stockholders. Malcomson decided to start yet another automobile company. But when it failed, he was forced to sell his other assets, including his shares in Ford. Henry Ford bought enough of them to assume a majority position. The most important stockholder outside of the Ford family was James Couzens, Malcomson's former clerk; as General Manager, then vice president and secretary-treasurer at the Ford Motor Company, he was effectively second-in-command throughout many of the Model T years.

The direction of the company toward even pricier models had bothered Henry Ford. He used his new power to curtail their production, a move that coincided with the Panic of 1907. This case of accidental good timing probably saved the company. Ford, insisting that high prices ultimately slowed market expansion, had decided in 1906 to introduce a new, cheaper model with a lower profit margin: the Model N. Many of his backers disagreed. While the N was only a tepid success, Ford nonetheless pressed forward with the design of the car he really wanted to build. The car that would be the Model T.

"I will build a motorcar for the great multitude," he proclaimed. Such a notion was revolutionary. Until then the automobile had been a status symbol painstakingly manufactured by craftsmen. But Ford set out to make the car a commodity. "Just like one pin is like another pin when it comes from the pin factory, or one match is like another match when it comes from the match factory," he said. This was but the first of several counterintuitive moves that Ford made throughout his unpredictable career. Prickly, brilliant, willfully eccentric, he relied more on instinct than business plans. As the eminent economist John Kenneth Galbraith later said: "If there is any certainty as to what a businessman is, he is assuredly the things Ford was not."

In the winter of 1906, Ford had secretly partitioned a twelve-by fifteen-foot room in his plant, on Piquette Avenue in Detroit. With a few colleagues, he devoted two years to the design and planning of the Model T. Early on, they made an extensive study of materials, the most valuable aspect of which began in an offhand way. During a car race in Florida, Ford examined the wreckage of a French car and noticed that many of its parts were of lighter-than-ordinary steel. The team on Piquette Avenue ascertained that the French steel was a vanadium alloy, but that no one in America knew how to make it. The finest steel alloys then used in American automaking provided 60,000 pounds of tensile strength. Ford learned that vanadium steel, which was much lighter, provided 170,000 pounds of tensile strength. As part of the pre-production for the new model, Ford imported a metallurgist and bankrolled a steel mill. As a result, the only cars in the world to utilize vanadium steel in the next five years would be French luxury cars and the Ford Model T. A Model T might break *down* every so often, but it would not break.

The car that finally emerged from Ford's secret design section at the factory would change America forever. For $825, a Model T customer could take home a car that was light, at about 1,200 pounds; relatively powerful, with a four-cylinder, twenty horsepower engine, and fairly easy to drive, with a two-speed, foot-controlled "planetary" transmission. Simple, sturdy, and versatile, the little car would excite the public imagination. It certainly fired up its inventor: when Henry Ford brought the prototype out of the factory for its first test drive, he was too excited to drive. An assistant had to take the wheel.

"Well, I guess we've got started," Ford observed at the time. The car went to the first customers on October 1, 1908. In its first year, over ten thousand were sold, a new record for an automobile model. Sales of the "Tin Lizzie," or "flivver," as the T was known, were boosted by promotional activities ranging from a black-tie "Ford Clinic" in New York, where a team of mechanics showcased the car, to Model T rodeos out west, in which cowboys riding in Fords tried to rope calves. In 1909, mining magnate Robert Guggenheim sponsored an auto race from New York to Seattle in which the only survivors were two Model T Fords.

"I believe Mr. Ford has the solution of the popular automobile," Guggenheim concluded.

In the early years, Model Ts were produced at Piquette Avenue in much the same way that all other cars were built. Growing demand for the new Ford overwhelmed the old method, though. Ford realized that he not only had to build a new factory, but a new system within that factory.

Throughout his tenure as the head of the company, Henry Ford believed in maintaining enormous cash reserves, a policy that allowed him to plan a new facility for production of the Model T without interference or outside pressure. The new Highland Park factory, which opened in 1910, was designed by the nation's leading industrial architect, Albert Kahn. It was unparalleled in scale, sprawling over sixty-two acres. John D. Rockefeller, whose Standard Oil refineries had always represented state-of-the-art design, called Highland Park "the industrial miracle of the age."

In its first few years, the four-story Highland Park factory was organized from top to bottom. Assembly wound downward, from the fourth floor, where body panels were hammered out, to the third floor, where workers placed tires on wheels and painted auto bodies. After assembly was completed on the second floor, new automobiles descended a final ramp past the first-floor offices. Production increased by approximately 100 percent in each of the first three years, from 19,000 in 1910, to 34,500 in 1911, to a staggering 78,440 in 1912. It was still only a start.

"I'm going to democratize the automobile," Henry Ford had said in 1909. "When I'm through, everybody will be able to afford one, and about everybody will have one." The means to this end was a continuous reduction in price. When it sold for $575 in 1912, the Model T for the first time cost less than the prevailing average annual wage in the United States. Ignoring conventional wisdom, Ford continually sacrificed profit margins to increase sales. In fact, profits per car did fall as he slashed prices from $220 in 1909 to $99 in 1914. But sales exploded, rising to 248,000 in 1913. Moreover, Ford demonstrated that a strategic, systematic lowering of prices could boost profits, as net income rose from $3 million in 1909 to $25 million in 1914. As Ford's U.S. market share rose from a respectable 9.4 percent in 1908 to a formidable 48 percent in 1914, the Model T dominated the world's leading market.

At Highland Park, Ford began to implement factory automation in 1910. But experimentation would continue every single day for the next seventeen years, under one of Ford's maxims: "Everything can always be done better than it is being done." Ford and his efficiency experts examined every aspect of assembly and tested new methods to increase productivity. The boss himself claimed to have found the inspiration for the greatest breakthrough of all, the moving assembly line, on a trip to Chicago: "The idea came in a general way from the overhead trolley that the Chicago packers use in dressing beef," Ford said. At the stockyards, butchers removed certain cuts as each carcass passed by, until nothing was left. Ford reversed the process. His use of the moving assembly line was complicated by the fact that parts, often made on subassembly lines, had to feed smoothly into the process. Timing was crucial: a clog along a smaller line would slow work farther along. The first moving line was tested with assembly of the flywheel magneto, showing a saving of six minutes, fifty seconds over the old method. As similar lines were implemented throughout Highland Park, the assembly time for a Model T chassis dropped from twelve hours, thirty minutes to five hours, fifty minutes.

The pace only accelerated, as Ford's production engineers experimented with work slides, rollways, conveyor belts, and hundreds of other ideas. The first and most effective assembly line in the automobile industry was continually upgraded. Those most affected were, of course, the workers. As early as January 1914, Ford developed an "endless chaindriven" conveyor to move the chassis from one workstation to another; workers remained stationary. Three months later, the company created a "man high" line—with all the parts and belts at waist level, so that workers could repeat their assigned tasks without having to move their feet.

In 1914, 13,000 workers at Ford made 260,720 cars. By comparison, in the rest of the industry, it took 66,350 workers to make 286,770. Critics charged that the division of the assembly process into mindless, repetitive tasks turned most of Ford's employees into unthinking automatons, and that manipulation of the pace of the line was tantamount to slave driving by remote control. The men who made cars no longer had to be mechanically inclined, as in the earlier days; they were just day laborers. Ford chose to see the bigger picture of the employment he offered. "I have heard it said, in fact, I believe it's quite a current thought, that we have taken skill out of work," he said. "We have not. We have put a higher skill into planning, management, and tool building, and the results of that skill are enjoyed by the man who is not skilled."

But the unskilled workers, many of them foreign born, didn't enjoy their work, earning a mediocre $2.38 for a nine-hour day. Indeed, the simplification of the jobs created a treacherous backlash: high turnover. Over the course of 1913, the company had to hire 963 workers for every 100 it needed to maintain on the payroll. To keep a workforce of 13,600 employees in the factory, Ford continually spent money on short-term training. Even though the company introduced a program of bonuses and generous benefits, including a medical clinic, athletic fields, and playgrounds for the families of workers, the problem persisted. The rest of the industry reluctantly accepted high turnover as part of the assembly-line system and passed the increasing labor costs into the prices of their cars. Henry Ford, however, did not want anything in the price of a Model T except good value. His solution was a bold stroke that reverberated through the entire nation.

On January 5, 1914, Henry Ford announced a new minimum wage of five dollars per eight-hour day, in addition to a profit-sharing plan. It was the talk of towns across the country; Ford was hailed as the friend of the worker, as an outright socialist, or as a madman bent on bankrupting his company. Many businessmen—including most of the remaining stockholders in the Ford Motor Company—regarded his solution as reckless. But he shrugged off all the criticism: "Well, you know when you pay men well you can talk to them," he said. Recognizing the human element in mass production, Ford knew that retaining more employees would lower costs, and that a happier workforce would inevitably lead to greater productivity. The numbers bore him out. Between 1914 and 1916, the company's profits doubled from $30 million to $60 million. "The payment of five dollars a day for an eight-hour day was one of the finest cost-cutting moves we ever made," he later said.

There were other ramifications, as well. A budding effort to unionize the Ford factory dissolved in the face of the Five-Dollar Day. Most cunning of all, Ford's new wage scale turned autoworkers into auto customers. The purchases they made returned at least some of those five dollars to Henry Ford, and helped raise production, which invariably helped to lower per-car costs.

The central role that the Model T had come to play in America's cultural, social and economic life elevated Henry Ford into a full-fledged folk hero. But Ford wasn't satisfied. Fancying himself a political pundit and all-around sage, he allowed himself to be drawn into national and even world affairs. Before the United States entered World War I, he despaired with many others over the horrors of the fighting; late in 1915, he chartered a "Peace Ship" and sailed with a private delegation of radicals for France in a naive attempt to end the war. In 1918, he lost a campaign for a U.S. Senate seat. The following year, he purchased a newspaper, the *Dearborn Independent*, which was to become the vehicle for his notorious anti-Semitism. The newspaper railed against the International Jew, and reported scurrilous conspiracy theories such as *The Protocols of the Elders of Zion*.

In 1915, James Couzens resigned from the Ford Motor Company, recognizing that it was Henry's company, and that no one else's opinion would ever matter as much. In 1916, Ford antagonized the other shareholders by declaring a paltry dividend, even in the face of record profits. In response, the shareholders sued, and in 1919 the Michigan Supreme Court upheld a lower court ruling that it was unreasonable to withhold fair dividends under the circumstances. The Ford Motor Company was forced to distribute $19 million in dividend payments. In his own response to the escalating feud, Henry threatened publicly to leave the company and form a new one. He even made plans and discussed the next car he would produce.

Fearing that the worth of Ford stock would plummet, the minority shareholders suddenly became eager to sell; agents working surreptitiously for Henry Ford quietly bought up lot after lot of shares. The sellers did not receive all that the shares were worth, because of the rumors, but they each emerged with a fortune. James Couzens, the most wily of the lot, received the highest price per share, and turned to a career in the U.S. Senate (he won his race, unlike the old boss) with $30 million in the bank. Ford gained complete control of the company at a cost of $125 million—$106 million of the stock, plus $19 million for the court-ordered dividend—a fantastic outlay that he financed with a $75 million loan from two eastern banks. On July 11, 1919, when he signed the last stock transfer agreement, the fifty-five-year-old mogul was so enthused that he danced a jig. The stock was divided up and placed in the names of Henry, Clara, and Edsel Ford.

In 1921, the Model T Ford held 60 percent of the new-car market. Plants around the world turned out flivvers as though they were subway tokens, and Henry Ford's only problem, as he often stated it, was figuring out how to make enough of them. As a concession to diversification, he purchased the Lincoln Motor Car Company in 1921. Company plans seemed to be in place for a long, predictable future and Ford was free to embark on a great new project: the design and construction of the world's largest and most efficient automobile factory at River Rouge, near Detroit. Arrayed over 2,000 acres, it would include 90 miles of railroad track and enough space for 75,000 employees to produce finished cars from raw material in the span of just forty-one hours. River Rouge had its own power plant, iron forges, and fabricating facilities. No detail was overlooked: wastepaper would be recycled into cardboard at the factory's own paper mill. River Rouge was built to produce Model T

Fords for decades to come, but by the time it was capable of full production later in the decade, a factory a tenth its size could have handled the demand for Model Ts.

THE MODEL T'S RIDE COMES TO AN END

On June 4, 1924, the ten millionth Model T Ford left the Highland Park factory, which would remain the main facility for T production. While the flivver outsold its nearest competitor by a six-to-one margin that year, its unbridled run was nearing an unforeseen conclusion. After years of conceding the low end of the market to Ford, another automaker was setting its sights on that very sector.

At the beginning of the decade, General Motors was an awkward conglomerate of car companies and parts suppliers, managed more for the sake of its whipsaw stock-price than for efficiencies in automaking. In the middle of the decade, though, a revitalized GM, under the brilliant leadership of Alfred P. Sloan, Jr., began to offer inexpensive Chevrolets with amenities that the Model T lacked. Instead of a herky-jerky crank start, a Chevy had an electric starter. Instead of the sturdy but antiquated planetary transmission, it had a smooth three-speed. The market began to shift; price and value ceased to be paramount factors. Styling and excitement suddenly counted to the customer. Even though the Model T cost a mere $290 in the mid-twenties, dealers clamored for a new Ford that would strike the fancy of the more demanding and sophisticated consumers.

But Henry Ford refused even to consider replacing his beloved Model T. Once, while he was away on vacation, employees built an updated Model T and surprised him with it on his return. Ford responded by kicking in the windshield and stomping on the roof. "We got the message," one of the employees said later, "As far as he was concerned, the Model T was god and we were to put away false images." Only one person persisted in warning him of the impending crisis: his son, Edsel, who had been installed as president of the Ford Motor Company during

AN EPIC LEGAL BATTLE

In 1879, a Rochester lawyer named George Selden applied for a U.S. patent for a road vehicle powered by a gasoline engine. Through his own delays and those of the government, however, a funny thing happened. Selden, who never built an actual automobile, received the patent on it in 1895, long after other people *were* building automobiles. In return for a percent of future revenues, Selden assigned the valuable patent to a group of New York financiers in 1897, and they defended it vigorously. In the first years of the century, they settled on a process by which automakers joined the Association of Licensed Automotive Manufacturers (ALAM), which served as a conduit for licensing fees of 1¼ percent on annual sales. Most of the country's automakers seemed reconciled to joining ALAM.

Even Henry Ford tried to join, in 1903, but the ALAM overstepped its bounds when it tried to dictate to him the price at which he could sell his cars. Ford refused to listen, refused to join the club, and certainly refused to pay the royalty. The ALAM brought suit. Even before the case was heard in court, the two sides battled each other through full-page newspaper advertisements. Ford's ads took the unusual step of offering to indemnify both buyers and sellers of his cars from any lawsuits claiming Selden patent infringement. (Only fifty customers were worried enough to accept the offer.)

In 1909, six years after the lawsuit started, it was finally heard by a federal judge in New York, who ruled that the patent was valid. Ford's entire enterprise seemed to be in danger, but he was defiant nonetheless. In 1911, the Court of Appeals overturned the decision, validating Selden's patent, but deeming it applicable only to vehicles substantially copied from the rickety contraption he had sketched back in 1879! The ruling not only freed Ford from the tyranny of the Selden patent, it freed all of America's other automakers, as well. Henry Ford had spent a great deal of money in legal fees, but he got his money's worth. As he said, "Probably nothing so well advertised the Ford car and the Ford Motor Company as did this suit."

the dividend trial and its aftermath in 1919. It was the first of many arguments that Edsel would lose, as the once adoring relationship between the two deteriorated into distrust and disrespect on Henry's part and woeful disillusionment on Edsel's.

The Chevrolet continued to take sales from the dour Model T. By 1926, T sales had plummeted, and the realities of the marketplace finally convinced Henry Ford that the end was at hand. On May 25, 1927, Ford abruptly announced the end of production for the Model T, and soon after closed the Highland Park factory for six months. The shutdown was not for retooling: there was no new model in the works. In history's worst case of product planning, Henry sent the workers home so that he could *start* to design his next model. Fortunately, Edsel had been quietly marshaling sketches from the company's designers, and he was ready and able to work closely with his father on producing plans for the new car, called the Model A. It was a success from its launch in December 1927, and placed the company on sound footing again. By the time it went into production, the River Rouge had become the main Ford manufacturing facility.

When the last Model T rolled off the assembly line, it was not the end of an era, it was still the very dawn of the one that the little car had inaugurated. Cars—more than half of them Model Ts—pervaded American culture. They jammed the streets of the great eastern cities and roamed newly laid roads in southern California. Adapted to haul everything from mail to machine guns to coffins to schoolchildren, automobiles represented an opportunity for change in practically everything. They also became a crucial factor in recasting a growing economy. Henry Ford had created a car for the multitudes and that car had created the basis of the car culture embraced by every subsequent generation.

The Ford Motor Company, having survived its own crisis in the twenties, was one of only forty-four U.S. automakers left in 1929, out of the hundreds that had entered the fray since the beginning of the century. That year, Ford, General Motors, and the newly formed

Chrysler Corporation—known then and now as the Big Three—accounted for 80 percent of the market.

Henry Ford died on April 7, 1947, at the age of eighty-three, having outlived the Model T by nearly twenty years. A century has passed since he took the first car he built for a ride. The world remains in large part the one set into motion by Henry Ford: a world in which cars are for everyone. As Will Rogers said, "It will take a hundred years to tell whether he helped us or hurt us, but he certainly didn't leave us where he found us."

Charles Merrill, co-founder of Merrill Lynch.

CHARLES MERRILL
AND THE DEMOCRATIZATION
OF STOCK OWNERSHIP

I n 1947, when a *Forbes* survey identified the nation's fifty out-standing business leaders, most of them ran large manufacturing concerns, like General Motors and U.S. Steel. Only Charles E. Merrill, a sixty-two-year-old college dropout, made his living on Wall Street. In the early twentieth century, Merrill turned the investment world on its head with the notion of selling stocks and bonds to middle-class retail customers. With Merrill as their champion, securities would become a consumer product that would hold as important a place in America's commercial culture as automobiles and life insurance policies.

After working on Wall Street for several years, Merrill started his own firm in January 1914. Several months later, he was joined by his friend, Edmund Lynch. As he became a specialist in under-writing public offerings for supermarket and department store chains, Merrill considered applying their merchandising methods to his financial products. Sensing an opportunity in the late 1930s, he merged with a large brokerage firm, E. A. Pierce & Co., and became a zealous advocate for the retailing of stocks. As Merrill worked hard to restore the public's shattered trust in the capital markets during the Depression, his firm's large army of account executives developed a populist image, for which they acquired the sobriquets "We the People" and "The Thundering Herd." And through a sustained campaign of public education and advertising, Merrill Lynch strived to fulfill its leader's long-standing goal to "bring Wall Street to Main Street."

Charles Merrill's crusade was validated only in the 1950s, when the New York Stock Exchange supported his efforts, mainly by allowing investors to buy stock on installments. While the investment world wasn't truly democratized until after his death in 1956, Charlie Merrill undeniably started it all. Today, his success can be measured by more than 30 million Americans who own stock through mutual funds, retirement accounts, and pension plans.

A YOUNG MAN FROM FLORIDA GAINS A FOOTHOLD ON WALL STREET

Charles E. Merrill was born in 1885 in the hamlet of Green Cove Springs, outside Jacksonville, Florida. His father, Charles Morton Merrill, was a country doctor who also ran the town's drugstore. Here young Charlie showed an early eye for shrewd merchandising, boosting the shop's milkshake sales by adding grain alcohol and hiking the price.

Merrill headed north for higher education after graduating from high school. But he had to drop out before earning his degree at Amherst College due to temporary family financial difficulties. He tried law school but quit and even played a season of semiprofessional baseball in Mississippi. Another job as a reporter on the West Palm Beach *Tropical Sun* gave him what he would later call "the best training I ever had. . . . [I] learned human nature."

Despite his wanderings, Merrill became engaged to a woman he'd met at Amherst. And when her father offered him a job as a $15-a-week office boy in his textile company, Patchogue-Plymouth Mills, Charles Merrill moved to New York. He arrived in Manhattan as the Panic of 1907 shook the commercial world, but the crisis proved to be an opportunity. With credit scarce in the wake of the panic, company owners were forced to resort to extraordinary measures to survive. In an act of desperation, Merrill's boss sent his twenty-two-year-old aide to try to obtain a loan from National Copper Bank. Displaying the force of personality and salesmanship that would later mark his career, Merrill finagled his way in to see the bank president, and purportedly coaxed from him a $300,000 loan.

"My two years [at Patchogue-Plymouth] turned out to be the equivalent of a university course in general, and credit, finance, cost accounting and administration in particular," he later said. But the job proved short-lived because the young bachelor found he wasn't ready for marriage. He preferred to frequent clubs and hang around the YMCA at 23rd Street where he met Edmund Lynch, a graduate of Johns Hopkins University, who made a living hawking soda fountain equipment. After Merrill broke off his engagement, he found it awkward to work for his ex-fiancée's father, so he took a job as the sole employee in the fledgling bond department of a Wall Street firm, George H. Burr & Company. He soon enlisted his friend Lynch.

It was at Burr & Co. that Merrill first articulated his innovative doctrine of securities marketing. Since Wall Street's typically wealthy clients were largely out of reach of an inexperienced broker without social connections, Merrill decided he would appeal to a different customer base. While Henry Ford was turning the Model T into the first democratic automobile, Merrill figured that bonds and stocks could be marketed as consumer products as well. In an attempt to reel in new prospects, he wrote an article entitled "Mr. Average Investor" in the November 1911 edition of *Leslie's Weekly*. "Having thousands of customers scattered throughout the United States is infinitely preferable to being dependent upon the fluctuating buying power of a smaller and perhaps on the whole wealthier group of investors in any one section," he wrote.

In 1912 the bond dealer became involved in another aspect of Wall Street business that would dictate his future strategy. George Burr wanted to underwrite a chain of stores run by Sebastian Kresge, and assigned his young executive the task of landing the client. Merrill not only won the account and helped Kresge sell $2 million in preferred stock, he also discovered a new retailing phenomenon in the process. Chain stores, groups of outlets owned by a single operator, were proliferating. By providing a wide selection of goods, the stores offered convenience, choice, and value. And within a matter of decades, they would change the way Americans shopped.

MERRILL BECOMES AN EXPERT IN CHAIN-STORE FINANCING

Propelled by a powerful impulse to be his own boss, Merrill set up his own shop at 7 Wall Street in January 1914. Edmund Lynch joined Merrill in July. They signed a co-partnership agreement and the firm's name became Merrill, Lynch & Co. The duo, both with little capital and experience but a lot of gumption, plunged head long into the financial services business. Following on his success with Kresge, Merrill sought and won a contract to underwrite the $6 million offering of a chain store called J. G. McCrory Co. Unfortunately, they were forced to postpone the issue when the Stock Exchange closed temporarily at

the outbreak of World War I. The partners finally brought the oversubscribed issue public in May 1915, and netted Merrill $300,000. The same
year, Merrill Lynch won the right to sell a secondary offering for Kresge.
To handle their growing business, the entrepreneurs hired new staffers,
among them Winthrop Smith, who would prove to be one of Merrill's
most successful acolytes.

While most Wall Street executives viewed the chain store as a
passing fad, Merrill recognized it as the future of American shopping.
"Chain stores were no mystery to the investing public we reached," he
wrote. "Their families frequented them daily and noticed the increasingly
large crowds that flocked to them. Yet [the stores'] securities didn't have
a broad market. I saw an opportunity to render a real public service and
at the same time to make a great deal of money."

Merrill adopted chain store-style marketing for the sale for securities. While he couldn't offer coupons or special sales, he did the next
best thing. In 1917, without the approval of the New York Stock Exchange (NYSE), he created the first advertisements ever run for Liberty
Bonds, offering to sell them "without profit or commission." He used
them as a kind of loss leader. "People who start buying bonds from
motives of patriotism will continue to do so because they are the most
convenient form of safe investment," he wrote, as quoted in Joseph
Nocera's book, A *Piece of the Action*. Although Liberty Bonds disappeared
when World War I ended, this early effort to merchandise securities was
a harbinger of Merrill's future business style.

In the post-war decade, his company specialized in the public sales
of grocery stores, department chain stores, and other retailers. And in
most instances, Charles Merrill exercised the underwriter's prerogative
to retain a large chunk of stock for himself. "If a stock is good enough
to sell, it's good enough to buy," he said. But it was more than a marketing technique. For as the stock appreciated Merrill became wealthy
indeed. And as a major shareholder he had a say in the companies'
development. Merrill even took control of a chain at one point: In 1926
his firm bought Safeway Stores and then arranged for a number of other

grocery companies to join the chain. The new Safeway company would go on to survive brutal competition and remains one of the largest and most successful food retailers.

A PROPHET OF DOOM WEATHERS THE DEPRESSION

As the long-running bull market approached its speculative climax in the late 1920s, Merrill sensed impending disaster. Displaying remarkable foresight, he sent a letter to clients, dated March 31, 1928. Merrill wrote: "Now is the time to get out of debt. Sell enough securities to lighten your obligations or pay them off entirely. . . . We do not urge that you sell securities indiscriminately, but we do advise in no uncertain terms that you take advantage of present high prices and put your own financial house in order." Like most prophets of doom, he was largely ignored. At the end of 1928, Merrill offered retiring President Calvin Coolidge a lucrative partnership in his firm on the condition that Coolidge speak out against rampant speculation. The president declined. Indeed, Merrill's foreboding view diverged so sharply from his colleagues' collective wisdom that he came to doubt his own sanity. But a visit to a psychiatrist cleared up any doubts. The doctor had already taken Merrill's advice and sold his holdings: "Charlie, if you're crazy, then so am I."

Merrill resumed his doomsaying. In 1929 he wrote a letter to Lynch explaining his desire to reduce the firm's exposure. "The financial skies are not clear. I do not like the outlook and I do not like the amount of money we owe," he wrote. "If I am wrong in insisting upon liquidation, then that is a luxury which I can afford and in which you and all of my partners should indulge me. . . ." Merrill's prophecies were vindicated in October 1929. While the Crash bankrupted many stock brokerage firms, Merrill Lynch remained solvent. But Merrill foresaw that a recovery would be a long time coming. In February 1930 he transferred the firm's customer accounts and much of his capital to the brokerage firm E. A. Pierce & Co., which had survived due to an unusually strong capital base.

Disentangled from the wreckage of Wall Street, Merrill weathered the remainder of the Depression looking after his own investments and participating in the management of the chain stores he had helped finance. He picked up the pieces of a company called MacMarr and merged its 1,300 stores into Safeway in 1931. With that, Safeway was larger than every food-store chain except A & P and Kroger. The following year, Merrill founded *Family Circle*, a mass-circulation magazine that was sold at his grocery stores. For all his success in retailing, in the 1930s, however, Wall Street was never far from his mind.

MERRILL BRINGS MERCHANDISING TO THE BROKERAGE INDUSTRY

As the economy slowly emerged from its paralysis, Merrill saw that the time was ripe to bring his gospel of merchandising back to the brokerage industry. In E. A. Pierce he saw a new pulpit. By acquiring troubled firms, Pierce had grown into America's largest brokerage house, with thirty-nine outlets sprinkled throughout the United States. Though economic conditions were improving, Pierce, which had over-extended itself, nonetheless was close to insolvency. In late 1939, Winthrop Smith told Merrill that the firm could turn a profit if it had some fresh capital.

Merrill was cautious. The Crash had soured the public on Wall Street's products. In November 1939, a Roper poll showed that one in eleven American citizens thought the Stock Exchange was a meat wholesaler. Furthermore, Wall Street remained what it had been for most of its history: an insider's club run by and for the benefit of its members and their select group of friends. The entire system was geared toward servicing large investors whose trades and assets could generate fat commissions. The larger firms, few of which had offices outside New York and other major cities, were simply not interested in pitching their services to small investors. As the *New York Times* noted in 1940, "Too few houses have been geared to handle the $1,000 account at a profit."

Among Wall Street's heavy hitters, only Merrill believed there was money to be made servicing small accounts. He had learned from his retail chain experience that Americans with modest means could provide a lucrative customer base. So he decided to gamble on E. A. Pierce. He engineered a merger of Merrill Lynch and Pierce in January 1940, gaining 56 percent ownership by injecting $2.5 million of his personal fortune into the new entity. The combined firm had its fiscal house in order, and already was an established presence in several major cities. The new partnership produced a powerhouse brokerage.

Merrill immediately started proselytizing for a transformation in the marketing of stocks and bonds. As Homer Shannon later wrote in *Forbes*, Merrill had realized "that the crash of 1929 and the decade of depression which followed called for complete reorientation on the part of the commodity and security dealer, and of the investment banker." The merger was announced in January 1940, but did not become operational until April 1, under the new name Merrill Lynch, E. A. Pierce & Cassatt. (Although Lynch had passed away in 1938, Merrill insisted that his name be included in the full title of the partnership.) When it opened for business, the company announced its consumer-oriented strategy. As Merrill put it: "We must bring Wall Street to Main Street— and we must use the efficient, mass merchandising methods of the chain store to do it."

The first imperative was to control costs. He looked at the labor-intensive process brokers followed to place and complete orders on the floor of the exchange. In 1940 it cost about fourteen dollars for each transaction, which in turn brought in only ten dollars in revenues to the firm: a losing proposition. Finding that 85 percent of business was conducted by telephone, Merrill decided "it is perfectly damned nonsense to maintain a gilded palace to take care of 15 percent." So he moved the company's headquarters to a lower-priced building (70 Pine

Street), and had murals painted on the walls depicting chain stores like Safeway, McCrory, and Kresge.

To rally the troops for the new crusade, Merrill held a two-day conference at the Waldorf-Astoria. But he realized that indoctrinating his employees with the new gospel was just a beginning. More important, Merrill had to convince the public of the efficacy of his new strategy. As he wrote in a 1940 letter to the firm's partners and managers: "We in the security business have a job to do—a job of re-establishing faith in the security markets as a place for sound investment. . . . There will be no secrets in our plans or operations."

The most visible manifestation of the new openness was the publication of an annual report. As the company's longtime division director in charge of sales wrote: "During the nine months of operations in 1940, we ended up with a loss of $308,000. Mr. Merrill decided that our customers were entitled to know how we had fared, so we published our First Annual Report." In 1941 the notion of a private partnership laying bare its balance sheets for all the world to see was unprecedented. Wall Street firms preferred to operate under a veil of secrecy. But Merrill viewed such public reports as a key to earning public trust. They also garnered valuable free publicity. Newspapers and magazines ran large articles on the company's earnings, and the public came to view the firm's operating results as a measure of Wall Street's overall performance, much as Wal-Mart's results serve as a barometer of the retail climate today.

Merrill's new way of doing business made him a heretic in the clubby world of lower Manhattan, but he was driven by a sense of mission: He loved to quote from the speech in Shakespeare's *Henry V* in which the young king addresses his brothers and cousin as "we few, we happy few, we band of brothers." But Merrill's band was aging. In 1944, when the firm conducted about 10 percent of the NYSE's volume, the average account executive was fifty-two years old. Merrill saw the entrenched brokers, schooled in Wall Street's older ways, as an obstacle, and decided he needed fresh, eager, young recruits whom he could train in his own image. So in 1945 the firm set up a school that would turn World War II veterans into brokers. Carefully selected students received stipends for enrolling in the six-month cram course. Upon graduation, the missionaries were sent off to branch offices in outposts like Omaha, where the hundredth office was opened in December 1949.

Merrill's was among the first Wall Street firms to open branches in smaller cities. It was also the first to pay the newly minted account executives straight salaries rather than commissions. This signaled to customers that brokers weren't seeking to make a quick buck by selling them bad securities.

Just as the campaign began to gather steam, its leader was forced to withdraw from the field of battle. After suffering several heart attacks in 1944, Merrill was prohibited by his doctors from going into the office. While operating control of the firm passed to managing partner Winthrop Smith, Charles Merrill remained the firm's animating spirit. He continued to monitor the brokerage chain's daily operations from his homes in Palm Beach, Southampton (Long Island), and Barbados, spending most days on the telephone, issuing commands to senior executives.

REACHING NEW CLIENTS THROUGH PROMOTIONS AND EDUCATION

Believing that educated consumers would be more willing to invest, the firm took its message to the masses through a variety of media: Merrill Lynch produced company and industry research reports, and its analysts churned out massive amounts of informational literature. The firm published easy-to-read pamphlets on topics like "Hedging" and "How to Read a Financial Report." In 1947, 75,000 free copies of the biweekly *Investor's Reader*, the equivalent of a grocery store circular, were distributed to potential clients. All the literature was available by mail and at the firm's many branch offices.

In a practice uncommon for a brokerage house, the firm plowed substantial amounts of revenue into advertising. In 1947, when it earned $6.2 million and was the nation's largest retailer of stocks, Merrill Lynch spent about $400,000 on advertising. The firm ran 2,774 separate advertisements in 288 different newspapers in 1949, decades before the "When E. F. Hutton talks, people listen" campaign became famous. "Merrill Lynch's advertising objectives are, first, to educate and, second, to attract people to the store," said Jack Adams, an executive at Albert Frank-Guenther Law, the advertising agency that managed Merrill Lynch's account. The ads ranged in size from small tombstone-like notices to massive treatises on investing. Many of them were written by Louis Engel, who joined the firm in 1946 as an advertising director. He ran a full-page ad in the *New York Times* entitled, "What Everybody Ought to Know About This Stock and Bond Business." It provided straightforward answers to questions like: What are stocks? What are bull and bear markets? How do you do business with a broker?

All these efforts earned Charles Merrill and his company the acclaim of the financial press. "As an individual, he has done more to make the business of marketing securities respected than any other person," *Forbes* wrote in 1947. But the public remained wary. A 1949 Federal Reserve Board Survey found that 69 percent of American families with incomes of over $3,000 a year were opposed to investments in common stocks. And in a 1949 consumer survey the St. Paul (Minnesota) *Dispatch-Pioneer Press* found that 90 percent of that city's residents in the top salary brackets had never purchased a share of stock or a corporate bond. Similar statistics could be found in cities across the country.

This exasperated Charles Merrill to no end. "Americans spent more than $9 billion last year for new automobiles, and yet were willing to invest only $580 million of new money for industry by the purchase of common stocks," he groused. The problem, as he saw it, existed because his colleagues in the securities industry had little interest in spreading the good word. In a 1950 letter to his customers, Merrill wrote: "The great majority of people in the securities business haven't lifted a finger to help in the public educational job that must be done." That year his firm's 106 offices and 3,389 employees serviced 104,800 accounts.

MERRILL'S DREAM MATERIALIZES WITH AN ASSIST FROM THE NYSE

The 1950s provided a nurturing environment for Merrill's experiment. Over the course of the decade the Dow Jones Industrial Average rose more than fivefold, from 120 to 679. Helped by American dominance in world trade, government programs like the GI Bill, and a steadily growing economy, a large segment of the nation's population began to attain middle-class financial security and unprecedented economic comfort. In 1952, 82 percent of families had life insurance; 52.8 percent maintained savings accounts; 41.9 percent had U.S. savings bonds; 20.9 percent had annuities and pensions. Despite these solid statistics, few had stocks. The Brookings Institution found that just 6.49 million Americans (or 4.2 percent of the population) owned stocks. And most of them were wealthy by the standards of the day; the 75 percent of the population making less than $5,000 per year accounted for just 32 percent of stock ownership.

But during the cold war, buying stock came to be seen—and promoted—as an act of patriotism, a powerful weapon in the nation's arsenal against Soviet expansionism. "Our goal should be to have every American a stockholder in business enterprise," said General Motors chairman Alfred Sloan. "Under such circumstances the trend toward socialism can be retarded. It might even be averted."

Such cold war rhetoric was echoed by New York Stock Exchange vice president Ruddick Lawrence in January 1954, when he introduced the Monthly Investment Plan (MIP) as part of a belated NYSE campaign to increase public confidence. The MIPs let consumers buy stock on installment. Under the plans, investors could inject a fixed amount of

THE MODERN CORPORATION

As the largest securities firm and the chief advocate of small investors, Merrill Lynch remained an industry pioneer in the decades after its founder's death. Charles Merrill, who dubbed partnerships "antiques," had long agitated for the New York Stock Exchange to let its broker-members to incorporate. Such a move would signify the full arrival of modern business practices to the loosely managed club of Wall Street. More importantly, it would improve the liquidity and financial stability of firms.

The NYSE finally allowed its members to incorporate in 1953. But legal difficulties followed, and Merrill's death three years later prevented the firm he had founded from taking advantage of the opportunity until 1958. In December of that year, with 117 partners, 126 branch offices and $43 million in capital, Merrill Lynch was the first major Wall Street partnership to incorporate.

Thirteen years later the company again pioneered corporate organization on Wall Street. In 1970 the New York Stock Exchange finally gave its member firms permission to do what they had been helping other companies do since the nineteenth century: sell their stock to the public. And in June, 1971, Merrill Lynch became the second brokerage firm to go public, selling four million shares to the public at $28 each. In the years since, virtually every major brokerage house has followed suit. Today, of Wall Street's major investment firms, only Goldman Sachs remains a private partnership.

money every month, from as little as $40 to as much as $999. The money went to buy shares of a single stock, even if only in fractional terms. Lawrence called the program "an idea for Democratic Capitalism—the conviction that Americans everywhere should have the opportunity to own their share of American business." MIPs, of course, played perfectly into Merrill's long-standing efforts to bring small investors through the doors of his branch offices. By April 1954 the firm had sold

40 percent of the 10,885 MIPs in place, because, like Safeway, it had branches all over the country and a recognizable brand name. In 1954 the NYSE's 608 member firms had 1,247 offices across the United States; Merrill owned 119 of them.

Merrill Lynch augmented the NYSE's campaign with its own. In 1954 the firm outfitted three blue-and-silver buses with desks, wireless telephones, stock market tickers listing prices of seventy stocks, and eager account executives. From bases in Chicago, Boston, and New York, they fanned out into the sprawling new suburbs, parked in the lots of supermarkets, train stations, and factories, and touted the wonders of dividends and capital appreciation throughout the heartland. This exercise, said Winthrop Smith, was "nothing more than a logical outgrowth of our belief that investment service has got to be made much more widely available. . . ." The idea was to make it seem as if stocks could be purchased as easily as potato chips.

No venue was too small or too big for Merrill Lynch's promotional juggernaut. In May 1955 the firm helped sponsor a "World's Fair of Investing," a kind of revival meeting, in Manhattan's cavernous 71st Infantry Regiment Armory on Park Avenue and 34th Street. After going through exhibits staged by blue-chip companies like General Motors and IBM, visitors were funneled into a Merrill Lynch "seminar on investing," an animated display of the mechanics of buying stocks and bonds. The following year Merrill Lynch set up a stock information and corporate exhibition center smack in the middle of bustling Grand Central Terminal, joining the newsstands, florists, and food stands that put their products where the crowds were.

MERRILL LYNCH BECOMES A WALL STREET INSTITUTION

The relentless promotion paid off. Merrill Lynch became the best-known brokerage firm in America and abroad. When members of the Soviet press came to visit New York City in October 1955, they stopped at two bastions of capitalism: the floor of the New York Stock Exchange and the headquarters of Merrill Lynch at 70 Pine Street.

As more and more Americans shifted assets out of low-interest savings accounts and into the stock and bond markets, the number of individual shareholders rose to 8.6 million by the end of 1956, a 33 percent increase over 1952. The NYSE census estimated that over 500,000 people were joining the American stockholder family each year. Between 1952 and 1956 the median income of shareowners actually fell from $7,100 to $6,200, and the estimated median age of the 2.14 million shareowners added between 1952 and 1956 was thirty-five. "The day of golf club contacts and rich classmate contacts is gone, what with the redistribution of wealth," Louis Engel said in 1954. "Now you sell ten shares and twenty shares to lots of people. We feel the broadening base of stock ownership is a damn good thing. We still have some big accounts, of course. Go after the Dooleys and you get the Stuyvesants, too," Engel said.

Charles Merrill didn't live to see the fulfillment of his prophecy. Determined to ignore physical limitations, he remained a legendary carouser into his eighth decade. And he was always game for a fresh challenge. In 1953 he underwent experimental treatment for his heart ailment, a treatment based on findings of the Atomic Research Project. His health improved somewhat, and he rallied the troops for what would be some of his last exhortations during a two-day executive meeting at the Hotel Statler. In the weeks before his death in October, 1956, it was only fitting that Merrill should insist on watching over the public disclosure of the firm's results in its annual report. One partner recalled that, "It could not be released until he approved every word and illustration."

David Sarnoff, president of RCA.

DAVID SARNOFF, RCA, AND THE RISE OF BROADCASTING

Brigadier General David Sarnoff commanded what radio pioneer Lee De Forest called, "an Invisible Empire of the Air, intangible, yet solid as granite." This invisible empire became, under Sarnoff's guidance and stewardship, the foundation for today's electronic mass media.

At the tender age of fifteen, David Sarnoff took a job as office boy for the firm that became the Radio Corporation of America (RCA). Quickly climbing the ranks to high-level management, he foresaw radio's commercial potential and helped it grow. After he ascended to the presidency of RCA in 1930, the post he held for the next forty years, Sarnoff fostered another new mass media technology: television.

Sarnoff chalked up some of his success to good fortune. "I was lucky that at an early age I hitched my wagon to the electron," he said in 1967. But timing wasn't everything. "The uniqueness of David Sarnoff lies in his combination of a visionary and determined builder and hard-headed industrial leader," wrote the MIT scientist Dr. Jerome Wiesner.

AN IMMIGRANT BOY IS PRESENT AT THE CREATION OF THE WIRELESS

David Sarnoff was born in 1891 in Uzlian, a tiny Jewish village near Minsk. When David was five, his father, Abraham Sarnoff (a house painter) immigrated to the United States, and his mother sent her precocious son off to a yeshiva in Borisov. David quit his study of the Talmud when, in 1900, Abraham had saved the $144 needed to book passage for his family's arduous journey to New York City's Lower East Side. "As an immigrant boy, I was tossed into the bewildering whirlpool of a metropolitan slum area, to sink or swim," Sarnoff recalled.

David hawked Yiddish newspapers like the *Tageblatt* and *Forverts* on the street and took on the responsibility of supporting his family when his father fell ill soon after the Sarnoff's arrival in America. David borrowed $200 and bought a newsstand at 10th Avenue and 46th Street. In 1906, when his father died, David Sarnoff decided he'd rather write for newspapers than sell them. He intended to present himself at the *New York Herald*. By mistake, he wandered into the offices of the Commercial Cable Company, a telegraph concern that rented space in the same building. "I don't know about the *Herald*, but we can use another messenger boy in our shop," said the manager.

The fifteen-year-old Sarnoff had stumbled into the communications industry at a propitious moment. Since the mid-nineteenth century, people had been sending messages over wires in Morse code. But at the turn of the century a revolutionary new mode of communications was beginning to percolate: the wireless telegraph. Throughout Europe and America, tinkerers were experimenting with ways to zap electronic impulses through the ether. In 1901 Guglielmo Marconi had successfully completed the first transatlantic wireless transmission. In a matter of seconds, an electronic impulse signifying the letter "S" traversed the same distance it had taken the Sarnoff family several weeks to travel.

While working as a five-dollar-a-week courier, Sarnoff learned to operate the telegraph. In an ironic piece of good luck the Commercial

Cable Co. fired him when he asked for three days off to attend Jewish high holiday services. He quickly found work as an office boy with the U.S. unit of British-owned Marconi Wireless Telegraph Co. In 1906 Sarnoff introduced himself to the great inventor. "We were on the same wavelength," he said. In the coming years, when Marconi would visit the office, Davey, as he was known, would act as his personal assistant, running errands and arranging trysts.

Having proved himself in New York, the seventeen-year-old Sarnoff was sent to work at the Marconi station on the then remote outpost of Nantucket in 1908. The position paid $70 a month and afforded him the use of the station's extensive library. Davey wasn't interested only in using the wireless radio as a tool. He wanted to know how and why it worked. As Jack Irwin, operator of the Nantucket station, later wrote of Sarnoff: "He was so enthusiastic about radio that he stood a great part of my watch, voluntarily, and thereby allowed me to play tennis and otherwise enjoy the summer advantages of Nantucket." And when he was off watch, the ambitious teenager worked on correspondence courses in mathematics.

In 1909 Sarnoff returned to New York to work at a Marconi station in Brooklyn, where he continued his education, devouring every scientific journal he could find at the New York Public Library and taking an advanced electrical engineering class at the Pratt Institute. After several months in Brooklyn, Sarnoff was promoted to run the wireless station atop the Wanamaker department store in Manhattan. On April 14, 1912, the *Titanic* began sending S.O.S. signals over its wireless system. Sarnoff rushed to his post, and listened anxiously as the rescue effort began, gleaning details relayed from a Marconi-equipped ship in the doomed liner's vicinity. He provided transcripts to William Randolph Hearst's *American*, which sensationalized the findings and mentioned Sarnoff's name. "The *Titanic* disaster brought radio to the front, and also me," he said.

RADIO AND SARNOFF EMERGE AS COMMERCIAL POWERHOUSES

Despite his early fascination with technology, Sarnoff decided to shift his career path toward radio as a business. As his collegue Robert Marriott later recalled, Sarnoff maintained in 1913 that "the place to make money is where the money is coming in. . . . I am going to solicit the sale of contracts and service that will bring money into the company."

In 1914 vice president Edward Nally transferred Sarnoff to the Marconi headquarters and gave him responsibility for inspecting wireless equipment on ships and shoreside facilities in New York Harbor, as well as the job of evaluating new wireless devices.

In the fall of 1916, Congress considered granting licenses to the Navy to operate radio stations in direct competition with privately operated stations. Nally took Sarnoff with him to Washington to protest the congressional move. Summoning up the immigrant's instinctive feel for American freedoms, he called such a measure "a continuous military inquisition into private correspondence, an undemocratic and dangerous institution." Sarnoff was only twenty-five years old, and already he had taken his first steps toward becoming the spokesperson for the new industry.

At this time, Sarnoff and a few other experimenters believed that the wireless could be used for another, more commercial purpose—public entertainment. In 1915 he wrote a prescient memo to company executives: "I have in mind a plan of development which would make a radio a 'household utility' in the same sense as the piano or the phonograph. The idea is to bring music into the home by wireless." The company, he recommended, should erect a powerful transmitter, and then sell small receivers, equipped with antennae and amplifying tubes, to receive different wavelengths. "Baseball scores can be transmitted in the air by the use of one set installed at the Polo Grounds," Sarnoff wrote. If just one in fifteen American families bought a $75 radio, he calculated, this product could quickly garner $75 million in sales.

Marconi executives shelved the memo. But as Sarnoff's plan sat idle, others were making waves with similar ideas. In 1916, the inventor Lee De Forest started his own primitive station, airing music and lectures. And after World War I, during which armies had attempted to use wireless in combat, there was a growing realization that radio could help wire the world together. "Do you not know the world is all now one single whispering gallery?" said President Woodrow Wilson in a 1919 speech in Des Moines. "The tongue of . . . with the wireless and the tongue of the telegraph, all the suggestions of disorder are spread through the world."

Since its inception in 1899, American Marconi had been a subsidiary of a British firm, the Wireless Telegraph and Signal Company, Ltd. This foreign ownership troubled the Wilson administration. So the government induced the dominant American electronics firm, General Electric, to buy a controlling interest in American Marconi. In 1919, GE rechristened the firm the Radio Corporation of America. While the GE executive Owen Young became RCA's chairman, much of the old Marconi staff remained intact. Sarnoff, who had been appointed commercial manager, stayed on with an $11,000 annual salary. His responsibilities now included supervising hundreds of employees at nearly 400 company outposts throughout the world.

With a gross income of just $2 million in 1920, RCA was a tiny piece of the $272-million General Electric. But RCA was destined for greater things, and the vehicle for its rise would be commercial radio. In 1920, after noting the small-scale successes of other radio pioneers, Sarnoff again pitched the radio "music box," this time in a twenty-eight-page memo to Young. "We must have suitable apparatus for sale before we can sell it in large quantities," he wrote. Fusing a visionary's capacity for dreaming with a keen eye for the bottom line, Sarnoff laid out a detailed business plan: The company would sell 100,000 radios for a total of $7.5 million in the first year; 300,000 for $22.5 million the next year; and 600,000 in the third year for $45 million.

After GE approved a $2,000 investment for a prototype, Sarnoff set to work producing a practical radio. He kept an eye on area scientists and investors who were developing radio technology, in particular, Dr. Alfred Goldsmith, a professor at City University of New York. RCA hired Goldsmith, on the recommendation of Sarnoff, to run the company's new research facility in the Bronx, and Sarnoff paid frequent visits to the laboratory, acting as liaison between corporate headquarters and the scientists. As Owen Young later said, "David had sensitive ears. . . . His ears were sensitive to the scientists."

But manufacturing a radio was only half the challenge. Radio had to find a public market. Realizing that companies would have to produce programs to which Americans would listen, Sarnoff arranged for RCA to broadcast a boxing match between Jack Dempsey and Georges Carpentier in Jersey City in July 1921. In what may have been the first major sports broadcast in the United States, an estimated 400,000 enraptured fans listened—on homemade radios and those in public arenas— as Dempsey knocked out his French opponent in the fourth round. With the success of this broadcast and others like it, radio broadcasting stations began to sprout up across the United States. The number of stations rose from 30 in 1922 to 556 in 1923. Such mass audiences made broadcasters realize they could sell air time to companies. And when WEAF, a New York station owned by AT&T, aired an advertisement by the Queensborough Corporation real estate firm in August 1922, commercial radio was born.

The radio emerged quickly as a popular consumer product. Industry-wide production rose from 100,000 sets in 1922 to 500,000 in 1923, when Sears Roebuck began to sell radios made by various manufacturers through its many outlets. To hasten the spread of radio and to avoid potential antitrust action from the government, RCA licensed its patents and sold components so rivals could produce their own versions. Company executives intuitively understood that the proliferation of radio devices would ultimately serve their interests. As a result, RCA did not monopolize the business. In 1922, for example, RCA was responsible for only about $11 million of the $60-million radio industry.

BINDING A NATION TOGETHER THROUGH A RADIO NETWORK

Sarnoff saw radio as far more than a means of transmitting blow-by-blow accounts of boxing matches. As *Forbes* noted in 1927: "Radio, to him, is a new dimension of human life. It must be compared, not with mere inventions such as the automobile and the flying machine, but with the discovery of fire or the advent of language in human affairs." Sarnoff believed that radio had the ability to change the way Americans related to each other and to their government. "For the first time in the history of an American Presidential election, rival Presidential candidates will appeal through the forum of the air to the American electorate." he predicted in April 1924, noting that radio had "made it possible for millions to follow every move in the convention hall."

But if radio were to provide common experiences for a nation, it would require a new mode of delivery. That mode, he decreed, would be a national radio network. In 1922, at Sarnoff's request, RCA had set up two stations in Manhattan, WJZ and WJY. Both could reach audiences within a thirty-mile radius of the city. But engineers quickly devised the means to pipe radio sounds through telephone lines to stations in other cities. So in 1926, when some five million American homes had radios, RCA stitched together a chain of stations to form the National Broadcasting Company. For the first time, a program created in a New York studio could be piped simultaneously to stations in Texas, California, and Maine.

As radio expanded nationwide, Sarnoff made increasingly extravagant projections: "Radio may end war, for its mission is to bring the whole world into friendly communication," he said. "Wars result from misunderstanding; when people understand each other, they are pretty likely to become friends." Sarnoff viewed such public musings as an important part of his role to promote and defend the new medium. In 1927, when H. G. Wells wrote a *New York Times* article calling radio an "inferior substitute for better systems of transmitting news or evoking sound," Sarnoff felt compelled to fire back: "The fundamental basis of broadcasting is a service to the many, not to the few."

Sarnoff's public activities elevated him to a major figure in the radio industry. ". . . Although still a young man, he now holds the position of vice president and general manager of the great Radio Corporation of America and is consulted constantly by the great leaders, not only in the world of business and industry, but in the world of science, too," *Forbes* wrote in 1927.

Stock in RCA, known simply as Radio, rose from $10 in the early 1920s to above $200 in June 1928. Throughout the decade, the company rarely paid dividends, preferring to plow cash back into research. Riding the crest of the radio wave, RCA posted a $15.9-million profit on sales of $176.5 million in 1929. David Sarnoff's stock rose too. When he was appointed executive vice president in 1929, radio was a $842-million business; unit sales rose from 650,000 in 1928 to 842,548 in 1929.

FORGING AHEAD WITH TELEVISION DURING THE DEPRESSION

As early as 1927, in yet another visionary forethought, Sarnoff had discussed the possibility of developing "theaters of the home." Just a decade after the radio was first conceived as a consumer product, scientists in separate laboratories were developing the means to transmit a picture through the air electronically. Sarnoff believed this breakthrough could add a new dimension to radio. In 1929, when the Russian scientist Vladimir Zworykin demonstrated the iconoscope (a scanning technology that formed the basis of early television), Sarnoff hired him and supplied him with research facilities. This marked the beginning of a twenty-year, $50-million drive to re-create RCA's radio success in the new medium.

In 1929, Sarnoff told the *New York Times*: "The world moves so quickly that it is hard to keep apace with the times." But the Depression brought the promising technological developments and expansive consumerism to a dead halt. Between 1930 and 1933, RCA's sales shriveled from $137 million to $62 million, and its bottom line collapsed. Profits eroded from $5.5 million in 1930 to a $582,000 loss in 1933. Amid the difficult times, however, radio proved its worth by broadcasting Franklin D. Roosevelt's vaunted "fireside chats" that helped sustain a troubled nation throughout the Depression.

It was during these hard times that Sarnoff came to the fore. When Owen Young stepped down to attend to personal financial difficulties in 1930, David Sarnoff rose to become president of RCA at age thirty-nine. He gained an even greater degree of independence in 1932, when, after extensive antitrust proceedings and negotiations, GE and Westinghouse were forced to divest their RCA shares. While the economic climate was far from healthy, Sarnoff found himself with a free rein to focus on the company's core business—radio and radio broadcasting—and to push into new areas, like television.

Sarnoff oversaw the effort from RCA's new offices on the fifty-third floor of 30 Rockefeller Center. Completed in 1933, the art deco complex was a temple to progress and technology. It was the world's largest office complex, featuring 2.7 million square feet of work space, murals depicting technology and commerce, speedy elevators, and a rooftop observatory. As the author Tom Lewis wrote in 1991: "To Sarnoff, Rockefeller Center physically embodied everything that was important about American business, especially businesses run the way he wished them to be, like the Radio Corporation of America."

With RCA's financial health restored in 1934—earning $4.29 million on $79 million in sales—the company continued to invest in television technology. In 1935, Sarnoff had laid out a plan to establish a transmitting station and manufacture a few receiving sets. He kept tabs on the company's development of television through frequent visits to RCA's laboratory in Camden, New Jersey. Despite his fascination with the future and infatuation with contemporary technology, Sarnoff favored an old-fashioned style of management. In 1936 a public relations consultant asked to see an organizational chart of RCA's top management. "This is a company of men, not of charts," Sarnoff replied. More probably, he considered it a company of one man. An "old-timer" in his late 40s, D. S., as Davey was now known, was the king of radio. In 1938, with 142 stations, RCA could reach more of the twenty-five million radio owners at one time than any other company. In twenty years it had risen from a tiny subsidiary of GE to a vertically integrated entertainment and communications powerhouse with revenues of $110.5 million and profits of $8 million in 1939.

Radio waves coursed everywhere, creating communication for people on ships, in cars, in their homes and offices. As the decade came to a close, however, Sarnoff stood on the verge of breaking open a new frontier. At the opening of the World's Fair in New York on April 30, 1939, Sarnoff spoke into a television camera at one of the nation's first live broadcasts. "Now we add radio sight to sound," he proclaimed. "It is with a feeling of humbleness that I come to the moment of announcing the birth in this country of a new art so important in its implications that it is bound to affect all society. It is an art which shines like a torch in a troubled world." That year, RCA started selling television receivers for $625 a set. But the outbreak of World War II diverted the resources, attention, and time of RCA's scientists and executives to more vital projects.

RCA PIONEERS TELEVISION AFTER WORLD WAR II

"In war, science dares the impossible; it must continue to dare the impossible in peace if a fuller life is to permeate society," Sarnoff said in 1946, when RCA introduced a television set priced at $375. Americans yearned to watch events like the World Series, political conventions, concerts, and other programs they had been hearing for decades. With the end of World War II, consumers were eager to indulge themselves with entertainment. Sales of televisions quickly soared, from 175,000 in 1947 to seven million in 1950, and nearly half of those carried RCA's name. In the 1952 calendar year alone, the number of TV sets owned by Americans rose from 15 million to 21 million. They had so permeated the market that in 1952 Sarnoff estimated 47 percent of American families had a television in their homes.

RCA stood ready to exploit this boom by providing programming as well. In 1953, the NBC television network began broadcasting. NBC filmed programming previously produced for radio, and beamed it through coaxial cables to the 238 affiliated stations that had cropped up all over the country.

In September 1951, RCA held a ceremony to honor Sarnoff's forty-five years in the business. But rather than rest on the company's laurels, he challenged its scientists to come up with three new products by his fiftieth anniversary in 1956: a true amplifier of light that would boost the quality of pictures; a device that could record video signals on inexpensive tape; a new electronic air conditioner for the home. "The housewife's dream of an all-automatic home will be realized," Sarnoff wrote in a 1956 *New York Times* article. "The days' chores in the house will be prescheduled, with each of the tasks performed electronically."

ADDING COLOR TO THE MAGIC OF TELEVISION

For years, RCA and NBC's long-time rival in the radio business, CBS, had been trying to develop a system that could deliver color pictures. The Federal Communications Commission (FCC), eager to establish a standard, approved a system devised by CBS in October 1950. In so doing, the FCC overlooked RCA's system, which was still, admittedly, in development. Sarnoff was undaunted by the setback. "We may have lost the battle, but we'll win the war," he said.

CBS didn't rush to manufacture color sets because color was not compatible with existing cables. And in 1953 CBS abandoned it entirely. Meanwhile, RCA's scientists continued to plug away at a system that could send color over existing cables to run on twenty-one-inch screens. RCA brought a twenty-one-inch color set to the market in 1954. Though relatively cheap—$795 in 1955—color television was slow to catch on. Black and white sets were still more affordable and color TV's quality was bad. Sarnoff had forecasted that sales would quickly grow to 75,000 in 1954 and to 3 million in 1957. But by 1958 just 325,000 color sets had been sold. Bob Hope joked that color television had "a tremendous audience—General Sarnoff and his wife."

Sales of black-and-white televisions continued to grow, however, and the company's TV network proved to be a smashing commercial success. As a result, RCA's revenues approached $1 billion in 1954. While the company had grown into a very large modern corporation, there remained an intense identification between David Sarnoff and RCA. In the 1950s the annual report was always issued on Sarnoff's birthday, February 27. "Have faith and confidence in Uncle Sam of the United States of America and in Daddy David of RCA," one shareholder said. Intent on keeping the family in the company's management, Sarnoff elevated his son, Robert, to president of NBC in 1955.

Robert took over at a time when the initial failure of color television stunted RCA's growth. Between 1952 and 1962 the company's sales rose 154 percent, but profits fell 24 percent. And for much of the latter half of the expansive 1950s, RCA's stock remained stuck in low gear, the result of its cumulative $130-million investment in color. But the investment began to pay dividends as the market finally began to come around. Sales of black-and-white sets declined from 7.4 million in 1955 to 5.1 million in 1958, as consumers slowly switched to color. In 1960, Walt Disney shifted his "Wonderful World of Disney" show to NBC so it could appear in color. The following year, color television grew to a $100-million industry. RCA, cornering nearly 70 percent of the market, had become the nation's twenty-sixth largest company with $1.54 billion in sales.

Even as he grew older, Sarnoff continued to dream. "Science and technology will advance more in the next thirty-six years than all the millennia since man's creation," he wrote in 1964. "By the century's end, man will have achieved a growing ascendancy over his physical being, his earth, and his planetary environs." Come the year 2000, he

PUTTING BUSINESS IN SERVICE OF THE NATION

RCA first introduced a television for commercial distribution in 1939. But World War II stopped the designers in their tracks. Possessed of an unflagging sense of duty, Sarnoff immediately put his great enterprise on hold in order to serve his adopted country in a time of crisis. On Dec. 7, 1941, he sent a radiogram to President Roosevelt. "All our facilities and personnel are ready and at your instant service. We await your commands."

RCA's 22,000 employees had a great deal to offer to the war effort. Ten months after Pearl Harbor, RCA opened its $2-million research center in Princeton, New Jersey. The scientists immediately went to work developing communications and technology that could be used by the armed forces. "More than ever before in history, this war is a contest between the brains and imagination and teamwork of the scientists, engineers, and production workers of one group of nations pitted against those of another group," said Sarnoff, who immediately went on active duty as a colonel in the Signal Corps, and was later promoted to Brigadier General. World War II was the first war in which radio was widely used by all combatants. Technology, whether it was the airplane, the Enigma encoding machine, or the atomic bomb, provided the margin of victory.

Sarnoff's personal contribution to the war effort was also significant. In 1944 he set up shop in London, where he coordinated broadcast, press, and internal army communications for the massive D-Day invasion.

---

foretold, the ocean would be cultivated for crops, electronic devices would regulate impaired human body organs, newspapers would appear in simultaneous editions all over the world, and overseas mail would be transmitted via satellite by means of facsimile reproduction.

Sarnoff finally retired from RCA at the age of seventy in 1969, the year Neil Armstrong took his first tentative steps on the moon and reported his progress back to an enraptured American audience via wireless. Despite Sarnoff's battle with a variety of illnesses, he could not let go of the company he had helped to build. "I cannot separate RCA and Bob and David Sarnoff," he said. When David died on December 12, 1971, the communications industry, which began with wireless technology scarcely a century before, had revolutionized human life and made an incredible impact on how people view the world. "The electron has lifted RCA from a small company with a humble beginning and with very modest means to the role of leader in a great industry," he said back in 1954. David Sarnoff may well have said the same about himself.

Walt Disney at his drawing board.

WALT DISNEY AND HIS FAMILY-ENTERTAINMENT EMPIRE

Walt Disney suffered a devastating setback in 1928, a blow so harsh that his career seemed about to disintegrate. The twenty-six-year-old animator lost his first successful cartoon creation, "Oswald the Lucky Rabbit," because he had naively signed away the ownership rights in a production deal with his New York distributor. Emerging empty-handed from the debacle, Disney didn't quit. In fact, the man who was called "the most significant figure in graphic art since Leonardo," by the British political cartoonist David Low, learned a great lesson from the early disappointment. Within the year he would take the entertainment industry by storm. Armed with a comprehensive understanding of intellectual property rights, and blessed with a natural genius for creating memorable characters and beguiling fantasy worlds, Disney masterminded a new kind of business empire.

As the head of his own studio, Disney not only used his own imagination but also created an atmosphere in which others could use theirs. He began with Mickey Mouse, the perky character who became an international phenomenon. By relying on a wide range of children's stories and fairy tales, like Pinocchio and Snow White, and by endowing his own characters with realistic human attributes and emotions, he appealed to adults and children alike. But Disney didn't rely solely on ticket sales for revenue. He mined his creations for maximum commercial advantage and found ways to cross-promote his characters in new media. Then, when it seemed he had fully exploited all existing means of distribution, Disney invented yet a new one: Disneyland.

Walt Disney was a complex man, not merely the genial "uncle" that he seemed to be as the host of his television series. Disney worked himself to the point of exhaustion, and yet he never reached the limit of his ambition. In nearly a half century, he created a corporation unique in both business terms and sociological terms. Disney brought to all of his projects an innate understanding of fantasy, as a means of blurring reality in order to see it all the more clearly. "Fantasy," he liked to say, "—that is, good acceptable fantasy—is really only fact with a whimsical twist."

A YOUNG INVENTOR ENTERS THE EARLY FILM INDUSTRY

Walt Disney was born on December 5, 1901, the fourth son of a middle-class American couple named Elias and Flora Disney of Chicago. The

Disneys also had a daughter, younger than Walt. The father was a restless and ornery man. When he moved the family to a farm in Missouri and proceeded to drive his boys like hired hands, the older two ran away. The farm failed after four years, and the Disneys moved to Kansas City, where Elias bought a newspaper distributorship and enlisted the two remaining boys, Roy and Walt, as paperboys. Both of them were beaten, not occasionally—as the practice of discipline might have indicated in the years around 1910—but often, as often as Elias lost his temper. Flora comforted her boys and they comforted each other, but, when Walt was ten, Roy left home too. Walt Disney's childhood, blessed with enjoyable times on the farm and at the family house in Kansas City, was also deeply scarred by the mean moods of his father and the unhappy way that each of his older brothers left.

As the man who would turn childhood into a veritable commodity, Walt Disney often referred to recollections of his own early fears and joys. Like many lonely children, Walt passed idle hours creating imaginary friends with pen and paper. When the family moved to Chicago, he found an outlet for this apparent talent, when he became the junior art editor of the McKinley High School newspaper. He began to realize that doodling could be more than simple whimsy by bartering caricatures for free haircuts. Meanwhile, America had entered World War I on the side of the Allies. At the age of sixteen, Disney volunteered as a driver with the American Red Cross Ambulance Corps. The war was over by the time he reached France, so he drove more trucks than ambulances. But once he settled into regular duty he continued to draw cartoons for the amusement of his fellows.

After the war, Disney returned home to Chicago and eventually settled in Kansas City, where his older brother Roy was working as a banker. He tried to make a career as a cartoonist, but after he was rejected for a job at the *Kansas City Star*, he opted to become a graphic artist for a local advertising firm, Pesmen-Rubin. At the same time, the eighteen-year-old began to take great interest in animated films, a new medium about to explode with the sudden popularity of a character called Felix the Cat. In 1920, Walt signed on as a $40-a-week illustrator with the Kansas City Film Ad Company, which made 60-second animated cartoon advertisements that were screened in movie theaters. Disney learned how to use the basic tool of animation, the stop-action camera, which captured a series of drawings to create the illusion of movement.

As Disney learned the fundamentals of film animation, he realized that he had little desire to make cartoons just to sell products. Having seen Felix the Cat, he wanted to use his talents for pure entertainment. At both Pesmen-Rubin and Kansas City Film, Disney worked closely with another artist, Ubbe Iwerks. In 1922 the two of them founded their own company, Laugh-O-gram, to make short animated films. Rather than create new characters, the animators took story material from well-known children's favorites like *Goldilocks and the Three Bears*. But their distributor went bankrupt even before they could release their first film. Then Disney began to explore commercial applications for some of his other ideas. He thought he'd invented an original variation on animation when he placed a real person into a cartoon. Though the technique had, in fact, been used before, it led to the first commercial acceptance for a Disney-Iwerks film. Disney began making *Alice's Adventures*, in which a child actress appeared in cartoon surroundings. Even though he ran out of money before he could complete the film, Disney had glimpsed his future.

In 1923, Walt Disney left Kansas City for a place where he had heard young filmmakers could find financial backing for their projects: Hollywood. With $40 in his pocket and an unfinished print of *Alice's Adventures*, Disney boarded a train heading west. When a fellow traveler asked about his intentions, he said, "I'm going to direct great Hollywood motion pictures."

Disney's dream was not far-fetched. Hollywood's burgeoning film industry needed talent, and the price of entry was nothing more than imagination and ambition. Still, it was difficult for Disney to get his foot in the door. Upon arriving in Los Angeles, he lived with his uncle

Robert and made the rounds of the studios, quickly finding out, though, that great directors were not necessarily hired off the street.

Without work, Disney did what he'd done under the same circumstances in Kansas City: he became an entrepreneur. As he put it, "When you can't get a job, you start your own business." Walt had two tangible assets: his brother Roy, a sharp businessman who was living in Los Angeles, recuperating from tuberculosis; and *Alice's Adventures*. In 1923 he wrote to Margaret Winkler, a successful distributor based in New York, claiming he had "just discovered something new and clever in animated cartoons! . . . a new idea that will appeal to all classes and is bound to be a winner . . . a clever combination of live characters and cartoons." Winkler watched *Alice*, offered suggestions for what there was of it, and encouraged Disney to finish it. With that, he and Roy set up an animation studio, Disney Brothers, in Uncle Robert's garage. In October 1923, Winkler ordered six *Alice* movies, at $1,500 each, and Disney was truly in business. Once the series was launched, Ubbe Iwerks also joined the new venture, at first as a contract cartoonist.

After completing the *Alice* films, Disney married Lillian Bounds, an inker at the studio. His distributor, Margaret Winkler, also got married at about the same time, and she handed over control of the distribution company to her new husband, Charles Mintz. He worked with Disney to create a recurring cartoon rabbit, like Felix the Cat. Walt sketched a bunny, and Mintz named it "Oswald the Lucky Rabbit." Though Oswald became the basis for a series of well-received "shorts," Disney's success was itself short-lived. In his naiveté, he had agreed to a production deal in which he would produce the cartoons but Mintz's company, along with Universal Studios, would own the character. In 1928, when Disney went to New York to renew his contract, Mintz laid out a stark scenario: he and Universal owned the rights to Oswald, and he had already talked to a cadre of Disney's top animators about jumping ship to work for him. The distributor literally cut Oswald's creator out of the picture. Burned by this experience, Disney made a vow: "Never again will I work for anybody else."

MICKEY MOUSE PROVIDES INDEPENDENCE

After the showdown with Mintz, Walt and Lillian Disney wearily boarded a train for the ride back to California. As the cars chugged westward, Walt realized that his new-born studio would quickly dissolve unless he invented a new character. His thoughts quickly turned to mice. "I do have a special feeling for mice," he liked to say later. "Mice gathered in my wastebasket when I worked late at night. I lifted them out and kept them in little cages on my desk. One of them was my particular friend."

Back in California, the first sketch that Walt produced of a new mouse character looked too much like a caricature of himself, so Ubbe Iwerks worked with him to produce something cute—something, it turned out, like Oswald with mouse ears. They decided to name the rodent Mickey Mouse. The first film to star Mickey Mouse was a cartoon entitled *Plane Crazy*, which depicted Mickey's misadventures in an airplane, and cost $1,800 to make. It was quickly followed by *The Gallopin' Gaucho*. But it was the third Mickey Mouse film, *Steamboat Willie*, that would change animation forever.

After the October 1927 premiere of *The Jazz Singer*, the first film to synchronize sound with action, Disney was convinced that Mickey would have to be heard as well as seen. If Al Jolson could speak on film, then so could Mickey. Because Disney insisted on making the sound mesh perfectly with the action, *Steamboat Willie* became an elaborate affair; Disney hired a full orchestra to record the music, and the sophisticated animation required about 20,000 hand-crafted frames. The company was running out of money and Walt had to sell his beloved sports car. But Disney was prepared to gamble. "I think this is Old Man Opportunity rapping at our door," he wrote to Roy from New York. "Slap a big mortgage on everything we got and let's go after this thing in the right manner." *Steamboat Willie* cost about $15,000 to produce, but the investment proved worthwhile. On November 18, 1928, when it premiered in New York as the opener for the movie *Gang War*, a commercial giant roared—or, rather, squeaked. When the world first listened to Mickey Mouse's high-pitched dialogue, it was Disney himself they heard, providing the rodent's voice in a falsetto pitch.

With the help of a smart press agent, Mickey Mouse was an overnight success, receiving rave reviews from reporters who were specially invited to the premiere. Mickey soon became a national fad, and not merely with children. With the success of *Steamboat Willie*, Disney was in demand. He began turning out new Mickey Mouse features at the rate of one per month. Several studios, including Universal, wanted to handle Disney's distribution or even to buy the company outright. But Disney, who often worked himself to the point of exhaustion, wasn't interested in being acquired. "I wanted to retain my individuality," he said. He tried to get around the studio system and distribute his cartoons to independent theaters, but he found that while Mickey was making a fortune, little money of it made its way back to Disney.

Finally, in 1930, after seven years in Hollywood, Disney capitulated and made a deal with a studio, signing a $7,000-per-film distribution agreement with Columbia Pictures; the two parties divided the money, but Disney kept the copyrights. "Mickey Mouse to me is the symbol of independence," he said in 1948. "Born of necessity, the little fellow literally freed us of immediate worry. He provided the means for expanding our organization to its present dimensions and for extending the medium of cartoon animation toward new entertainment levels."

TURNING A MOUSE INTO A COMMERCIAL POWERHOUSE

Columbia distributed Disney cartoons worldwide, and in 1930 the mouse became an instant worldwide phenomenon. Italians referred to him as *Topolino*; in Spain he was called *Miguel Ratoncito*; in Sweden, *Musse Pigg*. "Sometimes I've tried to figure out why Mickey appealed to the whole world. Everybody's tried to figure it out," Disney said in 1961. "So far as I know, nobody has. He's a pretty nice fellow who never does anybody any harm, who gets into scrapes through no fault of his own, but always manages to come up grinning."

It wasn't long before Disney realized the potential of his creation beyond the silver screen. Given the star's popularity, a host of companies were eager to help market Mickey. But Disney had his own ideas. At a time when "multimedia" had yet to enter the lexicon of American business, Disney grasped its essence, and he immediately moved to boost the mouse's image and widen his exposure. In 1930 he published *The Mickey Mouse Book*, and it sold 97,938 copies in its first year. He also entered an agreement with King Features to develop a Mickey Mouse comic strip that in turn led the company to encourage the proliferation of Mickey Mouse Clubs, which had begun to sprout up in the United States and abroad.

The cartoon rodent seemed to possess star quality and, as a result, Mickey became a celebrity endorser. In 1932, Disney hired New York businessman Kay Kamen to figure out ways to mine Mickey's commercial appeal. While licensing products and technology was a relatively common practice, Mickey rapidly rode the concept to new heights. Kamen's first act was to license the National Dairy Products Company to make Mickey Mouse ice cream cones; the company sold about 10 million cones in the first month.

By the end of 1932 companies ranging from RCA to General Foods were helping to sell the mouse, and Disney generally received about 5 percent of the wholesale price of the licensed products. Within Kamen's first year with the company, his deals had netted the company about $300,000, or nearly one-third of its revenues. The most enduring product of these early agreements was the Mickey Mouse watch. Introduced by the Ingersoll-Waterbury Company in 1933, it sold 2.5 million watches in its first two years.

Old Man Opportunity, whom Walt had heard knocking with the first Mickey Mouse talkie, seemed to be kicking the door down as the series took off. In response, Walt Disney tried to do too much: turning out a new Mickey Mouse film every month and exploiting business opportunities on all sides. He had a nervous breakdown and was found unconscious by his wife. When he returned to work after a long vacation, Disney was more obsessed than ever with building the company.

Increasing revenues in the early thirties enabled the Walt Disney Studio to invest in improving the quality of animation. While his licensees churned out merchandise based on his characters, Disney made it clear that his films were not merely commercial products, but a valid new art form. Thus, in 1932, his studio became the first to start its own school, where Disney could train young animators in his own methods. Procuring the latest in film technology, he gave them the highest quality materials with which to work. That same year, Disney released a film called *Flowers and Trees*. Set to the music of Schubert and Mendelssohn, it was the first cartoon ever filmed in the new process of Technicolor, and it won the first of forty-eight Oscars the studio would receive in Disney's lifetime.

The heightened quality coming out of the Disney Studio was apparent in the new series called Silly Symphonies—produced on the concept that dialogue was barely necessary if music was used effectively in a cartoon. In 1934, the Silly Symphony movie called *The Wise Little Hen* introduced Disney's second most enduring star: Donald Duck. The commercial success from Mickey Mouse proved to Disney that he could compound profits by creating even more proprietary characters. So he and his artists developed an ensemble "cast," including Donald Duck and dogs named Pluto and Goofy. To support the growing roster, Disney boosted his payroll to 187 by 1934. Since he saw his studio as an "idea factory," size was an advantage. "We can't run out of story material," said Disney, who worked cheek-by-jowl with a cadre of writers, drafts people, and composers. "As our creative organization grows in size and its individuals grow in ability, the flow of ideas will increase in volume and quality."

Despite the proliferation of new characters, it was clear that Mickey was still first in the heart of the boss. Walt Disney mounted a big Mickey

Mouse clock on his office wall and put an imprint of the mouse on company paychecks. And the man who provided Mickey's voice spoke of his creation as if he were a human being. "The little fellow seems to make friends regardless of race, color, or national boundaries," Disney said in 1935. Indeed, in Japan, where he was known as *Miki Kuchi*, the mouse was the most popular figure other than the emperor. And as Mickey's creator, Disney himself became a celebrity. When he traveled to England in 1937, he dined with the Queen of England and met H. G. Wells. The following year, he received honorary degrees from both Harvard and Yale. At times the line between the creator and the star was so blurred, it disappeared altogether. When Disney accepted an award from the League of Nations in Paris, he even spoke in the voice of Mickey Mouse.

SNOW WHITE LEADS THE WAY FOR ANIMATED FEATURE FILMS

In 1934, Disney decided to do something that nobody in Hollywood had ever done: make a full-length animated film. The subject was to be Snow White and the Seven Dwarfs. Disney took animation to a new level of sophistication with a greater sense of reality. For one sequence, he even hired a dancer to pose in costume, filmed her, and then re-created her movements frame by frame. Originally budgeted for $250,000, the film's costs quickly multiplied, in large part due to Disney's exacting standards. The animators drew some 250,000 separate pictures, while cinematographers employed a new multiplane camera that used layers of background to create a more lifelike setting. As the total budget surpassed $1 million, Disney's chief creditor, the Bank of America, grew jittery. The undertaking became known as "Disney's Folly," drawing the scorn of a chorus of naysayers. "It was prophesied that nobody would sit through a cartoon an hour and a half long," Disney remembered. "But we had decided there was only one way we could successfully do *Snow*

White. It was to go for broke, shoot the works. There could be no compromise on money, talent, or time."

Snow White and the Seven Dwarfs debuted on December 21, 1937. "All the Hollywood brass turned out for my cartoon!" Disney exulted. Across the country, audiences flocked to the theaters. *Snow White* quickly earned back its costs, grossing $8.5 million in its first release. (It has returned to theaters at regular intervals ever since, toting up even greater returns.) In 1939 the production received a special Academy Award, one large statue surrounded by seven smaller ones, presented by Shirley Temple. Once again, Disney did not allow the film's commercial appeal to be limited to theaters. The film featured several catchy songs, including "Whistle While You Work," which were marketed as single records.

Buoyed by their success, Walt and his brother Roy, who was the vice president of Walt Disney Productions, decided to spend $100,000 to buy fifty-one acres in Burbank, California. They built a sophisticated new animation studio on the property, which Walt liked to call "the house that *Snow White* built." It was planned as an ideal work environment, according to Walt's many theories. Among other things, he liked trees, small rooms, and tables (rather than desks); the overall effect was of a village, but a very busy one.

Disney, who insisted on being called Walt by all his employees, closely supervised the creative work, though he hadn't made any drawings himself since the mid-twenties. The atmosphere he created at the studio was supportive—without being congenial. He let his creative staff members come and go without set hours and provided them with new equipment and the best supplies. And yet Disney was feared too. "One day I boarded a studio elevator en route to the third floor," Disney writer Charles Shows wrote in his memoirs. "Unexpectedly, Walt stepped into the elevator with me. Fearing I might say something he didn't like, I punched the button marked '2' and fled through the doors the moment they opened—a whole floor short of my destination—just to get away from the Boss."

At this new campus-like studio, Disney devoted his full attention to making animated features. His second full-length animated film, *Pinocchio*, cost $2.6 million and was even more elaborate than *Snow White*. Disney had his crew make 175 separate models of Pinocchio before he found one he liked. There were, however, consequences for such exacting and expensive standards. Despite the popularity of most of its films, Walt Disney Productions was heavily in debt by the late thirties, due to high production costs and yet another hobbling distribution deal, this one with RKO, and the construction of Disney's Burbank Studio, which cost $3.8 million. By 1940 the studio had accumulated $4.5 million in debt. In an effort to reduce this figure, the company plotted a public offering. In April 1940, it sold $4 million worth of stock.

The influx of funds allowed Disney to pay down debt while helping to finance the production of three new features: *Pinocchio* (1940), *Fantasia* (1940), and *Bambi* (1942). *Fantasia*, Disney's most ambitious feature to date, didn't have dialogue, except as narration between separate segments; it featured speechless cartoons set to classical pieces like Stravinsky's *Rite of Spring* and Mussorgsky's *Night on Bald Mountain*. *Fantasia* cost $2.28 million and was the first feature-length movie in which Mickey Mouse appeared. Sparing no expense, Disney hired the famed conductor Leopold Stokowski to select music and synchronize it with the animation. Though it won critical acclaim, *Fantasia* was not a success at the box office. Neither was *Pinocchio*, nor *Bambi*.

Although none of the movies had been as successful as *Snow White*, they certainly brought attention to Walt Disney's incredible talent and constant innovation. Without pretty princesses or handsome princes, *Pinocchio* and *Bambi* contained disturbing themes and frightening sequences. Some critics even classify *Bambi* as a horror film, in its depiction of the forest and of the animals' fear of hunters and fire. Only in re-release would the three films earn back their production costs and, ultimately, much more. But Disney had attained his dream, in his own way: He was a great director. "It isn't that I deliberately set out to break movie traditions," he said of *Fantasia* in 1940. "But if someone didn't break loose with new things the movies wouldn't be where they are today. . . . Somebody's got to be a damn fool."

DIVERSIFYING IN WAR AND PEACE

Before the outbreak of World War II in 1939, about 45 percent of the income of Walt Disney Productions came from abroad. But the war choked off that flow. In the aftermath of the bombing of Pearl Harbor, the war arrived abruptly at the Disney studio in Burbank, when the U.S. Army confiscated much of the lot to use as a service center in the defense of a Lockhead plant near the studio against enemy attack. For most of 1942, the studio was constrained. After the army left, Disney was overwhelmed with government work, making training and propaganda films. Just as David Sarnoff put RCA's technological capabilities into the service of the nation, Disney applied the fruits of his imagination to the war effort.

Aside from producing animated instructional films Disney made *The New Spirit*, in which Donald Duck talked about the need to pay income taxes on time. When Treasury Secretary Henry Morgenthau, Jr. criticized the concept because he had expected to see a more respectable, human character representing Mr. Average Taxpayer, Disney grew angry. "I've given you Donald Duck. At our studio, that's the equivalent of giving you Clark Gable out of the MGM stable," he said.

During the war, Disney also created comic insignias for different military units. "It was here that we learned the true meaning of diversification," he said. And on D-Day, June 6, 1944, Mickey Mouse was one of many official passwords. The character had become so fully integrated in the national popular culture, even the war needed him.

One commercial entertainment feature the studio made during the war was about bombers, *Victory through Air Power*. As a cartoon feature, the subject did not appeal to the war-weary public. When the market for wartime instructional films petered out with the end of the war, the studio was deeply in debt. Disney decided to produce a new type of live-action documentary, as entertainment, in addition to a lineup of new cartoon features. With wild animals in the starring roles, the documentary films in the "True-Life Adventure" series were cheaper to make than animated productions. In 1948, the year in which the 5 millionth Mickey Mouse watch was sold, Disney introduced the first in the series, *Seal Island*. The film, which portrayed the lives of playful seals in Alaska's Pribilof Islands, won an Academy Award for best documentary and was a surprise hit at the box office. Disney quickly followed up with a series of thirty-minute nature documentaries.

As of 1953, Walt Disney had been in Hollywood for thirty years. Famous for having raised animation to true art, Disney was admired by filmmakers and applauded by parents. Children, of course, loved "Disney," and the great storytelling that the word itself came to represent. But Walt Disney Productions was still only scraping along financially. One step in the right direction was the establishment in 1953 of a distribution subsidiary, called Buena Vista, to replace the flagging relationship with RKO. In-house distribution worked efficiently for Disney and, for the first time, the studio could actually keep the money it earned in rentals.

In the mid-1950s, Disney began to sell into a rapidly developing new distribution channel: television. After making several experimental television shows, Disney signed an exclusive long-term contract with ABC in 1954, becoming the first leading Hollywood producer to do so. The *Disneyland* television show, hosted by Walt Disney and featuring cartoons and nature films, premiered in 1954. The Disney magic worked wonders on the small screen: In its first season, the show scored an astonishing 41 rating on Nielson's meters, meaning 30.8 million of 75 million possible viewers tuned in. The following year, Disney created *The Mickey Mouse Club*, a new television phenomenon that appealed to young children and adolescents alike. Aside from making stars of child-actor Mouseketeers like Annette Funicello, the show helped boost sales of licensed Disney products. At the height of the show's popularity in the mid-1950s, Mickey Mouse ears sold at a rate of 25,000 sets a day.

THE MAGIC KINGDOM: TOTAL IMMERSION IN A FANTASY WORLD

With everything he did, Disney offered a piece of his fantasy world to his audience. But he wanted a way to truly bring his vision to life. In an audacious departure from his media-based entertainment, he was determined to build a theme park. He conceived of the idea while watching his two daughters play on a merry-go-round. ". . . I felt that there should be something built, some kind of family park, where parents and children could have fun together," he recalled. In a 1948 memo he first described the prospects of a Mickey Mouse park. After commissioning the Stanford Research Institute to conduct a study on the ideal setting, he bought sixty acres of orange groves in Anaheim, twenty-five miles south of Los Angeles near the Santa Ana Freeway. His studio, controlled in part by Roy and other important stockholders, was hesitant to cooperate, and so Walt started a separate company to plan the venture, Walt Disney, Inc., and poured his life savings into launching it.

Once again Walt Disney's vision ran ahead of the business sense of his Hollywood colleagues. He found it difficult to find backers for the project, which was slated to cost $5 million and would eventually cost $17 million. "It was hard for anybody to visualize what I had in mind," he said. "I wanted to do all the basic things amusement parks do, but in a new way." As part of the television contract, ABC had agreed to invest $500,000, but extracted a 35 percent equity stake in return.

As Disneyland took shape, however, companies began to realize the commercial possibilities of the theme park and paid either to obtain concessions where they could sell their own products or to have their names associated with certain rides for the sake of public relations. The money was crucial, because construction of the park went over budget. When the fantasyland opened on July 17, 1955, complete with live-television coverage, it was an instant sensation. In the first week, over 170,000 visitors anted up the one-dollar admission for adults and the fifty-cent ticket for children.

Disneyland was the nation's largest entertainment complex, offering Americans their first experience with a total theme park environment. More significantly, it was a sort of interactive display case for Disney's inventions of the previous thirty years. Visitors could stroll down Main Street, pose with actors dressed as Mickey and Minnie Mouse, and walk through a replica of Sleeping Beauty's castle. Sections like Frontierland echoed themes from television programs and contained dozens of rides, while Adventureland offered a jungle cruise, and Tomorrowland featured a ride that simulated trips to the moon. Like Disney's animated films, the family-friendly park strived for the closest possible approximation to reality. Indeed, it was a marvel of authentic pretense.

Disney's family haven opened at exactly the right time. America was in the midst of the Baby Boom, with 76.4 million children born between 1946 and 1964. Hordes of them, 10,000 per day, streamed into Disneyland with their parents. By the time the 10 millionth visitor entered on the last day of 1957, the typical day tourist spent $2.70 for rides and admission, $2 on food, and 18¢ on souvenirs. Such numbers translated into impressive profits as Disney's artificial world quickly surpassed America's natural wonders as a tourist destination. In 1959, Disneyland drew 5 million people—more than the Grand Canyon and Yellowstone and Yosemite National Parks combined. The appeal stretched beyond America's borders too. On his famous visit to the United States in 1959, Soviet Premier Nikita Khrushchev grew infuriated when the State Department canceled his visit to Disneyland, for security concerns.

INTEGRATING THE EMPIRE OF MAKE-BELIEVE

Selling the same characters in so many different ways, Walt Disney Productions earned profits every year during the fifties. By 1962, when the Walt Disney Company had produced over 500 television shows and the theme park was a huge success, its aging founder said, "Our business is still making motion pictures." But that wasn't quite true. The films

CONTINUOUS RELEASE

Before the advent of video rentals, most movies were released once and then consigned to history. Studios brought big hits, like *Gone with the Wind,* back into first-run movie houses, but the real money was usually made in the first release.

Disney, however, soon learned that successive generations could rediscover a family movie, as if it were brand new. For cartoon audiences, he established a "generation" at about seven years.

In its original 1937 release, *Snow White* more than earned back its costs, grossing $8.5 million. But that was just the beginning. In the United States alone, it was re-released six times by 1993. Dubbed into ten languages and distributed in forty-six countries, it has grossed $100 million. *Fantasia*, which barely broke even on its first release in 1940, was distributed widely in the 1960s and finally became a hit. It was most recently released in 1990, it's fiftieth anniversary. In controlling titles, the Walt Disney Company has also established a unique policy in video sales: placing movies on the market only for a limited period, to generate buying excitement to be repeated at another interval in the future. Video only reinforced Walt Disney's long-standing contention that animated figures could lead far richer commercial lives than their flesh-and-blood counterparts: Cartoons don't grow out of date and their stars never age or retire.

his factory continued to turn out were just the beginning of an integrated marketing process that Disney had expanded brilliantly over the years. Each new addition to the Disney family created a ripple effect in many different pools. In 1962, for example, the studio was preparing to release a new animated story called *The Sword in the Stone*, based on the legend of King Arthur. As part of the film's marketing push, Disney licensed publishers to produce comics and hardcover books based on the movie. Songs from the musical were released as records and sold in sheet music form. At factories across the country, several of the more than 100 Disney licensees labored to stamp out King Arthur swords and other products based on the film. And Disney made sure the film was introduced through all of his own commercial venues: advertisements ran during his television shows. On the strength of the shrewd packaging and repackaging of original material, Walt Disney's company had evolved into a sprawling giant, with about half of its revenues coming from motion pictures, one-third from Disneyland, and 5 percent from television and the remaining from merchandise licensing. Before the park opened, Walt Disney Productions took a one-third stake in Disneyland and soon after absorbed it completely.

Two projects received Walt Disney's full attention in the last years of his life. When critics complained in the early sixties that Disney movies had lost their high level of quality, with one-dimensional movies like *The Sword in the Stone* and *The Absent-Minded Professor*, Disney personally supervised *Mary Poppins* (1964). He oversaw every aspect of the picture, and the award-winning hit became one of the high points of his career.

The second project was more time-consuming. Even though some 50 million people had visited Disneyland by 1965, Disney wasn't satisfied. "Disneyland will never be completed as long as there is imagination left in the world," he liked to say. As the lead booster of Disneyland, Walt remained frustrated that the theme park just wasn't easily accessible to the majority of Americans, who lived in the east. Seeking to expand his empire's reach, he began to plan Disney World in 1958. He chose a site in 1965, purchasing 27,000 acres outside Orlando, Florida, for about $5 million. This swampy land in the center of the state would become the site of the new park, a veritable tomorrowland of family entertainment. "It's the biggest entire project we've tackled in forty-two years," Disney proclaimed. "We want something educational, something to keep the family together that would be a credit to the community, to the country as a whole." The $400-million park, which opened in 1971, was not merely an East Coast copy of Disneyland. It had aspirations as a model of city planning, featuring on-site resorts, hotels, and, ultimately, EPCOT (Experimental Prototype Community of Tomorrow) Center—a futuristic educational environment that featured pavilions representing different countries.

Walt Disney didn't live to see the completion of Disney World (or "Walt Disney World," as it was officially renamed in memoriam). A victim of lung cancer, he died at the age of sixty-five December 15, 1966. He left a company as his monument, a company that became an integral part of the American family.

Disney's innovations in animation and in business sprang from the same restless aspect of his character. "By nature I'm an experimenter," he said two months before his death, while accepting the Showman of the Year award. "To this day, I don't believe in sequels."

John H. Johnson and his daughter Linda Johnson Rice.

JOHN H. JOHNSON: FINDING THE BLACK CONSUMER

n 1995, *Ebony* magazine turned fifty years old. While its founder isn't as well known as other civil rights pioneers, perhaps he should be. With nothing more tangible than raw business talent, a tenacious belief in his own ideas, and the power of persistence, John H. Johnson pulled himself up from poverty in segregated Arkansas to a coveted spot on the *Forbes 400*. In 1942, at the age of twenty-four, Johnson published *Negro Digest*, the first successful consumer magazine to reach a mass audience of African Americans. From there, this great-grandson of slaves proceeded to forge an immense and varied enterprise focused upon the needs of black America. His complex of holdings, which includes *Ebony* and *Jet* magazines and two cosmetics companies is as significant for hundreds of black professionals it employs as it is for the services and products it offers to black consumers. Through his business achievements, he demonstrated the moral and economic benefits of reaching out to all races.

Long before experts spoke about the glories of niche marketing, Johnson recognized the economic potential of the black American market. Corporate America was skeptical. It took Johnson nearly three decades to convince the business establishment that there was a viable market for his and their firms' products.

DISCOVERING A MARKET WITHIN A MARKET

In November 1965 a glamorous crowd of 800, including chief executives and political figures, gathered for lunch at the Waldorf-Astoria's Starlight Roof to celebrate *Ebony* magazine's twentieth anniversary. Among those assembled were a galaxy of stars from the realms of politics, entertainment, and sports: Jackie Robinson, Lena Horne, Ossie Davis, then-U.S. Solicitor General Thurgood Marshall, the newspaper columnist Carl Rowan, the halfback James Brown, Muhammad Ali, Duke Ellington, and Sammy Davis, Jr. As a reporter commented: "The men and women in the room seemed to symbolize the progress Negroes had made in areas of American life once closed to them."

The nation's black aristocracy had gathered to celebrate the twentieth anniversary of a monthly magazine that covered a part of America that had largely been ignored by the mainstream national press. *Ebony*, adhering to its founding mission, "expressed the brighter side of Negro life and highlighted Negro achievement," Johnson boasted. But the world had changed. "Achievement in the old era was measured, to a great extent, by material things. . . . Today achievement is measured in terms of whatever a man sets out to do."

By either measure, John Johnson had already reached great heights. The Waldorf-Astoria was a long way from the tin-roofed house in Arkansas City, Arkansas, where he was born in 1918. His father, Leroy, died in 1926 in a sawmill accident, leaving his mother, Gertrude Johnson, to support her son and daughter as a cook and washerwoman.

The future was bleak for African Americans in the Depression-era Deep South. Arkansas City didn't fund a black high school, and there were few jobs outside of menial labor open to African Americans. Like millions of her peers throughout the South, Gertrude Johnson looked to the North for redemption from the hopelessness of her situation. After years of skimping and saving, she trundled her son and her belongings on a Chicago-bound train in 1933. "Chicago," John Johnson later wrote in his autobiography, *Succeeding Against the Odds*, "was to the Southern blacks of my generation what Mecca was to the Moslems and what Jerusalem was to the Jews: a place of magic and mirrors and dreams." The African-American migration had already transformed the South Side of Chicago into a segregated but fully functioning black metropolis—home to the nation's largest black-owned bank, to black-owned insurance companies, newspapers, and nightclubs, and to black-run political clubs. "Black Chicago, then and now, was a city within a city," Johnson wrote in 1986.

He thrived at the all-black DuSable High School, where he joined the yearbook staff and became editor in chief of the school paper. At night he pored over such self-improvement books as Dale Carnegie's *How to Win Friends and Influence People*.

At an assembly for honors students, Johnson drew up the courage to introduce himself to one of the speakers: Harry H. Pace, the president of Supreme Liberty Life Insurance Company, the most prominent black-owned business in the North. "I want to go to college," Johnson said, "but I don't have enough money." Pace told him to show up at his office the following September. With characteristic confidence, Johnson did just that, without an appointment, and announced: "The president is expecting me." Pace hired Johnson as an office assistant in 1936. Johnson worked part-time while attending the University of Chicago.

At Supreme Life, surrounded by well-dressed professional blacks, Johnson found a new home and further inspiration. Here was a rare company whose entire customer base and staff was black. "Until that moment, the height and color of my dream had been set by the ceiling and color of the Black preachers, teachers, and lawyers I'd seen," he said. "Now, suddenly, I was surrounded by Black clerks, salesmen, and money managers."

By 1939 Johnson was promoted to editor of the company's in-house monthly magazine, *The Guardian*. This was a compendium of articles about blacks culled from national publications of the day. Clipping articles at his desk, Johnson recognized his destiny. "It occurred to me that I was looking at a black gold mine," he said. Black America needed a magazine of its own. While local black newspapers thrived in virtually every major city, there was no national black consumer magazine. Johnson decided to found a black *Reader's Digest* entitled *Negro Digest*, a serious, national, text-based magazine that would run articles from prominent black and white writers on topics of interest to African Americans.

UNCONVENTIONAL TACTICS

With World War II raging, it was not an optimal moment for a twenty-four-year-old with little experience, black or white, to start a new magazine. The nation had only just emerged from the Depression. Johnson, having married Eunice Walker in 1941, had a wife to support. Nonetheless, he went to New York to seek the advice and blessing of Roy Wilkins, the editor of the National Association for the Advancement of Colored People's respected nonprofit magazine, *The Crisis*. Wilkins dismissed his idea. "Save your money, young man," he said. "Save your energy. Save yourself a lot of disappointment."

Johnson ignored Wilkins's warning. He believed that his magazine would succeed because it would meet a sizable demand. "In 1942, black men and women were struggling all over America for the right to be called 'Mr.' and 'Mrs.' In that year, we couldn't try on hats in department stores in Baltimore, and we couldn't try on shoes and dresses in Atlanta," Johnson said. "It was a world where the primary need, almost as demanding as oxygen, was recognition and respect." Johnson knew that his magazine could supply that vital air.

Harry Pace had offered to give Johnson access to Supreme Life's mailing list, a roster of 20,000 black consumers. Johnson anticipated that a few thousand of them would front the annual two-dollar subscription fee, which would provide the necessary start-up funds. But he quickly ran into his first roadblock—20,000 letters would cost $500 in postage. When Johnson applied for a loan, an officer at the First National Bank of Chicago laughed at him. "Boy, we don't make any loans to colored people," the man said. Johnson finally found a willing lender in the white-owned Citizens Loan Corporation, but it insisted on some collateral. The only security he could offer was his mother's furniture, but she first had to agree to it. "For three or four days, we prayed together and cried together," John Johnson recalled. Finally Gertrude said, "I think the Lord wants me to do it." From this point, there was no turning back. Johnson saw *Negro Digest* as more than a publication; it was his future. "I'm saying that I had decided once and for all. I was going to make it, or die," he wrote. He mailed out his 20,000 letters.

The mass mailing elicited some 3,000 founding subscribers, bringing in $6,000, enough to print an inaugural issue. Working in an office in the Supreme Life building, Johnson cobbled together the debut issue of *Negro Digest*, subtitled "A Magazine of Negro Comment," and brought it to market on November 1, 1942. The premiere issue included reprinted articles by such luminaries as Carl Sandburg and the NAACP director Walter White, along with a smattering of original pieces.

Soon after publication, Johnson pulled off the first of many marketing coups. Having printed 5,000 magazines, he was stuck with 2,000 extra copies. Most newsstands wouldn't carry them, "because colored books don't sell," the distributor Joseph Levy told him. Johnson devised a clever strategy to achieve his goal. He enlisted friends to ask repeatedly for *Negro Digest* at Levy's Chicago-area outlets. Responding to the grass-roots demand, Levy bought two thousand copies. Johnson then used these funds to reimburse his friends who had bought the magazine at Levy's newsstands.

Within eight months, *Negro Digest* had a national circulation of

50,000, mostly in Chicago and other cities with large black populations. Readers liked the magazine because its articles elevated blacks' self-image and because Johnson openly confronted racism, a topic rarely addressed in black or white publications. Johnson ran a regular feature entitled, "If I Were a Negro," in which prominent whites were asked to offer their thoughts on racial issues. Johnson eventually persuaded Eleanor Roosevelt to write one of these columns. "If I were Negro, I would have great bitterness," she wrote in an October, 1943 cover story that garnered national attention and helped boost *Negro Digest's* circulation to 100,000.

EXPANDING WITHIN THE BLACK MARKET

With *Negro Digest* bringing in profits during its first year, Johnson sought to expand. After buying a street-level storefront on the South Side for $4,000 in 1943 to serve as his office, he began searching for new opportunities. When the artist/cartoonist Jay Jackson and the writer Ben Burns approached him with the idea of starting a black-oriented entertainment magazine, Johnson was intrigued and agreed to fund the venture. Just as *Negro Digest* was modeled after *Reader's Digest*, Johnson would now create a magazine in the image of Henry Luce's hugely successful *Life*. Less concerned with politics and topical issues than *Negro Digest*, this new magazine would offer intimate glimpses into the lives of black achievers and celebrities. "We wanted to emphasize the positive aspects of Black life. We wanted to highlight achievements and make Blacks proud of themselves," Johnson said. "From the beginning, I considered the company as a vehicle for building and projecting the image of Black people in America, an image that had been distorted by media oriented primarily to nonblacks."

The first issue of *Ebony* (his wife, Eunice, came up with the name) appeared on newsstands on November 1, 1945, and it had a 25,000-copy press run. Within hours those copies were sold and Johnson printed another 25,000 copies. Relying on writers he had met through *Negro*

Digest, Johnson ran a mix of features. The cover story was a first-person account by a New York pastor who took Harlem kids to Vermont farms. There was also a profile on the writer Richard Wright. Johnson delighted in putting the images of beautiful black women on *Ebony*'s cover. In March 1946, the first four-color cover featured Lena Horne; it sold 275,000 copies. The following year *Ebony* became the first black magazine tracked by the Audit Bureau of Circulation, and it registered a circulation of 309,715.

REACHING WHITE ADVERTISERS

While subscriptions provided a solid financial foundation, *Ebony*, like all magazines, needed advertising revenue to sustain itself. Johnson refused to compromise quality, insisting on the same standards that white audiences might find in *Life*; but slick paper, high-quality presses, and lots of photographs made *Ebony* an expensive proposition. And since Johnson ran it at a loss, the bigger the magazine grew, the more money he lost. "My problem was not the editorial content of the magazine—the readers were yelling for more. My problem was not circulation—I couldn't print enough copies. My problem was advertising or, to come right out with it, the lack of advertising."

Just as blacks were largely prohibited from conducting business with white companies—indeed, were generally barred from other aspects of white life—white advertisers did not buy space in black magazines. The legal and social segregation of mid-century America made it more difficult for Johnson to obtain the basic goods and services that any business requires to function. Amenities other business people took for granted, such as lodging, weren't always available to him. On a business trip to Washington, Johnson was denied a room at the Shoreham Hotel. (To this day, he refuses to stay there.) He had problems acquiring office space as well. When he realized the building owner wouldn't sell to a black man, Johnson posed as the janitor for an alleged white purchaser, and inspected the building dressed in overalls. (He later bought the building through an intermediary.)

While the publisher continually butted his head against the wall of racial prejudice, he refused to limit his ambitions. "When I see a barrier, I cry and I curse, and then I get a ladder and climb over it," he said. As *Forbes* observed: "Such an attitude can make for a tenacious salesman." Putting Dale Carnegie's lessons to use, Johnson tried to sell executives from various companies on the idea that their advertising dollars would be well spent in *Ebony*.

When Fairfax Cone, the head of the powerful Chicago advertising agency Foote, Cone & Belding, declined to see him, Johnson learned from a sympathetic secretary that Cone would be riding a particular train from Chicago to New York. Johnson made sure he was on that train, and he cornered Cone in the club car. Before the train pulled into New York, Johnson had himself a customer—and an important long-term relationship.

Johnson reasoned that since most blacks owned radios, and since Zenith, a leading manufacturer, had its headquarters in Chicago, *Ebony* would be a natural outlet for Zenith advertising. But before he approached Commander Eugene McDonald, the company's chairman, Johnson laid some necessary groundwork. Learning that McDonald had trekked to the North Pole, Johnson tracked down Matthew Henson, an African-American explorer who had actually beaten the pioneering American explorer Commodore Robert Peary to the Pole. Johnson had Henson inscribe a copy of a book Henson had written and also ran a four-page article on the explorer in *Ebony*'s July 1947 issue. At Zenith, Johnson steered the conversation to polar exploration, which wasn't hard, since McDonald displayed on his wall a pair of snowshoes given him by Matt Henson. "Young man," said McDonald as if on cue, "if you were putting out any kind of a magazine you would have something on Matt Henson." Johnson then showed him the published article. "I don't see why we shouldn't be advertising in this magazine," McDonald concluded.

Johnson's confidence in the potential of the black consumer market paid off. He demonstrated to prospective corporate clients that African Americans bought more U.S. goods than Canadians did, and that they were an economic force that deserved attention. With each success, Johnson proved that profit motive was stronger than racism. By early 1948 he had enlisted Pepsi-Cola, Colgate, Beech-Nut, Seagram, and Remington Rand as advertisers for the magazine.

However, selling advertisements to one executive at a time was far too time-consuming and inefficient. The publisher realized that the long-term viability of his operations hinged on his ability to attract advertisers en masse. So he used mass media to inform large numbers of corporate decision-makers about the commercial possibilities in the undiscovered Negro consumer market. To that end, Johnson began to write occasional pieces in his own magazine and trade publications. As early as 1947 he wrote in *Ebony*, "big advertisers of consumer items fail to recognize the immensity of the Negro market." In 1952 he wrote in *Advertising Age* that the black consumer market, $15 billion strong, was "ripe and ready."

After its early success, *Negro Digest* began to lose money and Johnson recognized that the magazine must give way to more dynamic and original publications. He shut it down in 1951. At the same time, he raided the staffs of black newspapers to start *Hue*, a pocket-sized feature magazine, and *Jet*, a news magazine. The cover of the first *Jet* on November 1, 1951, featured Edna Robinson, the wife of Sugar Ray Robinson. Within six months its circulation grew to 300,000 copies a week.

As the business grew, the Johnson Publishing Company evolved from a one-man shop into a publishing enterprise with offices in Chicago, New York, and Washington D.C. A vast majority of the more than one hundred employees were black. By November 1955, when his magazines had a combined circulation of 2.6 million, the publisher had become a real force in black America. Johnson was appointed to the boards of the Tuskegee Institute and the National Urban League. In 1957 after buying 1,000 shares of the life insurance stock, he accepted an invitation to join the board of directors of Supreme Liberty Life Insurance, the company that had given him his first job. Over the next several years, Johnson regularly purchased stock in the company, and by 1964 he was the largest shareholder.

JOINING THE MAINSTREAM IN TURBULENT TIMES

Johnson had shrewdly positioned his products in the marketplace in the 1950s, and his foresight paid off handsomely in the 1960s. Rather than use the personal appeals and trade magazine articles of the past, the Johnson Publishing Company began to adopt more sophisticated tactics to convince white corporations of the promise of the African-American market. With the help of Fairfax Cone, who had become a crucial business partner, *Ebony* produced two promotional films—*There's Gold in Your Backyard* and *The Secret of Selling the Negro*—that served as how-to guides for potential advertisers. Dr. Frank Davis, hired by Johnson to serve as research director, released numbers to the press showing that black purchasing power would top $20 billion in 1961, and that the black population in the United States was rising at 3 percent a year, compared with the 2 percent growth rate for whites. As blacks continued to stream from low-paying jobs in the South to higher wages in northern urban centers, their incomes grew. The average family income for Southern blacks was less than $2,000 a year in 1960, compared with nearly $4,000 for their Northern counterparts.

Blacks' sense of empowerment was rising along with their incomes. And Johnson's magazines rode the crest of the burgeoning civil rights movement and the swelling wave of black power. In the 1950s he endured criticism from blacks who said he wasn't sufficiently militant on the crucial issues of the day. However, both *Ebony* and *Jet* had consistently covered civil rights issues, from Little Rock in 1957 to the March on Washington in 1963, and Martin Luther King, Jr. was a contributor to both magazines. Johnson walked a tightrope: he balanced the need to report the news of radical change with the desire to appeal to his subscribers who were drawn largely from the more moderate, affluent segments of black America. A 1967 survey showed *Ebony* families had a median income of $6,648, placing them near the top 20 percent of black families.

Over the course of the 1960s, however, Johnson and his magazines came to reflect the changes sweeping through their audiences. "We were moderate when the Negro population was moderate, and we became militant when our readers became more militant," he said. In 1966, *Ebony* ran a piece entitled, "The White Problem in America," which laid much of the blame for black America's problems at the feet of the white majority. Another provocative piece, written by the magazine's senior editor Lerone Bennett, Jr. in 1968, asked the question: "Was Abraham Lincoln a White Supremacist?" While running such articles posed the risk of alienating hard-won white advertisers, Johnson didn't flinch. "It's no good carrying advertising unless we have the confidence of our readers." And the readers continued to express their confidence. *Ebony*'s circulation, which stood at 623,000 in 1960, first passed the one-million mark in October 1967, helping push the company's revenues to the $10-million mark.

Furthermore, Johnson's aggressive editorial stance did not, in fact, alienate his colleagues in corporate America. As the moral strength of Dr. King's message was increasingly embraced by political leaders, white executives began opening up to the idea of an integrated nation. "I don't want to destroy the system—I want to get into it," he said. As the nation's leading African-American businessman and a major publisher, Johnson rubbed shoulders with presidents, including John F. Kennedy and Richard Nixon, and even posed for a photograph with Lyndon Johnson holding an issue of *Jet*. John Johnson joined the corporate boards of high-profile companies, such as Zenith and 20th Century Fox, and bought a house on a mountaintop in the celebrity haven of Palm Springs. By 1968, eighty of the nation's top 100 advertisers could be found on *Ebony*'s client roster. After three decades of relentlessly serving and promoting the powerful black community, Johnson had gained the recognition of the white establishment.

By virtually any measure, the man who had been laughed out of a loan office in 1942 was by 1970 a member of the nation's elite. The most visible manifestation of Johnson's arrival was an $11-million, eleven-story headquarters building built in 1972 for the firm's several hundred employees. While it featured black American and African art, a cafeteria, and a 15,000-volume library, the building's most notable feature was its address: 820 South Michigan Avenue. Squarely within the confines of Chicago's blue-chip business district, Johnson's headquarters were, as UPI noted, "the first Chicago Loop building exclusively designed and constructed by a black-owned corporation."

NICHE MARKETING
IN AN INTEGRATED SOCIETY

Even as he gained acceptance and recognition in white America, Johnson remained unapologetically focused on the African-American market. He knew that any legislative reforms would not immediately alter the social reality that had informed his original business plan. "We are moving in a crisis of identity," he said in 1973. "Everyone wants to identify with his own." And so when Johnson Publishing Company diversified in the 1970s, it sought to provide new services and products for its core market. Johnson bought two radio stations with black music formats, started *Ebony Jr!* in 1973, and sponsored television shows like the *Ebony Music Awards* and the *American Black Achievement Awards*. In 1974 he also gained complete control of Supreme Liberty Life Insurance and folded that company into his publishing corporation. Though the Johnson Publishing Company now a diversified powerhouse, *Ebony* and *Jet* remained the pillars of its prosperity. In 1983 when, by *Forbes*'s estimation, "Johnson's magazines reach nearly half the U.S. adult black popula-

SUPREME LIBERTY LIFE: FROM OFFICE BOY TO CHAIRMAN OF THE BOARD

I don't invest in anything I can't control" is one of John Johnson's favorite maxims, one reflected in his relationship with Supreme Liberty Life Insurance Company, the black-owned insurance firm where Johnson went to work as an office assistant in 1936.

In the 1950s, as Johnson's magazines began to generate profits, he invested excess cash in the privately held Supreme Liberty Life. When he purchased 1,000 shares for $30,000 in 1957, Johnson was named to the board of directors. As *Ebony* and *Jet* grew, Johnson continued to increase his holdings. By 1964 he was the largest shareholder, and in 1974, having invested a totai of about $2.5 million, Johnson was elected chairman and chief executive officer of the firm.

Johnson's control of Supreme Liberty Life has enabled him to maintain sole ownership of his publishing empire. Rather than sell shares or bonds to the public to raise funds, Johnson used the insurance company's consistent cash flow to finance new ventures, ranging from a cosmetics company to radio stations. In the early 1990s, he sold Supreme Liberty to another insurance company, United of America.

tion," the $118-million company unseated Motown Industries to become the top of *Black Enterprise* magazine's list of black-owned corporations.

Throughout the years, Johnson resisted the temptation to cash out his holdings by selling shares in the company to the public. Rather, he relied on the cash flow from the magazines and from Supreme Life to finance expansion. As the sole owner and proprietor of the booming company, John Johnson reaped the windfall. Continuing to break the race barrier, in 1982 he became the first black man to land on the *Forbes 400*.

The founder continued to run the company as the stern father of a growing family, albeit with the aide of his daughter and designated heir, Linda Johnson Rice. Upon receiving her MBA from Northwestern's Kellogg School, she was named president and chief operating officer at the age of twenty-nine.

The man whom *Forbes* called "perhaps the richest and certainly the most powerful black businessman in the country" is still intensely aware of the reasons for his success: the ability to connect with black consumers. "I'm at the top, but not a day goes by without someone reminding me in some way that I am black," he wrote in *Succeeding Against the Odds*. When Johnson started in business, his race was a tremendous liability. His genius has been to turn that liability into a profitable advantage.

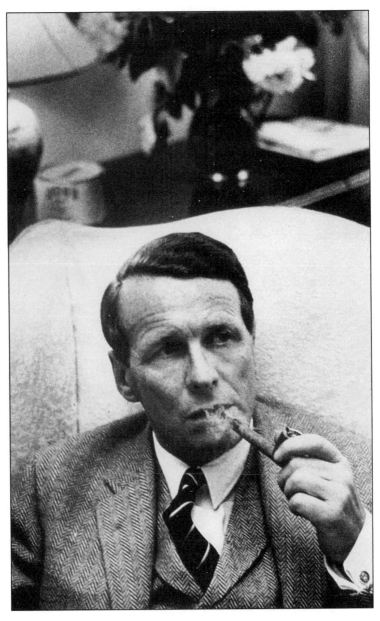

David Ogilvy, chairman of Ogilvy & Mather, in 1963.

DAVID OGILVY AND THE CREATION OF MODERN ADVERTISING

mong the countless stories of newcomers finding fame and fortune in America, few are as entertaining and unusual as David Ogilvy's. An unconventional Englishman who made American conventions his life's study, the Oxford dropout was a flamboyant and successful advertising man. The firm he founded in 1948 quickly grew into one of the world's largest advertising agencies. And by combining research with willful self-promotion, Ogilvy became, in the words of the writer Martin Mayer, "one of the more likable and legitimately odd figures in the American business scene." The widely imitated ads his firm produced, and the theories that lay behind them, helped change the face of advertising. In the process, David Ogilvy became known as a sort of philosopher of advertising—and *Ogilvy on Advertising*, the book he wrote in 1983, was his *magnum opus*.

At the beginning of his varied career, Ogilvy became fluent in the scientific testing and measuring of public opinion by working for the Gallup organization. His innovation was to bring the dispassionate science of popular opinion to bear on advertising, an industry thought to be governed more by emotion than by fact. In an effort to translate theory into practice, Ogilvy started his own firm—a bold move considering he had almost no experience. He quickly made a name for himself by devising risky, off-beat campaigns that created well-known brand images for companies. But when trying to conjure up sizzle and buzz for his clients' products, Ogilvy didn't rely solely on catchy phrases or sexy images. Rather, he used cold, hard facts. Gleaning statistics from polling data to determine the style and content of his advertisements, Ogilvy created exacting formulas that specified the ideal mixture of copy and images. His campaigns were wildly successful, as time and again he proved that facts can indeed translate into sales power.

By the time Ogilvy withdrew from the daily operations of his firm in the 1960s, Ogilvy & Mather was among the largest advertising firms in the world, and much of the advertising industry had adopted the scientific methods David Ogilvy had pioneered. He showed that a pitch based on painstaking research, packaged with flair, and placed in a few carefully chosen venues can have a greater effect than an unfocused advertising blitz.

A RESTLESS ENGLISHMAN MAKES HIS WAY TO AMERICA

As a child in the 1910s, David Ogilvy lived in a house once occupied by Lewis Carroll in the English countryside. But his upbringing was somewhat less fanciful than that imagined by the creator of *Alice in Wonderland*. Ogilvy's father, a classical scholar turned stockbroker, was financially ruined by World War I. Despite his misfortunes, he managed to send his son to the prestigious Fettes School in Scotland. Even though David was not among the school's top students, he won a scholarship to Christ Church, Oxford, to study history. "I would rather have been a historian than an advertising man," he later recalled in a rare moment of humility. "But I didn't have the brains to be a historian."

A restless youth in search of adventure, Ogilvy eventually exchanged the shaded cloisters of Oxford for Paris, where he found work as an assistant chef in the Hotel Majestic. He became bored in France and returned to England to sell Aga cooking stoves, a new brand of institutional oven. Ogilvy called upon schools and great houses, trying to sell English cooks on the virtues of the large ovens, and proved so successful at it that the company asked him to write a manual for its sales force. In 1935 he wrote a treatise on the product, entitled "The Theory and Practice of Selling the Aga Cooker." Jam-packed with facts about the cooker, it contained advice on which sorts of pitches would work best with different kinds of customers.

Ogilvy sent a copy of the brochure to his brother Francis, the managing director at the venerable London-based advertising firm of Mather & Crowther. Impressed, Francis immediately hired David as a trainee. For the next three years David Ogilvy enjoyed the life of a young man about town. "I went to concerts and balls which lasted until dawn. . . . I skylarked with girls," he recalled. "But it was during this period that I acquired the habit of hard work. And when my salary was doubled, I tasted blood." During this time, he was already starting to develop his own theories about advertising. In a 1936 presentation to colleagues at M & C, he laid out six governing theses. "Every word in the copy must count," read one. "Concrete figures must be substituted for atmospheric claims; clichés must give way to facts, and empty exhortations to alluring offers." Coming from a twenty-five-year-old with little experience, these suggestions might have seemed the musings of a precocious young man. Yet they became pillars of his theory of advertising, ideas that would make him among the most successful ad men of the century.

One of David Ogilvy's responsibilities was to monitor American advertising campaigns sent over by a clipping service. The research made him eager to learn more about America, and he sought a way to cross the Atlantic, "partly because I wanted to prove that I could succeed on my own, without the patronage of my brother." In 1938, still relying on his brother's patronage, he persuaded the firm to send him to the United States so he could study American advertising. Ogilvy made the trans-Atlantic journey in style, and upon arriving in New York he continued his high living. He fell in with the writer and drama critic Alexander Woollcott and his circle—which included Harpo Marx and Ethel Barrymore—thanks to introductions from his cousin, the author Rebecca West.

After making a report to his employers in 1939, Ogilvy quit his job and went to Princeton to attend his own version of graduate school. Eager to expand his inquiry into American consumer habits, Ogilvy landed a job with Dr. George Gallup, the great theorist of modern polling, whose company was located in the New Jersey college town. (Gallup was that rare breed of academic who could spin a scientific theory into lucrative practice. After working as Young & Rubicam's research director, he set up his own company to provide polling services.) Gallup put Ogilvy to work on a project Ogilvy called the "Audit of Marquee Values." Ogilvy's task was to conduct interviews that would measure public responses to stars' names and movie titles on theater marquees. While the job paid only $40 a week, the experience it afforded was invaluable. Ogilvy learned that consumers' preferences could be divined through their responses to carefully formulated questions. And he learned a great deal about American tastes. "If you ever decide to seek your fortune in a foreign country, the best thing you can do is to get a job with the local Gallup Poll. It will teach you what the natives want out of life, what they think about the main issues of the day, what their habits are."

When World War II broke out, Ogilvy left Gallup to work for British intelligence in Washington. During the war years he visited Amish country in Lancaster, Pennsylvania. Although the exuberant Englishman must have seemed out of place among the so-called Plain People, he became enchanted by their simple lives. After the war he leased several acres, and tried his hand at tobacco farming. "The years we spent in Lancaster County were the richest of my life," he recalled. "But it became apparent that I could never earn my living as a farmer."

FOUNDING A NEW ADVERTISING FIRM

After a few years in the quiet Pennsylvania countryside, Ogilvy was eager to return to the excitement of a big city like New York. At the age of thirty-eight, however, he was no longer a bright young whip just off the ship from Britain. He wanted to get back into advertising, and initially thought about seeking a job with Young & Rubicam. "But I never thought that Y & R would hire me—I didn't think I had any credentials," he said in a 1976 interview. "So the only thing I could do was start up on my own." It was an audacious act: he had only $6,000, no clients, no ads to show prospective clients, and no experience working in American advertising. But he felt he had something that really mattered: the appropriate theoretical training. "Dr. Gallup had taught me what he had discovered about the factors which make advertisements succeed or fail. . . . And I had read all the books about advertising, such as they were."

In an industry that values hands-on experience over book learning, Ogilvy did have one concrete asset: his brother. While David was in America, Francis had risen to managing director at Mather & Crowther.

Eager to help his brilliant younger brother, Francis persuaded his partners to finance David with $45,000 and let him use their name. He also enlisted another British advertising firm, S. H. Benson Ltd., to contribute $45,000 to form a joint venture that would, they hoped, establish a British beachhead in North America. As a condition for their investments, the British firms demanded that Ogilvy find an American to run the new venture. "They did not believe that one of their fellow countrymen could persuade American manufacturers to give him any business," he wrote. So he hired Anderson Hewitt, a well-connected J. Walter Thompson executive, and made him a partner.

In 1948 the firm of Hewitt, Ogilvy, Benson & Mather opened its doors. The proprietor of the new shop had no intention of building slowly. On the second day of business Ogilvy made a list of the five clients he most desired: General Foods, Bristol-Myers, Campbell Soup, Lever Brothers, and Shell Oil. "To pick such blue-chip targets was an act of mad presumption," he later conceded.

Ogilvy's first campaign was for his own newborn firm. He informed the trade press of his existence and sent unsolicited progress reports to hundreds of executives, although there wasn't much progress to report. With the help of his London connections, he landed a few small British clients like Guinness Ale and Wedgwood China (who spent just $40,000 a year on advertising). Otherwise, the response was generally underwhelming. After all, Ogilvy's firm was one of 3,000 American agencies vying for major accounts in a business where conservative companies worked with established firms they had known for years. "Six weeks after I started my agency, I was so desperate for business that I offered a young man of my acquaintance 10 percent of our stock if he brought in a vacuum-cleaner account which he had in his pocket," he later said. Fortunately for Ogilvy, the man refused.

Hewitt saved the day when, after five months, the partners had run through three-quarters of their capital. Hewitt's uncle, the chairman of J. P. Morgan & Co., arranged to lend the fledgling business $100,000 with no security. More importantly, Hewitt lassoed the Sun Oil

Company, a $3-million account. Upon landing this blue-chip client, the tiny firm was in business.

Although he worked in an industry that was generally bureaucratic, Ogilvy was a jack-of-all-trades. "The best fun I ever had was in the early days of Ogilvy & Mather, when I was both research director and creative director. On Friday afternoons I wrote research reports to the creative director. On Monday mornings I changed hats, read my reports, and decided what to do about them—if anything."

An early account with Hathaway, a small Maine-based shirtmaker, helped put Ogilvy on the map. Dwarfed by Arrow, the dominant shirtmaker, Hathaway sought to raise its profile with an advertising campaign. But it only wanted to spend about $30,000 a year. Arrow spent about $2 million on its advertising program, which was run by the established firm of Young & Rubicam. Yet Ogilvy believed he had a shot at beating Goliath. Large firms like Young & Rubicam tended to become conservative. They were vulnerable to nimble companies possessed of bold ideas.

Ogilvy was primed to offer low-profile clients with modest budgets a brand of advertising they wouldn't receive from more established firms. In the 1940s most ads were illustrated with drawings accompanied by attention-grabbing slogans. But based on his experience with Gallup, Ogilvy believed photographs would make a more compelling case for the product. He also knew from his research that endowing a photograph with "story appeal"—some unique, attention-grabbing feature—would pique the reader's curiosity.

Casting about for some sort of "hook," Ogilvy found inspiration in a drugstore he passed on his way to the Hathaway photo shoot. Acting on impulse, he purchased a $1.50 eyepatch featured in the store's window display, placed the patch on a mustachioed male model, and created a series of advertisements in which the Man from Hathaway engaged in activities ranging from driving a tractor to purchasing a Renoir painting. The campaign attracted a great deal of attention and was widely copied overseas. "Exactly why it turned out to be so successful, I shall never know," Ogilvy wrote of the campaign. The jaunty, European-looking

Hathaway model bore more than a superficial resemblance to its creator. From the beginning, Ogilvy had conflated his own personality with that of the firm: now; it almost seemed he did the same with the campaigns his agency produced. The Hathaway man campaign became a classic in the annals of advertising, and it helped establish the firm, which by 1953 had $10 million in billings.

The Hathaway eyepatch represented Ogilvy's first major attempt at creating brand image, one of his singular contributions to the industry. "Every advertisement should be thought of as a contribution to the complex symbol which is the brand image," he wrote. Ogilvy was far from the first to make this observation. But he was the first to develop it into a practical philosophy that allowed a brand image to evolve.

Ogilvy had an opportunity to apply the brand-image thesis to other products when a Puerto Rican economic development agency hired the firm to do a tourism campaign in 1954. He realized the client's main problem was the generally negative image people had of the Common-wealth. "We must substitute a lovely image of Puerto Rico for the squalid image which now exists in the minds of most mainlanders," he said. He devised a campaign that highlighted Puerto Rico's history and portrayed it as an island in renaissance. By his own immodest admission, "[The campaign] has had a profound effect on the fortunes of Puerto Rico. It is, I believe, the only instance of an advertising campaign changing the image of a country."

He further developed the theory of brand image with the firm's next major client, Schweppes, which he landed in 1955. Ogilvy turned Commander Edward Whitehead, the manager of the British beverage company's U.S. unit, into the star of the commercials. As *Forbes* later noted: "His was the memorable campaign that introduced Schweppes to this country, playing on America's fascination with British snobbery by featuring distinguished, bearded Commander Edward Whitehead." U.S. sales of Schweppes rose 500 percent in the nine years after the introduction of the campaign. Proving the point about consistency and brand image, Whitehead appeared in the advertisements for eighteen years.

Ogilvy also labored to create a brand image for himself. With dashing good looks and the ability to toss off quotes from writers and historical figures with ease, he pegged himself as "conservatively flamboyant." The *New York Times* noted in 1958: "For one thing, the forty-seven-year-old Mr. Ogilvy's dress and manner cause him to stand out, particularly among ad men, many of whom follow a pattern in their getup." In an industry where men (and they were virtually all men) donned the uniform of dark suits and red ties, he wore tweeds and light-colored suits with a foulard. His glasses hung down by the end of the nose, and he often sported a pipe.

While Ogilvy excelled at managing his own image, he didn't have the same success in dealing with the administrative details at Ogilvy, Benson & Mather. (The "Hewitt" was dropped when Anderson Hewitt left the firm in the mid-1950s). Realizing that the firm was growing beyond his capabilities to manage it, he recruited Esty Stowell, a former executive at Benton & Bowles, to become executive vice president in 1957. Stowell had a strong reputation as a marketing expert, and helped the agency acquire a reputation for strength in all departments. Stowell also took responsibility for managing the growing agency. "With a sigh of relief I turned over to him the management of every department in the agency except the creative departments. From that point on our agency began to grow in bigger chunks." Stowell had the experience and clout to attract important new clients, like Maxwell House Coffee (for whom the firm later created the enduring "Good to the Last Drop" campaign).

Though a relative newcomer to the scene, Ogilvy had become a huge hit in less than a decade. And nobody was more aware of this status than he. "I doubt whether any copywriter has ever produced so many winners in such a short period," the Briton wrote in 1978, with typical immodesty. "They made Ogilvy & Mather so hot that getting clients was like shooting fish in a barrel." The success also made the firm an attractive acquisition target for larger established agencies. Starting in 1955 Ogilvy had to rebuff larger firms who sought to acquire the outfit.

SELLING PRODUCTS WITH PLAIN FACTS

Not every move Ogilvy made proved a stroke of genius. He advised a client to pay Eleanor Roosevelt $35,000 to endorse Good Luck margarine in television commercials. This investment proved a bust, since people remembered the pitchwoman more than the pitch. "In those days I did not know that it is a mistake to use celebrities," Ogilvy said. "They are remembered but the product is forgotten."

This bit of Ogilvy wisdom has yet to become conventional. But his conclusion about celebrities led to a key evolution in his theory of advertising. As he would later put it, "make your product the hero of the commercial." Ogilvy came to believe the product should stand front and center because his experience with polling taught him that the consumer was an independent thinker. "The consumer isn't a moron; she is your wife. You insult her intelligence if you assume that a mere slogan and a few vapid adjectives will persuade her to buy anything. She wants all the information you can give her," he said.

Ogilvy's longstanding views on facts in advertising got their earliest full expression in 1958 with the advertisements he created for yet another British company, Rolls-Royce. After getting the assignment Ogilvy spent three weeks reading everything he could about the luxury automobile. "We made a list of every fact that we could get about the car and then boiled this down for the ad," he said. "We then wrote twenty-five headlines and had the copy supervisors decide on the best one." The result was a full-page advertisement with thirteen points containing 719 carefully measured words about the $14,000 car. The headline read: "At 60 Miles an Hour the Loudest Noise in This New Rolls-Royce Comes from the Electric Clock." "In my Rolls-Royce advertisement I gave nothing but facts. No adjectives, 'no gracious living.'" This approach proved enormously successful. The ad ran in only two newspapers and two magazines and cost $25,000, but it garnered an immense amount of attention.

Well-written, persuasive, and free from hustle, it emerged as a kind of template for future works.

As he continued to devise campaigns for an expanding roster of clients, including American Express and Shell Oil (another of his original dream clients), Ogilvy began to imbue his campaigns with scientific methodology. Having concluded the efficacy of a fact-based approach, the question remained as to which facts about a product mattered most. Gallup and other pollsters had conducted research on the factors that made people read advertisements and the factors that make people remember them. Increasingly, Ogilvy sought to apply the findings to determine the precise combination of images and information that would best sell a product. In preparation for a Helena Rubinstein campaign in the late 1950s he asked consumers what asset or capability of a facial-care product would make them most likely to buy. The research revealed that "cleans deep into pores" notched the highest score. As a result, the product was named Deep Cleanser. Ogilvy undertook this kind of pre-testing because he believed it was the agency's responsibility to create concrete results. By conducting research before writing copy, the advertising agency gave its client crucial marketing advice. "At our agency we accept the responsibility for selling things. Either we help sales or we are fired," he said.

In 1963 his firm had $55 million in annual billings to nineteen clients, including all five blue-chip firms he had identified as must-haves back in 1948. And the agency had spread to Chicago and Los Angeles. That year, Ogilvy published a book, called *Confessions of an Advertising Man*, which ultimately sold 800,000 copies in twelve different languages and made him a quasicelebrity. It may as well have been entitled "Advertisements for Myself," as it contained much self-congratulation, name-dropping, and puffery; he referred to his firm as "my atelier." Coming from an American, such antics would have seemed affected, but they fit into the prevailing brand image of the British. Besides, Ogilvy regarded such self-promotion as a necessity. "I can only plead that if I had behaved in a more professional way, it would have taken me twenty years to arrive," he wrote. "I had neither the time nor the money to wait."

In the book, aside from describing his own stunning rise on Madison Avenue, Ogilvy laid out in detail his developing philosophy on advertising, including fifteen rules on how to be a good client.

Advertisements, he taught, could be constructed with the exacting specifications of a jet engine. And their performance could be measured just as precisely, based on studies made by the firm and by polling groups. Headlines were crucial because "Five times as many people read the headline as read the body copy." And since research proved it was dangerous to use negatives in headlines, he urged copywriters to speak to readers' self-interest by employing phrases like "how to." As for the text, "Research shows that readership falls off rapidly up to fifty words of copy, but drops very little between fifty and 500 words." And he advised a focus on advice or service, since this approach "hooks about 75 percent more readers than copy which deals entirely with the product." Through experimentation, Ogilvy had even developed formulas for the successful advertisement. "If you start your body copy with a large initial letter, you will increase readership by an average of 13 percent," he advised. "If you use leading between paragraphs, you increase readership by an average of 12 percent." Yet he warned ad people not to use research "as a drunkard uses a lamp post, for support rather than for illumination."

Confessions achieved for Ogilvy the visibility he craved. Indeed, in 1964 he was even offered the leading role in a Broadway play entitled *Roar Like a Dove*. He refused, in part because the business of the agency came to occupy more of his time.

AN ESTABLISHED FIRM GOES PUBLIC AND GROWS GLOBALLY

The British firms that gave Ogilvy his start had slowly sold their stakes to him. By the end of 1964 Mather & Crowther's stake fell to 8 percent,

Benson's was eliminated altogether, and David Ogilvy personally owned 31 percent of the stock. Meanwhile, Mather & Crowther had grown quickly, largely under the leadership of Francis Ogilvy. Its billings rose from $8 million to $53 million between 1954 and 1964. After Francis died in March 1964, David Ogilvy entered discussions with the firm where he had first learned his trade. In January 1965 the two firms merged to create Ogilvy & Mather, or O & M as it was often known. Upon the merger's completion, Ogilvy presided over a firm with 600 staffers and a strong presence on two continents. Of its combined 1965 billings totaling more than $120 million, 59 percent were from North America, 28 percent from Britain, and 13 percent from Europe.

But the philosopher turned philosopher-king realized he was better equipped to be the brains rather than the muscle behind the enterprise, and he shunned the executive suite. "I am not an administrator. I do not wish to be an administrator. I will not be an administrator," he declared. A company biographical sketch from the 1960s said: "David Ogilvy is a copywriter at Ogilvy, Benson & Mather. He is also Chairman of the Board." In December 1965 Ogilvy promoted a colleague, John (Jock) Elliott Jr., to Chief Executive so Ogilvy himself could focus on the firm's creative work.

But Ogilvy was not entirely aloof from matters financial. He took the company public in April 1966. Ogilvy & Mather sold 349,883 shares at $22 each, becoming the sixth ad firm to go public. At the time, it was the ninth largest in the world, with billings of $150 million. Ogilvy, who owned 161,000 shares, sold 61,000 in the offering and still had a substantial stake in the firm. He spent some of the money raised in the public offering on a second home, a magnificent twelfth-century chateau called Touffou, perched atop a cliff overlooking a tributary of the Loire in the south of France. He began spending increasing amounts of time there, so much so that in 1975 he formally relinquished his day-to-day creative control.

With the guidance of the managers Ogilvy had hired and nurtured, the firm continued to grow. "In a wickedly erratic business, O & M stands out like a prime-time show without commercial breaks," *Forbes* wrote in 1977. "It hasn't had a down year since going public in 1966." In 1976, it earned $7.7 million on revenues of $112 million and its billings approached $800 million. Even more remarkable than a lengthy string of rising dividends was the loyalty of some of the firm's customers in an industry where fickle clients are the norm. American Express, which came on board in 1962 with a $1-million account, remained an O & M client as it grew. By 1984 American Express was spending $70 million a year on advertising.

OGILVY MELLOWS INTO A SAGE

By 1981 the agency had grown to include a hundred offices in thirty-five countries, 1,600 clients, and billings of $1.7 billion. From virtual retirement, David Ogilvy kept watch on his expanding empire and wrote the *magnum opus* that would distill a half-century of experience in advertising. Characteristically injecting his name and ego into the mix, he titled the 1983 textbook *Ogilvy on Advertising*. With this grand synthesis of years of thought and experiment, the cocky young self-promoter had completed his metamorphosis into a wise elder statesman. Chockablock with such Ogilvyisms as "Ads with news are recalled by 22 percent more people than ads without news," *Ogilvy on Advertising* has remained in print continuously and is widely used as a college-level text.

The sage of Touffou entertained his visitors in style and offered informal seminars to journalists and colleagues. Adopting the pose of an elderly crank, he periodically fulminated about the vulgarity of contemporary advertising, singling out in particular television. "Every ten or fifteen years, advertising gets a disease called entertainment," he told *Forbes* in 1988. "It's very bad, because the people who do it have

BREAKING AWAY FROM COMMISSIONS

In 1960, with a growing roster of blue-chip clients and a burgeoning reputation, David Ogilvy seemed well on his way to joining the exclusive club of top advertising men. Yet Ogilvy insisted on maintaining an iconoclastic posture by undercutting one of the industry's most-cherished and longstanding business practices: the 15 percent commission. For as long as anyone in the industry could remember, companies had paid agencies 15 percent of the total cost of their campaigns, regardless of their size, quality, or effectiveness. The commission had become enshrined as one of the foundations of the business, so basic that few questioned it.

Those few dissenters included Ogilvy. "We believe that the commission system is an anachronism," he wrote in response to a list of questions sent out by a company that was shopping its $15-million account. "It seems to us that the client-agency relationship is most satisfactory when the agency's emoluments are not related to the amount of money it can persuade the client to spend on advertising." He believed that a flat fee would permit the agency to dole out truly impartial advice on promotional campaigns.

The company that was looking for a new agency was Shell Oil. And its management agreed with Ogilvy. "We had come to regard it as downright unethical, like paying a doctor 15 percent on the cost of drugs he prescribes or the hospital bill he makes you run up," said Shell advertising manager Cyril Martineau. In November 1960, Shell stunned the advertising world by shifting its account from J. Walter Thompson to Ogilvy, Benson & Mather and by announcing it would pay OB & M a fee rather than a commission.

In offering Shell a flat fee Ogilvy did what he did best: attracted attention. But the move also proved a more profitable arrangement for his firm. Ogilvy arrived at the fee by estimating his firm's costs for servicing the Shell account and adding 25 percent as his profit. By contrast, advertising firms generally realized about a 21 percent profit under the commission system.

absolutely no interest in selling anything. They don't think of themselves as salesmen. They think of themselves as entertainers and geniuses."

As a sort of professor emeritus, Ogilvy remains an advisory presence in the firm's many offices, which he occasionally visits. In 1988, O & M started an early internal on-line information bank, called "Ogilvy Online." Among its features were notes, letters, and other missives from the founder. As vice president Suzan Nanfeldt told *Advertising Age*: "The machine is to let us know what David's up to."

The powerful independent streak that led David Ogilvy to build his own firm did not atrophy as O & M took its place among the world's largest agencies. Ogilvy was critical of the wave of consolidation and acquisitions that swept through the advertising industry in the 1980s. "Megamergers are for megalomaniacs," he said. "These big mergers do nothing for the people in the agency. It's quite the opposite." In 1989, to his chagrin, the London-based WPP Group PLC launched a hostile takeover bid. When the two agencies ultimately agreed to terms, WPP paid $864 million for the company that David Ogilvy had founded forty years before with $6,000 and a bunch of untested theories.

When the Ogilvy Group ceased functioning as an independent entity, the advertising world had evolved far beyond the one David Ogilvy dominated in the 1950s and 1960s. When Ogilvy set up shop, newspapers and magazines were the primary media for advertising. But by the late 1980s advertising pervaded every aspect of American life. Advertisements could be found not only in newspapers and magazines and billboards but also on hundreds of television channels, thousands of radio stations, in subways, and on the sides of buses—even in cyberspace. Advertising firms were even more sophisticated in their use of research, regularly employing focus groups of consumers to test products and using computers to sift through an ever increasing amount of data on the habits, tastes, and preferences of American consumers. Advertising had entered a brave new world in which some of the octogenarian's theories may have seemed dated. But the modern era's sophistication was also a logical outgrowth of the advertising world David Ogilvy helped create.

Ray Kroc, in front of one of his ubiquitous McDonald's restaurants.

RAY KROC, McDONALD'S, AND THE FAST-FOOD INDUSTRY

I n 1954, a fifty-two-year-old milk-shake machine salesman saw a hamburger stand in San Bernardino, California, and envisioned a massive new industry: fast food. In what should have been his golden years, Raymond Kroc, the founder and builder of McDonald's Corporation, proved himself an industrial pioneer no less capable than Henry Ford. He revolutionized the American restaurant industry by imposing discipline on the production of hamburgers, french fries, and milk shakes. By developing a sophisticated operating and delivery system, he insured that the french fries customers bought in Topeka would be the same as the ones purchased in New York City. Such consistency made McDonald's the brand name that defined American fast food.

By 1960, there were more than 200 McDonald's outlets across the country, a rapid expansion fueled by low franchising fees. Ray Kroc had created one of the most compelling brands of all time. But he was barely turning a profit. Ultimately, it was his decision to use real estate as a financial lever that made McDonald's a viable operation. In 1956, Kroc set up the Franchise Realty

Corporation, buying up tracts of land and acting as a landlord to eager franchisees. With this step, McDonald's began to generate real income, and the company took off. Kroc then introduced national advertising programs to support the rapidly proliferating franchises, and when it appeared that growth in the company's home territory was slowing in the early 1970s, he started an energetic and successful push to make McDonald's a global presence. Throughout the company's spectacular growth, Kroc maintained a delicate balancing act, imposing rigorous system-wide standards while encouraging an entrepreneurial spirit that welcomed ideas from all levels. Many of these ideas contributed to the company's astonishing success.

In amassing a $500-million fortune, the king of the hamburger transformed the nation's cultural landscape and forged an industry that is among America's greatest exports. The widely imitated success of McDonald's offers an excellent example for today's managers and executives searching for greater production efficiencies. By putting the humble hamburger on the assembly line, Kroc showed the world how to apply sophisticated process management to the most prosaic endeavors. To succeed the McDonald's way, companies must define the basic premise of the service they offer, break the labor into constituent parts, and then continually reassemble and fine tune the many steps until the system works without a hitch. Today, companies engaged in delivering pizzas, processing insurance claims, or selling toys benefit from the kinds of systems that Ray Kroc pioneered. To the degree that such operations maintain quality control, and cherish customer satisfaction, profits may flow.

DISCOVERING THE FUTURE IN SAN BERNARDINO

As a milk-shake machine salesman, Raymond Kroc routinely paid visits to clients. But when the fifty-two-year-old salesman traveled from his home near Chicago to southern California to meet two of his biggest clients, the result was anything but routine.

Maurice and Richard McDonald had left New Hampshire in 1930, seeking to make their fortune in Hollywood. Unable to strike it big in Tinseltown, the brothers wound up as proprietors of a drive-in restaurant in San Bernardino, a dusty outpost fifty-five miles east of Los Angeles.

While most restaurants bought one or two Prince Castle Multimixers, which could mix five shakes at once, the McDonalds had purchased eight. And Kroc was curious to see what kind of operation needed the capacity to churn forty milk shakes at one time. So he trekked to San Bernardino, and what he saw there changed his life. Kroc stood in the shadows of the stand's two radiant golden arches, which lit up the sky at dusk, and saw lines of people snaking outside the octagonal restaurant. Through the building's all-glass walls, he watched the male crew, clad in white paper hats and white uniforms, hustle about the squeaky-clean restaurant, dishing out burgers, fries, and shakes to the working-class families that drove up. "Something was definitely happening here, I told myself," Kroc later wrote in his autobiography, *Grinding It Out*. "This had to be the most amazing merchandising operation I'd ever seen."

Unlike so many food-service operations Kroc had come across, this joint hummed like a finely tuned engine. As *Forbes* put it: "In short, the brothers brought efficiency to a slap-dash business." They offered a nine-item menu—burgers, french fries, shakes, and pies—eliminated seating, and used paper and plastic utensils instead of glass and china. They had also devised the rudiments of a hamburger assembly line so they could deliver orders in less than sixty seconds. And the prices were remarkably low: fifteen-cent burgers and ten-cent fries. Kroc instantly knew he had seen the future. "When I saw it working that day in 1954, I felt like some latter-day Newton who'd just had an Idaho potato caromed off his skull," Kroc said. "That night in my motel room I did a lot of heavy thinking about what I'd seen during the day. Visions of McDonald's restaurants dotting crossroads all over the country paraded through my brain."

Kroc had seen his destiny. In 1906, Kroc's father had taken four-year-old Raymond to see a phrenologist—a practitioner of a nineteenth-century "medicine" that divined insights into a person's character and capabilities from the skull's shape and size. After groping and probing the bumps on the youngster's head, the phrenologist pronounced that the child would work in the food-service industry.

Kroc had an intuitive feel for the restaurant business. He also possessed a more practical working knowledge of the industry, having spent the past thirty years selling paper products and milk-shake machines to restaurants all over the nation. In his journeys, Kroc saw an astonishing variety of operations—coffee shops, mom-and-pop dinettes, diners, burger stands, and ice-cream chains like Tastee-Freez—and became something of an expert on the low end of the American restaurant scene. Kroc concluded that too many of his clients were hamstrung by haphazard, unscientific management. And to their great chagrin, Kroc took to offering unsolicited advice on how they could improve their businesses. "I considered myself a connoisseur of kitchens," he said. "I prided myself on being able to tell which operations would appeal to the public and which would fail."

Kroc felt sure the McDonald brothers' operation could succeed wildly if it expanded. So the next day, he offered them a proposition.

"Why don't you open a series of units like this?" he asked. The brothers demurred. They had already sold franchises in Phoenix and Sacramento for very little money, and had reaped no great benefits. At root, they were indifferent businessmen, satisfied with the $100,000 they earned annually and unwilling to invest the energy to build a chain. But Kroc was a veteran salesman with more than thirty years of experience. Using every ounce of persuasion he could muster, he finally convinced the brothers to cut a deal: Kroc would sell McDonald's franchises for the low price of $950. In exchange, he would keep 1.4 percent of all sales and funnel 0.5 percent back to the brothers. Because franchisees kicked back such a meager percentage of total sales—just 1.9 percent—the corporate parent made very little money.

This arrangement was far more favorable to the McDonalds' than to Kroc, for that small slice of revenues would have to account for Kroc's overhead and marketing costs—and profits. But it was the act of a desperate man. While Kroc made $12,000 a year from Multimixer sales, the business was marked for extinction due to heavy competition from Hamilton Beach-brand mixers. Too old to start again from scratch, the middle-aged salesman believed the comfortable existence he and his wife, Ethel, led in suburban Arlington Heights, Illinois, would vanish if this venture failed. "If I lost out on McDonald's, I'd have no place to go," he said.

BRANDING A SERVICE AND AN OPERATING SYSTEM

With the deal in hand, Kroc set about fulfilling his vision of McDonald's restaurants blooming from coast to coast. He started by building the chain's first link—an experimental model in Des Plaines, Illinois, outside Chicago, that featured the same low prices, limited menu, and rapid service as the San Bernardino stand. Opening on April 15, 1955, the store rang up a respectable $366.12 in sales, and quickly became profitable. Kroc watched over the store with the vigilance of a new mother, personally overseeing the kitchen and scraping gum off the parking lot with a putty knife.

For Kroc, duplicating the McDonald brothers' single store was just the beginning. To build a chain, Kroc knew that he had to impose discipline on the loosely run restaurant industry. And that meant refining standardized operating procedures into easily replicable processes. Forty years earlier, Henry Ford had realized that the mass production of automobiles required the marriage of precision parts to an efficient assembly process. Kroc's insight was to apply the same rigor to the construction of sandwiches. Espousing the idea that "there is a science to making and serving a hamburger," Kroc endowed his beef patties with exacting specifications—fat content: below 19 percent; weight: 1.6 ounces; diameter: 3.875 inches; onions: ¼ ounce. Kroc even built a laboratory in suburban Chicago to devise a method for making the perfect fried potato in the late 1950s.

The upstart company became an obsession for Kroc. "I believe in God, family, and McDonald's—and in the office, that order is reversed," he liked to say. But it seemed McDonald's always came first. Kroc's sales experience taught him that business was a Darwinian proposition, in which those least fit and adaptable would go the way of the dinosaur. Apparently, Kroc's marriage was not strong enough to survive the challenges of starting a new business. Ethel didn't share her husband's visceral feel for the restaurant business, and angered by Ray's late-life gamble, she resented the way the new company had taken over her husband's life. "This was a veritable Wagnerian opera of strife," Kroc wrote. "It closed the door between us." The thirty-nine-year marriage would finally end in divorce in 1961.

In seeking to build a chain, Kroc knew that McDonald's did not have the field to itself. When he opened for business in 1955, A&W, Dairy Queen, Tastee-Freez, and Big Boy were all modestly established chains, and the first Burger King (known then as InstaBurger King) had just opened in Miami. Consequently Kroc took great pains to differentiate McDonald's from these players—for competitive and intellectual reasons.

The crucial difference between Kroc and his rivals was one of world view. He saw franchisees as business partners, not as mere customers. In his travels selling the Multimixer, he had observed the way franchisers milked franchisees for profits without concern for their long-term viability. Kroc vowed not to fall into that lucrative but ultimately unproductive trap. "My belief was that I had to help the individual operator succeed in every way I could. His success would insure my success. But I couldn't do that and, at the same time, treat him as a customer," he said.

Instead of simply supplying franchisees with milk-shake formula and ice cream, Kroc wanted to sell his new partners an operating system. In other words, he branded a service. And this was the revolutionary means McDonald's would use to create a chain in which a store in Delaware and a store in Nevada could serve burgers of the exact same size and quality, each containing the same number of pickle slices and topped with the same-size dollops of mustard and ketchup, each arrayed on a similar tray alongside potatoes deep-fried for the exact same length of time. As Kroc recalled, "Perfection is very difficult to achieve, and perfection was what I wanted in McDonald's. Everything else was secondary for me." But the exacting demands served a strategic goal. "Our aim, of course, was to insure repeat business based on the system's reputation rather than on the quality of a single store or operator," Kroc said.

Among Kroc's first partners were fellow members of the Rolling Green Country Club who had seen Kroc's busy flagship store, which was a great advertisement for success. By 1958, Kroc had sold seventy-nine franchises, some of them to Rolling Green golfing buddies. Many customers, their curiosity piqued by a pleasant dining experience, knocked on Kroc's door. Still other prospective operators answered Kroc's newspaper ads. One of them was twenty-three-year-old Fred Turner, whom Kroc hired as a dollar-an-hour burger flipper in 1955. Turner shared his boss's fascination for the mechanics of burger-making, and quickly became a favorite of Kroc, who had only a daughter. "I have a son—his name is Fred Turner," wrote Kroc. Turner became Kroc's top assistant and joined two other key employees in the central office: June Martino, who had been Kroc's secretary from his Multimixer days; and Harry Sonneborn, a former Tastee-Freez finance executive who offered to come work for McDonald's for the low salary of $100 a week in 1955.

REAL ESTATE AS A FINANCIAL ENGINE

Although McDonald's franchises sprouted up across the Midwest and West like wildflowers after a spring rain, the company's success appeared to be short lived. While the original deal he had struck with the McDonald brothers endeared Kroc to early franchisees, it also set his fledgling enterprise on a direct course to insolvency. Through 1960, when the chain's restaurants racked up $75 million in sales, McDonald's earnings were a mere $159,000. "In short, Kroc's concept for building McDonald's was financially bankrupt," wrote McDonald's historian John Love. And Kroc's dream house of cards began to collapse under its own weight. Unable to give valued employees like Martino and Sonneborn raises, Kroc paid them by granting them 30 percent of the company. He further diluted his equity by ceding 22 percent of McDonald's stock to two insurance companies to get a $1.5-million loan in 1961.

Even this loan, obtained at remarkably onerous terms, only temporarily slaked the firm's thirst for capital: Kroc needed to raise a huge chunk of money—$2.7 million—to buy out the McDonald brothers. His relationship with them was a continuing source of irritation. They did not meet his precise standards at the McDonald's franchises they had sold in California. Worse in Kroc's eyes, they took the liberty of selling a McDonald's franchise to a competitor in Cook County, Illinois, Kroc's home territory. Such actions intensified Kroc's desire to manage the growing enterprise on his own. However much he came to rue his connection with the McDonald brothers, Kroc realized the value of product identification created by the more than 200 outlets bearing their name. "I needed the name," Kroc lamented. "How far could I go on Kroc burgers?" Desperate for ultimate control of the McDonald's name, in

1961 he mortgaged the company's future again. A New York money manager arranged a $2.7-million loan from several college endowment and pension funds, the interest payments on which were calculated as a percentage of McDonald's sales.

Deep in hock and with no profit growth in sight, Kroc faced a classic dilemma. He couldn't afford to expand. And he couldn't afford to tread water. Fortunately, Harry Sonneborn came up with a solution. He thought McDonald's could make money by leasing or buying potential store sites and then subleasing them to franchisees initially at a 20 percent markup, and then at a 40 percent markup. Under this plan, McDonald's would scout out sites and sign twenty-year leases at fixed rates. Franchisees would then pay McDonald's either a minimum rate or a percentage of sales, whichever was greater. As sales and prices inevitably rose over the years, the company would collect more and more rent as its costs remained virtually constant.

Embracing Sonneborn's idea, in 1956 Kroc set up a subsidiary, the Franchise Realty Corporation, to execute the new strategy. In the years thereafter, he flew around the country in a small airplane, scouting suburban neighborhoods dotted with tract housing, schools, and churches— which he regarded as fertile ground for the planting of new "Golden Arches." In this pre-strip-mall era, real estate along well-traveled byways was both cheap and plentiful. And in a short period of time, the real estate operation became a high-margin contributor to McDonald's bottom line. As Kroc noted: "This was the beginning of real income for McDonald's."

The real estate strategy played perfectly into Kroc's larger goal of control. Rather than sell blanket geographic franchises, which would grant the holder the right to build as many or as few stores as he chose in a particular area, Kroc sold only individual franchises, for a low fee of $950. This insured that operators unwilling to play by his rules could open no more than one outlet. As a landlord, Kroc could compose legal documents guaranteeing further control. And by writing leases that would force tenants to conform to corporate policy, he could more easily insure that the look, feel, and taste of McDonald's would be identical in Bangor, Maine, and Butte, Montana.

Leaving the company's stabilized finances in the capable hands of Harry Sonneborn, Kroc set about expanding and professionalizing the growing industrial empire. Under his novel conception, each franchisee and operator was like a plant manager. Knowing that the hallmark of any sophisticated industrial complex is professional management, Kroc in 1961 launched a training program—later called Hamburger University—at a new store at Elk Grove Village, Illinois. There, the faculty trained franchisees and operators in the scientific methods of running a successful McDonald's and drilled them in the Kroc gospel of Quality, Service, Cleanliness, and Value. "I put the hamburger on the assembly line," Kroc liked to say. Hamburger U also contained a research and development laboratory to develop new cooking, freezing, storing, and serving mechanisms.

While Kroc dictated the size and shape of burgers, he gave franchisees wide latitude in other areas. He knew that McDonald's had to simultaneously unleash the entrepreneurial energies of hundreds of operators while maintaining the standards and regulations crucial to the efficient operation of a far-flung industrial enterprise. As McDonald's chronicler John Love wrote: "Ray Kroc's genius was building a system that requires all of its members to follow corporate-like rules but at the same time rewards them for expressing their individual creativity."

GOING PUBLIC THROUGH ADVERTISING AND A STOCK OFFERING

Nowhere was the dichotomy between central control and operating autonomy more evident than in advertising. At Christmas in the late 1950s, Turner and other managers would tour the Chicago Loop in the "Santa Wagon," an ice-cream truck converted into a rolling likeness of a McDonald's drive-in. But despite this penchant for old-fashioned hucksterism, McDonald's had no company-wide advertising strategy. Instead, when Minneapolis operator Jim Zein saw his sales explode in 1959

after running radio ads, Kroc encouraged operators to take to the air-
waves with their own campaigns. Following this directive, two Washington, D.C., franchisees, John Gibson and Oscar Goldstein, decided to
target kids by sponsoring a local children's show, Bozo's Circus. When
the station canceled the show in 1963, the franchisees hired the head-
liner, a twenty-five-year-old television announcer named Willard Scott,
to create a new clown persona for local ads. Thus was born one of
advertising's most enduring icons: Ronald McDonald.

Successful advertising helped spur even greater growth. And in
1965, with 710 McDonald's spread throughout forty-four states, $171
million in sales, and a relatively tidy balance sheet, McDonald's finally
blossomed. The company went public on April 15, ten years to the day
after Kroc opened the Des Plaines store, selling 300,000 shares priced
at $22.50 each. Many of the shares were offered by Kroc, who reaped
$3 million on the sale, as well as by Sonneborn and June Martino. As
investors jumped on the McDonald's bandwagon, the stock jumped to
$30 on its first day of trading and soared to $49 soon after.

Kroc deployed the cash to expand and fend off rapidly proliferating
rivals, for the company's success had spawned a slew of imitators seeking
to cash in on the growing industrialization of fast food. In 1965, there
were already 1,000 Kentucky Fried Chickens, 325 Burger Chefs, and 100
Burger Kings in operation. Each chain, fortified by cash infusions, expanded rapidly in the late 1960s, so much so that by 1970, fast food
had grown to a $6.2-billion business garnering 17.8 percent of all money
spent in restaurants.

In such an environment, standing still was tantamount to shrinking.
"A laurel rested upon quickly wilts" was a favorite Kroc-ism. So aside
from opening new restaurants at a breakneck pace, McDonald's added a
new weapon to its arsenal: national advertising. Having labored mightily
to create uniform standards throughout the system, Kroc expended capital to forge a uniform image. In 1967, McDonald's spent $2.3 million,
or about 1 percent of its sales, on its first national advertising campaign,
which was an unheard amount for a fast-food chain. "What small busi-

nessman wouldn't cheerfully give up 1 percent of his gross to get our kind of commercials and things like sponsorship of *The Sound of Music* on network television to promote his store?" Kroc asked rhetorically. Expanding the Ronald McDonald campaign created by the Washington franchisees, the company outfitted the clown with a gaggle of kid-friendly characters such as the Hamburglar, Mayor McCheese, and Grimace, a large purple creature who craved shakes and french fries. "We're not in the hamburger business; we're in show business," Kroc liked to say.

Kroc backed up the advertising blitzkrieg with several new products, many of which were created by franchisees. Pittsburgh operator Jim Delligatti, seeking to bolster sales, in 1967 began testing a new double-decker hamburger that he dubbed the Big Mac. McDonald's introduced the sandwich throughout the chain in less than a year, and it has since become the firm's enduring signature product. Other new menu items, ranging from the Filet-o-Fish to the Egg McMuffin, also sprouted from the fertile imaginations of McDonald's operators and were similarly welcomed by Hamburger Central, as the headquarters came to be known.

BECOMING A GLOBAL INSTITUTION

Through rapid growth and extensive advertising, McDonald's in the early 1970s became the nation's largest fast-food chain and an easily recognizable feature of the American cultural landscape. And the supreme ruler of McDonaldland, Ray Kroc, became a figure of national stature. In 1972, when more than 2,200 McDonald's outlets racked up $1 billion in sales, Kroc received the Horatio Alger award from Norman Vincent Peale. As the value of his stock holdings rose to about $500 million, the septuagenarian acquired certain trappings of wealth: a house in Beverly Hills, a mansion in Florida whose doorbell chimed "You Deserve a Break Today," and the San Diego Padres baseball team. But Kroc remained at heart a simple man, who spoke proudly of "the peasant bones of my Bohemian ancestors." Unlike so many other newly rich captains of industry, he developed no taste for great art or society events. Instead, he continued to find beauty in the simple bun. "It requires a certain kind of mind to see beauty in a hamburger bun," Kroc rhapsodized. "Yet, is it any more unusual to find grace in the texture and softly curved silhouette of a bun than to reflect lovingly on the hackles of a favorite fishing fly?"

Just as the Ford Motor Company aroused the scrutiny of muckraking journalists and reforming politicians, Ray Kroc's high-profile industrial juggernaut attracted attention from many quarters. As McDonald's fare became a staple of the American diet, it aroused the snobbery of the food industry elite. *New York* Magazine's Mimi Sheraton proclaimed: "McDonald's food is irredeemably horrible, with no saving graces whatever." Nor did the nutritionists take kindly to McDonald's offerings. As Dr. Jean Mayer, a Harvard professor, wrote: "The typical McDonald's meal—hamburgers, french fries, and a malted—doesn't give you much nutrition. . . . It's typical of the diet that raises the cholesterol count and leads to heart disease."

Politicians took note, too. In 1974, when the company's market value surpassed that of lumbering U.S. Steel, Senator Lloyd Bentsen complained: "Something is wrong with our economy when the stock market is long on hamburgers and short on steel." But the future Secretary of the Treasury ignored the fact that burgers had become an industrial product nearly as significant as rolled steel, for the McDonald's industrial complex was a prodigious consumer of raw materials. It bought about 1 percent of all beef wholesaled in the United States and a huge quantity of potatoes besides. Each store was an opportunity-generating machine—providing one out of fifteen young Americans with a point of entry into the workplace. To broadcast its booming output, McDonald's made a practice of posting its latest chain-wide total sales figures on the Golden Arches. And the mounting billions were monitored in the highest offices in the land. President Richard Nixon, upon meeting Kroc in the early 1970s, asked him: "What is it now, eight or nine billion?" Kroc replied: "Mr. President, it's twelve billion."

Many analysts viewed McDonald's rampant growth as unsustainable.

But Kroc believed the company needed to continue to expand in order to survive. "I don't believe in saturation," he said. "We're thinking and talking worldwide." Kroc envisioned a world in which 12,000 sets of Golden Arches would stand as outposts of a mighty commercial empire. Sure, there was one store for every 90,000 citizens of the United States in 1972. But there were three billion people outside America's borders who had never wrapped their mouths around a Big Mac. So just as Henry Ford sought foreign markets for the Model T, Ray Kroc embarked upon an ambitious campaign. McDonald's started by invading former Axis powers Japan and Germany in 1971. And in 1977, it introduced the fast-food sandwich to the land of Sandwich, opening the company's 3,000th store in London. "With all the fervor of the Pilgrims returned, McDonald's set out to introduce Europe to the joys of the real American hamburger," *Forbes* noted.

Establishing beachheads in European capitals was just the beginning. Over the course of the decade, the thousand stores that the company opened overseas fueled its 27 percent annual growth rate. Golden Arches sprouted from the soil in virtually every continent—in South America, in Europe, and in Asia. The chain became so universally recognized as a symbol of American enterprise and influence that, when Marxist guerrillas blew up a McDonald's in San Salvador in 1979, they proclaimed the terrorist act a lethal blow against "imperialist America."

Although Kroc stepped down as chief executive in 1968, giving way to Fred Turner, he remained a vital symbol of the company's roots, and an enduring influence over day-to-day operations. The founder reviewed first-day results from each new store, and kept watch over the company-owned McDonald's outlet from his office in southern California. "Despite McDonald's success, and his personal wealth of $340 million, he always worries," *Forbes* wrote in 1975. "When Kroc travels, he insists that his chauffeur take him to at least six McDonald's for surprise inspections."

Though he killed the competition, the competition didn't kill Ray

ADAPTING TO FOREIGN CLIMATES

One key to McDonald's continued growth is international expansion. With operations in more than 65 countries, McDonald's now opens about one-third of its new restaurants outside of the United States. In the early 1990s, Fred Turner predicted that international sales would eventually surpass U.S. sales.

While foreign markets can sometimes offer new obstacles for the American company, like hostile government bureaucracies and unreliable local suppliers, McDonald's faces an even greater overall challenge. In each country, from Belgium to Brunei, the company is forced to walk the tightrope of selling its uniquely American product, while simultaneously catering to local tastes.

Although McDonald's always insisted on planting its rigid operating system in foreign soil, when it came to other aspects of the restaurants' operation, the company was more flexible. For example, to make the chain's name more easily pronounceable for Japanese consumers, it was changed to *Makudonaldo*, and its mascot became Donald McDonald. Hamburger Central also allowed local operators to devise unique promotional campaigns. "Our name may be American, but we're all Irish," ran one promotional campaign for outlets in Dublin.

Today, even the menus at McDonald's restaurants in foreign locations clearly reflect differences that do not exist at the company's American outlets. While the stores offer fare like hamburgers, french fries and milk shakes, there have been some additions: for example, when McDonald's restaurants opened in Germany in the early 1970s, they started serving beer; in the Philippines they offer McSpaghetti noodles, while Norwegian franchises offer a salmon fillet sandwich, the MacLak.

Kroc. He passed away from old age in January 1984, at the age of eighty-one, just ten months before McDonald's sold its 50-billionth hamburger.

Ray Kroc didn't live to see his company's ultimate triumph. The Dow Jones Industrial Average, the best daily barometer of the nation's economy, consists of the nation's thirty most important companies. In 1985, when the value of McDonald's $4.16-billion real estate portfolio surpassed that of Sears, the New York Stock Exchange added McDonald's to the Dow. With this stroke, Wall Street validated Ray Kroc's contention that beef patties could be placed on the assembly line. The once-humble hamburger finally took its rightful place among planes, trains, and automobiles as a titan of American industry.

Joseph Wilson, president of Xerox.

BETTING THE COMPANY: JOSEPH WILSON AND THE XEROX 914

ince the editors of *Forbes* are pretty fast when it comes to criticizing other people's business blunders, we'll use this space to tell a beauty on ourselves," the magazine's editors wrote in 1965. They recalled that in 1957 Joseph Wilson, then president of the Haloid Corporation, had visited their offices to tell them of his company's plans to create a new kind of copier. "The *Forbes* men were impressed," the magazine continued. "The president was a sincere, enthusiastic, extremely articulate man. He believed in what [the company was] doing. He had the facts and figures right at his fingertips. He understood finance and he understood technology. The president handled all our questions beautifully, professionally. And what did *Forbes* do with the story? Nothing."

There was good reason for that: At the time, Haloid was a small manufacturer of photographic papers, with minimal earnings and few employees. Its plans to "found a whole new industry" seemed wildly optimistic. In fact, virtually no one predicted the staggering success that the company, which was renamed Xerox in 1961, would achieve. Not even Joseph Wilson.

By 1957, Wilson and his colleagues had spent a decade developing the commercial possibilities of the then-primitive copying technology that had been rejected by many of the country's largest companies. As it developed the technology, the company protected the exclusivity of its rights by trading stock and anticipated revenues for access to its patents. Years before Haloid was ready to market its product, management had risked millions of dollars and years of their lives on an uncertain future.

In 1959 the gamble started to pay off: the company introduced the 914 copying machine. Weighing in at 648 pounds, the first modern copier occupied the floor space of a large desk, ground out copies at the excruciatingly slow pace of six per minute, and cost a whopping $29,500. But the 914 left existing copying machines in its dust and, just as the visionary Wilson promised, marked the beginning of a brand-new industry. Yet it wasn't technology alone that turned the 914 into the most successful commercial product of the 1960s. Haloid implemented a creative sales strategy that made the 914 affordable and worry free: the company decided to lease and maintain the machines rather than sell them.

FRUSTRATION LEADS TO INNOVATION

When the 914 was introduced, there were other copying devices on the market. Thomas Edison himself had invented a mimeograph machine, and the A.B. Dick Company had a copier of sorts on the market as early as 1887. But mimeography was a far cry from modern duplication. It involved typing a document on carbon paper, placing the carbon in a machine, and "running off" copies in a laborious, messy process. The state of the art improved somewhat in the 1930s with the proliferation of offset printing presses, but they were massive, expensive, slow, and impractical for average businesses.

An imaginative and restless patent attorney changed all this. Chester Carlson was frustrated by how long it took to make photocopies of patent documents. "There must be a quicker, better way of making these copies," he said.

The twenty-nine-year-old Carlson, who had studied physics at the California Institute of Technology before going into law, started tinkering with photographic technology in 1935. Like another technology pioneer, David Sarnoff, Carlson turned first to one of the world's great research resources: the New York Public Library. There he learned about a Hungarian scientist who used powder and static electricity to duplicate pictures. Believing he could use these discoveries as a basis for an efficient paper copying process, Carlson set up a makeshift laboratory in an apartment above a bar in Astoria, Queens and began his own experiments with "electrophotography." With the help of Otto Kornei, a physicist and German refugee, Carlson spent the better part of three years mixing chemicals and testing different methods. After a great deal of trial and error, he ultimately devised a complex five-part process that used electric charges, powder, and heat to create images. It was revolutionary because it required no chemical reaction and could be done without messy ink. On October 22, 1938, he successfully tested his new process by making an image of a piece of paper bearing the words "10-22-38 Astoria."

Carlson tried to peddle his discovery to the giants of American technology, but executives at companies like IBM, Kodak, and RCA regarded the young inventor more as a home-spun mad scientist than a prospective titan of industry. Twenty-odd companies backed away. "How difficult it was to convince anyone that my tiny plates and rough image held the key to a tremendous new industry," Carlson later said.

Finally, someone listened. Dr. R. M. Schaffert, the head of the Graphic Arts Division at Battelle Memorial Institute, a nonprofit research outfit in Columbus, Ohio, saw the potential of Carlson's process: "Mr. Carlson's invention on electrophotography appears to have possibilities, and if it can be made to work in a usable manner, broad commercial application can be expected. This process looks like a good research gamble." Battelle bought a 60 percent interest in Carlson's findings and in 1944 Carlson, now working with a team of Battelle scientists, began to further develop the technology.

OUT OF THE LAB, INTO THE MARKETPLACE

In 1944 the Haloid Corporation in Rochester, New York, faced a crisis. Founded in 1906 to sell photographic paper and supplies to companies like Eastman-Kodak, Haloid had experienced steady growth over the years. During World War II, when the army's extensive use of reconnaissance photography sparked a boom in the photographic paper industry, Haloid thrived. By 1947, it was a modestly profitable company with revenues of over $7 million and earnings of $138,000. But demand for its products diminished as the war wound down, and the company was left to fight for a share of the smaller market.

Joseph C. Wilson, a grandson of one of Haloid's founders and son of the man who was the company's president when it went public in 1935, ascended to the position of president in 1945. He realized that the company had to diversify in order to survive. "We've got to stop relying wholly on photographic paper," he said. "We've got to come up with new products for the market." Ideas surfaced for new kinds of photographic paper and for developing products for seismic recordings, among other things, but none had the breakthrough potential Haloid needed.

John Dessauer, Haloid's head of Research and Engineering Division, scoured hundreds of technical journals in search of new possibilities. In an article in Kodak's *Monthly Abstract Bulletin*, Dessauer found a summary of an article about Battelle's work on electrophotography. Because the process was akin to photography and used treated paper, Dessauer saw a potential new area of business. Wilson was immediately intrigued: "It was crude, but to me it had extra exciting potential."

The two men immediately set off for Columbus. They liked what they saw when they got there. "Of course, it's got a million miles to go before it will be marketable. But when it does become marketable, we've got to be in the picture," Wilson said. The man was nothing if not a big thinker. An inveterate reader, he peppered his speeches and presentations with quotations from philosophers and poets. He saw business as a noble quest and urged his colleagues to press on with lofty rhetoric. Perhaps this gave him the endurance and determination to travel the "million miles" between the Battelle laboratory and commercial success.

Wilson called Sol Linowitz, a Rochester lawyer who had long sought Haloid's business. In their first collaboration, they negotiated for the rights to the technology that so many other larger firms had rejected. In 1946 they reached an agreement: Haloid would pay $25,000 to Battelle each year, plus 8 percent of future electrophotography revenues, in exchange for the right to develop Carlson's technology.

PATIENCE, PATENTS, AND PREDICTIONS

Knowing a long, expensive, and massive research and development process was necessary to achieve their goal, Wilson and his team focused on short-term objectives. First, the process needed a name. In 1948 a Battelle researcher and an Ohio State University classics professor coined a new word: *xerography*, from the Greek meaning "dry writing." The executives at Haloid liked the word. "It was short, startling, unlike anything else ever seen in advertisements," John Dessauer later wrote.

In an effort to show the public that it had tapped into an exciting new development, Wilson hastened to set a deadline for xerography's first demonstration: October 22, 1948, the tenth anniversary of Carlson's first copying effort. On that date, at a conference of the Optical Society of America in Detroit, Wilson, along with Battelle scientists, explained the process and displayed a red box that produced a single copy within a minute. Soon after, Wilson's father, Joseph R. Wilson, made a bold prediction: "The first commercial adaptation of xerography, the XeroX Copier Machine, Model A, will be made in 1950."

But this prediction proved fanciful. Haloid scientists couldn't produce a workable machine by 1950—or even by 1955. Each of xerography's many steps proved complex, and getting them to work in a foolproof, seamless, and reliable process was difficult. As his company labored toward the larger goal, Joseph C. Wilson took several steps to insure its short-term survival. In 1950, Linowitz and Wilson renegotiated Haloid's contract with Battelle to become the sole licensee, thereby prohibiting other companies from gaining access to Carlson's discoveries. But that didn't allay the company's fears. Carlson's basic patent was set to expire in 1957, at which time firms with greater resources than Haloid would be able to use the technology with impunity. Wilson soon realized that the only way to guarantee Haloid's investment and any future was to boost research and development and gain new patents. "If we own the rights to the new facets of xerography, our position will be less vulnerable," he said. In 1953 alone, Haloid received ten new patents in xerography. The following year Linowitz, the lawyer originally hired for a one-shot deal, became vice president in charge of a new department of licenses and patents.

Since they were unable to produce a functioning copier quickly, Wilson and Haloid's scientists contented themselves with incremental progress. The research yielded profitable applications in the form of new products, based at least in part on the xerographic technology. In 1955, for example, Haloid introduced Copyflo, the first totally automated xerographic machine, a tool that could make prints from microfilm.

MONEY AND MORALE

Between 1947 and 1960, Haloid spent $75 million—twice its operational earnings—on xerography research. To raise funds, the executives borrowed, issued stock, and generally scraped by. In 1951, the company borrowed one million dollars from Lincoln Alliance Bank, and many employees bought stock as an expression of support. "The members of our team were all gambling on the project," Dessauer told the *New Yorker* in 1967. "I even mortgaged my house." And Wilson insured that those who didn't purchase stock also had a personal stake in the company's future: he started a profit-sharing plan in 1945. As Dessauer later wrote, "The challenge of the administrator is to channel the effort of the revolutionary into productive endeavors that advance corporate objectives."

Although there was a strong family-like feel to Haloid, the 1950s were difficult years for the company. "Various members of our own group would come in and tell me that the damn thing would never work," said John Dessauer. Maintaining morale among the crucial research staff became a difficult task. But Wilson held the enterprise together. "Haloid is on a soul-size search," he liked to say. He remained intently focused on his goal and showed a remarkable loyalty to his employees, refusing to fire or lay off people.

The chief executive also monitored the research closely. "Wilson had a capacity for viewing projects and problems in their broadest context, yet he seldom neglected the details in small print," wrote former Xerox employee Blake McKelvey in an unpublished biography of Wilson. "After each of their frequent trips to Battelle, he would prepare, or ask Dessauer to prepare, a summary report of the matters discussed, the decisions reached, and the actions planned."

Keeping on top of the company's progress was necessary because larger outfits, like Kodak, 3M, American Photocopy Equipment, and Smith-Corona Marchant, were all developing and producing copying machines. But thanks to Haloid's patent strategy, none of the others employed xerography. Haloid believed this crucial difference would prove its ace in the hole.

Staking his company's future on the process, Wilson kept Haloid independent rather than enlisting larger firms as partners. He wanted to reap the entire windfall should xerography prove profitable. As a result, Haloid was forced to borrow and barter in order to gain crucial necessities. In 1954 the company received a $3-million loan from Massachusetts Mutual Life Insurance Company to build a new factory on the 100 acres of land Haloid had purchased in Webster, a rural farming town about fifteen miles outside of Rochester. Two years later, in 1956, Haloid bought the four basic xerography patents and licensing rights on improvements of them from Battelle. It paid for this transaction with the only currency it had: some cash, its stock, and its promise. Battelle received 25,000 shares, $500,000 cash for each of the next three years, plus a guarantee of 3 percent of xerographic sales through 1965.

PREPARING THE GROUND FOR THE 914

In the mid-1950s the mythical copier, dubbed the 914 because it could duplicate copies on paper up to nine inches by fourteen inches long, was still a few years away. Even though other products were entering the steadily growing copying market, Wilson didn't rush the 914, for he knew his product had to be perfect. In 1958, Haloid spent nearly $2 million of its $27.5-million revenues on continuing research. Officially changing its name to Haloid-Xerox, Inc., the company issued a promising report: "During the next few years, we will market copying devices, microfilm enlargers, computer printers. A continuing flow of xerographic products is anticipated for many years to come." In 1956 the company created a partnership with the Rank Organization, a British conglomerate. Rank-Xerox, as it came to be known, would sell xerographic products outside North America. Meanwhile, Wilson began to lay the groundwork for the 914's debut. But the efforts sometimes literally backfired. When Wilson and other Haloid executives took a prototype for a demonstration in London, the copier started to smoke and nearly caused a fire at the Piccadilly Hotel.

Even while the 914's imminent availability was announced, Haloid's scientists continued to toil in the firm's laboratories. The 914 ultimately required 1,260 components, all of which had to move together in harmony. At the push of a button, a bar of light would scan a document and then transmit the reflected image to a selenium-coated revolving drum charged with static electricity; the drum, having been charged in a pattern identical to the image on the document, rotated through a chamber of powdered ink (or toner) which clung to the charged image; then, the drum pressed the image onto paper; and finally, heat and the pressure of a roller sealed the image neatly.

Simply describing this process would not turn customers on to the new machine. So Wilson invested the 914 with a great deal of importance. In 1959, speaking before the Philadelphia Securities Association, Wilson called xerography "a fundamental new way of visual communications."

THE 914 CREATES AN INDUSTRY

In August 1959, Wilson wrote an exhortatory letter to division heads, "We are about to give birth, either to our greatest success or to our greatest failure—the 914."

The paistakingly developed product Haloid-Xerox had an initial sticker price of $29,500—an enormous sum for a piece of office equipment. Realizing that such a price would prohibit mass sales, Haloid-Xerox adopted the strategy that made the product successful. It would lease the machines rather than sell them. Xerox set a monthly rental rate of $95, which included 2,000 free copies. Clients would then pay four cents for each copy beyond the initial 2,000, which were tabulated on meters installed on every machine. Wilson described the leasing tactic as "the most important decision we ever made—except for backing xerography itself."

In addition, Haloid-Xerox guaranteed maintenance of the 914s, which, despite the years of research and testing, could be temperamental creatures. As the business chronicler John Brooks later wrote: "It has to be fed and curried; it is intimidating but can be tamed; it is subject to unpredictable bursts of misbehavior; and, generally speaking, it responds in kind to its treatment."

The first 914, shipped on March 1, 1960, entered a crowded field. Thirty companies, among them 3M and Eastman Kodak, were vying for positions in what had grown to become a $200-million market. But the 914 was simpler and faster than its competitors, and it was much easier to use. Instead of creating a master page, users could place the document to be copied face down on the 914's glass surface. Moreover, it produced copies on ordinary paper, while many of the others only copied onto treated paper. The 914 was a different animal. "What other copying machines were to carbon paper, the 914 is to other copying machines," trumpeted a piece of promotional literature.

Through clever marketing moves, like a demonstration in New York's Grand Central Terminal, the product became an immediate success. The company's revenues almost doubled from $31 million in 1959 to $59 million in 1961. By 1961, 10,000 copiers had been installed. Peter McColough, who had risen to vice president of sales, rapidly expanded the existing sales and maintenance staffs, opening new offices in major cities across the country. And on April 18, 1961, just weeks before the company's stock began to trade on the prestigious New York Stock Exchange, its shareholders approved an official name change to the Xerox Corporation.

The following year, when sales surged to $176 million, *Forbes* heralded not only the company's arrival, but its future. "Potentially, Xerox is not so much a company as an industry." By 1962 the office copying business was worth $400 million, up from $40 million a decade before. And the 914 was, as *Financial World* put it, "the Cadillac of the copier machines."

The virtual overnight success of the 914 didn't change Joe Wilson. Rather, the company's success created a more visible platform for his unique business style. In 1961 a *New York Times* reporter covering his appearance before a group of securities analysts noted, "Wilson sounded more like a college professor lecturing a fairly advanced class rather than a salesman making a pitch. He quoted at considerable length from Lord Byron's *Don Juan* . . . and reminded his forum of various perceptions of Dostoyevski and Montaigne."

Many chief executives would have been content to sit back and watch their product take off. Not Wilson. "Ours is a business with infinite potentialities, because we serve all industries, all professions, every kind of enterprise," he said. Indeed, the company regarded itself as its own greatest competition. "Our philosophy is that no product line of any company, including ours, is going to last forever," said Peter McColough. "We feel we should be the ones to obsolete our products ourselves, not leave it to someone else."

Even as the 914 gained widespread acceptance, Xerox's scientists labored to replace it. The next card Xerox dealt was the 813, which could make copies on paper measuring eight inches by thirteen inches. The machine itself, developed at a cost of $20 million, was smaller than the 914. With the 813, which was more expensive than the 914, Xerox essentially used the same technology and process employed to such great effect in the 914, but it compacted the parts so the package could fit on a desktop.

Despite the introduction of new products like the 813, which was also leased, the convenient and affordable 914 was still Xerox's mainstay. And by 1965 it had helped the company become one of the nation's largest. But Xerox's top officers didn't behave much like their counterparts at other blue-chip firms. "Unlike other half-billion-dollar companies, Xerox is still run at the very top by entrepreneurs, the risk-takers who built it up from next to nothing," *Forbes* said in 1965. Joe Wilson remained at the helm until 1968, always striving to maintain a sense that his company marched to the beat of a different drummer. He remained on a first-name basis with most employees and took a full day around the Christmas holidays to shake hands with every Xerox worker.

In 1964, Wilson quoted Robert Frost in a speech before a Rochester civic group, which accurately summed up his management style: "Two roads diverged in a wood, and I—/I took the one less traveled by,/ And that has made all the difference." The same philosophy that helped sustain him while he made xerography a commercial reality led Wilson to form a unique vision of the world. "Businessmen must stop casting themselves as salesmen for business and start revealing themselves as people who are as interested in the affairs and programs of mankind as the teacher, the scientist, or the welfare worker," he said. Having played a central role in local organizations like the University of Rochester (an early investor in Haloid), Wilson transformed Xerox into a model corporate citizen. Wilson and other top executives spoke forcefully on improving social conditions. Long before other companies began to do so, Xerox made efforts to hire minority workers. It also gave employees paid leave to do volunteer work.

STAYING ON TOP THROUGH CUSTOMER SERVICE AND RESEARCH

Wilson could not have afforded to be such a solid citizen if not for the sound and efficient business organization he had built. By 1965, Xerox employed a 4,000-person sales force spread throughout eighty-five cities, which worked closely with headquarters and maintenance staff to keep customers happy. To give its sales force the incentive to stay in touch with customers, the company dictated that salespeople receive an initial commission on sales plus a continuing interest in the annual rental fees. In addition, the company had a profitable formula. In 1965 it spent about $2,400 to manufacture a machine. By then, customers were charged only a $25 monthly rental fee, plus four cents per copy for a minimum of 2,000. Since the average user made about 8,000 copies monthly and Xerox sold paper and other supplies to customers, it collected about $4,500 in annual revenues on every copier in place.

Customer satisfaction assumed a higher priority as Xerox's success attracted potential rivals like Pitney-Bowes, Litton Industries, and Olivetti Underwood. In all, some forty companies offered copiers by the mid-1960s. But their offerings could not produce copies as efficiently as the 914. In 1965, some 60,000 914s had been installed, earning 62 percent of Xerox's $392.6 million in revenues. The following year, when sales topped $500 million, Xerox owned 61 percent of the total duplication market—an amazing figure given the number of competitors.

Wilson adapted to the transformation of the marketplace with typical savvy. Recognizing the competition, he and Dessauer continued to authorize massive research expenditures. As Sol Linowitz said in 1965, "Patents are our guts, rather than just an appendage." In 1966, when it was awarded its 500th U.S. patent relating to xerographic products, the firm spent fully $40 million of its $500 million in annual revenues on research into new products. And the investment paid off. In 1965, Xerox introduced the high-volume 2400 (it could crank out 2,400 copies an hour). Like the 914, the 2400 was leased, not bought, and copies were paid for on a similar sliding scale, with the per-copy cost eventually falling to a half cent.

Xerox was a cultural phenomenon. As the estimated number of copies made in the United States rose from 20 million in the mid-1950s to 14 billion in 1966, the words "Xerox" and "copy" became interchangeable. Cheap and reliable copying allowed for the rapid dissemination of information. But even as it revolutionized communications, the copier inspired spasms of fear and loathing in certain quarters. "Xerography is bringing a reign of terror into the world of publishing, because it means that every reader can become both author and publisher," the media critic Marshall McLuhan wrote in 1966.

Still, Xerox managed to boost its profile, locally and nationally. In 1967 it completed work on Xerox Square, a thirty-story office complex in downtown Rochester, complete with sunken ice-skating rink in the middle, à la Rockefeller Center. The building lent an air of urban glamour to a company already accorded such status in the marketplace. Between 1960 and 1970, Xerox boasted an astonishing 47 percent annual increase in earnings per share. In the same period, the stock rose to a value of sixty-six times that of its 1960 price. As it soared, a whole class of "Xerox millionaires" was created. Not all of them were company executives, though. In 1942 a Rochester cab driver invested $1,000 in Haloid; thirty years later, that stake was worth more than $2 million. In 1969, Xerox had 38,000 employees, and its total stock market value was $8.2 billion. Virtually the entire increase in shareholder value could be ascribed to the 914.

A STRUGGLE TO DUPLICATE EARLY SUCCESS

Wilson realized the good times couldn't last. If Xerox continued to grow at the rapid pace it had set in the 1960s, its sales would exceed the U.S. gross national product in a few decades. At the 1966 annual meeting Wilson announced: "Our future from this point forward depends on what we do in fields other than copying."

Xerox had started to diversify as early as 1962 when it moved into the education business by acquiring University Microfilms Inc. And in the following years, the company added several profitable textbook publishers to its holdings. But it was left to Peter McColough to lead the company into uncharted and choppy waters. He took over as chief executive when Joseph Wilson stepped down in 1968 and sought to move the now-established company in several new directions simultaneously. McColough moved the headquarters from Rochester, New York, to

MAKING AN EXPENSIVE PRODUCT AFFORDABLE

Xerox's decision to lease, rather than sell, the 914 was both crucial and controversial. Some company executives felt that selling the machines, which retailed at $29,500, would bring huge revenues into the undercapitalized company. But Joseph Wilson typically took a longer view. He had observed the success of other companies—like IBM—that leased office machines, and he realized that any short-term gains reaped from sales would be offset by a slower rate of proliferation. And events showed that his intuition was correct. The pricing strategy allowed the machines to spread quickly throughout companies large and small, establishing the 914 as an office necessity.

In addition, Xerox was able to take advantage of favorable tax provisions. The tax code permits companies to take deductions for depreciation of machines and equipment they own. Since Xerox maintained ownership of all the machines it produced, the company could amortize the cost of all its production.

This strategy proved profitable. Thousands of Xerox copiers were leased to clients in the 1960s, and each year, Xerox could subtract a percentage of each machine's total value from its taxable income. By 1967, when an estimated 190,000 Xerox machines were in use, the company reported $239 million worth of rental equipment and related inventories. Xerox was thus able to reduce its taxable income substantially and boost its cash flow, which in turn allowed it to invest even more money into research and new products.

Stamford, Connecticut, because he believed the company's headquarters needed to be closer to New York, the nation's technological and financial capital.

And when IBM began to develop a commercial copier, McColough foolishly decided to tackle Big Blue on its home turf: computers. Rather than replicate Xerox's successful but painstaking development of the

914, McColough sought the easier route of buying an existing company. In 1969, Xerox acquired Scientific Data Systems (SDS), a mainframe computer company, for $900 million in stock. But SDS's best days were behind it, and six years later Xerox shut down SDS, and wrote off the entire investment as a loss. McColough also set up a research center in Silicon Valley in California to develop new computer technology. In the mid-1970s, the brilliant computer scientists assembled there created what could have been among the first major personal computers to hit the market. But the executives at headquarters, who had grown distant from the researchers, decided against introducing the machine, thus missing a crucial opportunity. What they abandoned contained the seeds that would later grow into the Apple Macintosh.

Aside from facing failures in these new areas, Xerox had a hard time with its traditional business. Its next-generation copier, the 9200, was developed at a cost of $300 million, and was introduced in 1971. But this time the Xerox product was not markedly better than new products made by competitors, and its sales were disappointing. Even so, in 1972, the Federal Trade Commission (FTC) charged Xerox with illegally monopolizing the office-copier business. According to the FTC, Xerox accounted for 86 percent of the $1.1-billion worldwide office-copier market. The company spent three years fighting off the charges and eventually reached a settlement. The FTC charges seemed particularly gratuitous given how Japanese companies like Canon, Minolta, Ricoh, and Sharp flooded the U.S. market with high-quality, low-cost office copiers in the 1970s. These imports were so successful that by 1982 Xerox's share of worldwide copier revenues had shrunk to 41 percent.

David Kearns took over Xerox's helm in 1977 and went on to engineer a comeback. Focusing on its core copying businesses, and backing away from computers, the ailing company fought back and regained a sizable market share. Today, Xerox remains the major power in the copier industry. In 1994 the corporation had $17.8 billion in revenues,

$15.1 billion of which came from business areas related to document processing. The technology Chester Carlson cooked up in a Queens apartment today brings the company revenues equivalent to the gross national product of Guatemala.

.

Howard Clark, Chief Executive Officer of American Express.

AMERICAN EXPRESS AND THE CHARGE CARD

Around the world at gas pumps, restaurants, and airline ticket counters consumers face the inevitable query: "Cash or charge?" It's a question that was rarely asked fifty years ago, but now we are on the verge of being a cashless society. Consumers and businesses routinely buy billions of dollars worth of services and goods without so much as a thin dime changing hands. The product that led this transformation was the American Express card, or, as *Forbes* called it: "the late-twentieth-century piece of magic that replaced checks, money, and charge accounts."

The American Express card, and every other charge card, evolved from the company's greatest invention, the traveler's check, which was introduced in 1891. With an American Express traveler's check in hand, a visitor otherwise unknown in Rotterdam, Quito, or Adelaide could obtain hard cash in a matter of moments. It was a whole new concept—selling people the honor of being trusted—and it caught on. Ever since, American Express has understood that concept better than any other company.

The company itself tried to engender trust at every opportunity. For example, the staff in its offices worldwide were instructed to help travelers, however possible. Expanding on its success and expertise, it grew to become the largest travel company in the United States. With worldwide connections, a thorough understanding of finance, and a clubby attitude, the company was on a firm foundation when it entered the burgeoning credit card field in 1958.

Part of the corporate culture of American Express, since its founding in 1850, has been to keep a quiet, even bland facade. With few exceptions, its chief executives have been content to stand in the background, behind the one name that has to mean something, if the names, and signatures, of its customers are to mean something all around the world. American Express executives through the first hundred years were so conservative, in fact, that many innovations were inadvertent or even unauthorized. Meanwhile, the company set aside ample cash reserves, guarded over its core businesses (or "tended its knitting," as one president put it), and stayed the most certain course in good times and bad. Steady management and a "safety-first" attitude toward finance surely resulted in American Express celebrating a hundredth birthday in 1950. But, at that same time, they nearly kept the company from entering the charge card business, which was to become its most important source of revenue.

The staying power of American Express can be ascribed to its understanding, as *Forbes* put it in 1989, that "A credit card, in short, is not a mere commodity, [but] it says something about the person who uses it." The company understood that the card could be considered much more than a financial accessory; it could be a status symbol in its own right.

A DELIVERY GIANT EVOLVES INTO THE DOMINANT TRAVEL FIRM

American Express was formed in 1850 as a temporary solution to a bitter feud among express companies in New York. The express business emerged in the 1840s in response to improvements in transportation and logistics exactly as it re-emerged in the 1970s, through companies like Federal Express. In both eras, companies got a good start by catering to individuals and businesses that were willing to pay extra for speedier, more reliable service than the U.S. Postal Service offered.

Henry Wells had built his express company, Wells & Company, in the 1840s by taking advantage of a new rail link just completed from Albany to Buffalo. He was a decent, likable man, and a humanitarian (he would later start one of the nation's first colleges for women, Wells College in New York State). In 1842, he offered a good opportunity in his company to a railroad freight agent named William G. Fargo. The two didn't always get along while Fargo was working his way up in the firm, but they would create a number of new ventures, including one of the most storied names in the history of U.S. business: Wells Fargo & Company.

Both men sensed that the more America spread out, the more it needed to be connected. Fargo had already expanded the company's express service to Chicago, when another upstate New Yorker, a tough wheeler-dealer named John Butterfield, built his network of stagecoach lines into serious competition. The two firms couldn't beat each other commercially, despite the bitter rivalry that grew between them. The agonizing truth, apparent to all concerned, was that the firms had no choice but to merge before they drove each other out of business.

In 1850, Henry Wells, John Butterfield, William Fargo, William and John Livingston, James Wasson and an attorney James McKay met in Buffalo, New York, to discuss terms. Days later, they reached an agreement and founded a new company—the American Express Company. However, the agreement had a catch: a clause in the charter they signed dictated that the company would automatically dissolve after ten years.

For ten years, the partners watched each other like hawks, with little whole-hearted agreement on anything. When Wells and Fargo suggested a further expansion of operations to California, Butterfield naturally disapproved. The opportunity was certainly too great to resist— though neither Wells nor Fargo probably realized then just how great— and so Wells, Fargo & Company was created in 1852, as a separate cousin company to American Express. It would become famous for the Pony Express, and for bringing well-capitalized banking to the American West.

The strains within the American Express board of directors led to factions within management and a generally tense, secretive atmosphere. Despite such problems, the firm managed its affairs with competence and grew into one of the most admired companies of the nineteenth century. From the company headquarters, initially in Buffalo and later in New York City, American Express slowly built up a network of offices along railroad spurs all over the country; the exceptions included the New England coast and a few other places staked out by friendly competitors.

After ten years, the company was making so much money that the partners finally agreed on something important: They didn't want to let the company dissolve. They found a way to circumvent the dissolution clause: selling off all company's assets, except for the name, and re-creating a new company around that name. By 1880, American Express maintained more than 4,000 offices in nineteen states. Customers, in complete confidence, could send packages, letters, or envelopes containing cash.

The firm now faced a challenge from the U.S. Post Office, which had started selling money orders in 1864. That allowed people to send money without shipping cash. In 1881, William Fargo's brother, J. C., was named president of the American Express Company. He was an irascible man, who wouldn't even consider issuing money orders at first, because they could be easily altered. When a brilliant employee named Marcellus Berry devised a way to safeguard the checks against tampering, American Express began to issue its own money orders at a price that was slightly lower than the post office's. The company subsequently made its first foray into the international side of the business, striking deals with firms like Kidder, Peabody & Company and Baring Brothers to guarantee payment of American Express money orders at banks in several foreign countries.

In the late 1880s, J. C. Fargo took a trip to Europe. Like any other well-heeled tourist, he arrived with a letter of credit from a major U.S. bank. A "letter of credit" was something like a bank book, in that designated banks in foreign cities would advance cash to the holder and then note on the letter the amount taken and the new total available. But letters of credit were a nuisance, even for a Fargo. "I had a lot of trouble cashing my letters of credit," J. C. complained to Marcellus Berry upon his return. "The moment I got off the beaten path they were no more use to me than so much wet wrapping paper. If the president of American Express has that sort of trouble, just think what ordinary travelers face. Something has got to be done about it."

That "something" was to be a remarkably enduring product that emerged as the first step in creating a cashless society: the traveler's check. Marcellus Berry designed it, too, and his version was almost exactly the same as the one still in use. The checks came in denominations of $100, $50, $20, and $10. For security purposes, purchasers signed each one in the upper left corner at the place of issuance and then signed it again when cashing it at an American Express office or foreign bank. One difference between the nineteenth-century check and today's edition is that, in those days of stable currencies, the checks included a handy scale for calculating exchange rates, which American Express guaranteed would be honored at any point in the future.

The traveler's check business began quietly: the company sold just 248 (worth $9,120) in 1891, the first year on the market. The concept was slightly flawed, since the checks could be cashed only at American Express offices, too few of which were established at the time. The company solved the problem by contracting with banks and hotels that would cash the checks. By 1892, when check sales boomed to $483,490, American Express offered a fourteen-page brochure listing of establishments that would accept them. Annual sales rose to $23 million by 1909.

Many fortunes have been made in the last hundred years by making various accoutrements of upper-class life available to the middle class. American Express created a miniature letter of credit when it issued the first traveler's check, granting a measure of worldly assurance to anyone with so little as $10, plus commission.

Overseeing the whole company, J. C. Fargo made no secret of the fact that he preferred carrying freight to serving tourists. The traveler's check couldn't be scorned, though. It was a unique product that not only generated cash flow but neatly diverted some cash flow into collecting pools as well: all those people who bought traveler's checks and never cashed them made a donation to the American Express Company. Even people who bought them and then delayed cashing them made the company a free loan. As these pools of cash grew, Fargo realized that traveler's checks were literally money in the bank for American Express. Fargo developed the business to the fullest, but when several executives suggested that the company put its worldwide connections to work in a travel service (in direct competition with Britain's Thomas Cook & Son), Fargo demurred. To him, American Express was fast becoming a financial services company, while still operating successfully as a freight company.

To a greater extent than almost any other company, American Express has been in a constant state of evolution. Wherever Americans went, the company was there to greet them, on the lonely frontier or on the even lonelier—for a busted Yankee—boulevards of Europe. The company's specific products and services could change, without its straying from its roots, and each successive CEO could see American Express as a completely different sort of company, without being wrong.

After J. C. Fargo retired, the company branched out. In 1915, American Express finally started its tourist service. "When you sell tickets to a prospective traveler, you can't just go down to the boat with a bunch of roses and say good-bye," said Frederick Small, who assumed the company's reins in 1923. "He has to be serviced all the way." The company offered to book tours, arrange trans-oceanic travel, and exchange currency for clients at offices in the United States and abroad. It quickly became the country's largest travel agency. "Romance had ambushed the American Express Company under the sober business guise of travelers cheques," *Forbes* wrote in 1929.

During World War II, the travel business virtually shut down and most of the company's European offices were shuttered. Yet American Express weathered the difficult times on the strength of the checks, which it sold in large quantities to U.S. soldiers. In the midst of the war, Small turned the company over to one of his protégés, Ralph Reed, a Wharton graduate who had joined American Express in 1919 as assistant to the comptroller. Reed was an Amex man all the way, according to the historian Peter Z. Grossman: "Like Small, he believed that Amexco was not just a company but a family, and he forgave everything except disloyalty." It was Reed who, late in his sixteen-year-tenure as president of American Express, would reluctantly introduce the American Express Card.

After the war, American Express rebuilt much of its travel service network, and was poised to cash in on the recovering tourist market. In the 1950s, pent-up demand for European travel burst out, encouraged by a strong dollar and growing prosperity at home. American Express offices resumed their stature as a "home away from home" for travelers. At the Paris office, at 11 Rue Scribe, up to 12,000 tourists stopped in each day, gathering mail, offering advice, booking trains or tours, and cashing traveler's checks. American Express was booming, and gross revenues rose fivefold between 1945 and 1957, when the company notched profits of $6.9 million on revenues of $54.7 million.

AMERICAN EXPRESS WATCHES A GROWING CREDIT CARD INDUSTRY

The charge card was not a new invention in the early 1950s, but it came onto the scene in a new form and turned into a major distraction for executives at American Express. Credit cards had first come into use at retail establishments in 1914, according to credit card historian Lewis Mandell. Although merchants saw them primarily as a convenience for major customers, it soon became clear that such cards could be profitable operations in their own right. In the 1940s, department stores like Gimbel's began offering store charge cards with revolving credit. Customers could use them to purchase items and were assessed interest charges on the outstanding balances. Restaurants and gas stations also offered charge cards. However, most early credit cards (all early cards were known as such, whether they offered revolving credit or not) could be used only at one particular store or at a single chain.

In 1950, Frank McNamara and Ralph Schneider, two businessmen, started Diners Club, the first of what came to be known as "travel and entertainment" cards. For a $3 annual membership fee, members received a card and could charge meals at restaurants, which took their payment—less five to ten percent—through Diners Club. This percentage came to be known as the "merchant discount." Although the arrangement meant lower profits on meals charged with the card, restauranteurs signed up in the belief the card would bring in more business. In starting Diners Club, McNamara and Schneider were positioning themselves as middlemen between restauranteurs and consumers. They guaranteed payment to the restaurants and collected from the cardholders.

American Express would ultimately follow Diners Club in starting its own credit card. As early as 1946, American Express executives floated a plan to start a highly conservative program under which clients could deposit money and then draw on the balance as they used the card. (Today, such an arrangement is referred to as a "debit card.") Reed rejected it. More specifically, he placed it "in indefinite suspense."

To Ralph Reed, American Express was a travel company—the preeminent one in the world. Each year more Americans seem to be traveling on trips planned by American Express and secured by Amex traveler's checks. Reed knew it firsthand, because he was the quintessential American tourist. In fact, he was everything that J. C. Fargo would have disdained: a man of humble birth—a comptroller on holiday—off to Europe each and every year to show the folks back home how easily he mixed with grandees and miscellaneous royalty. He was the quintessential tourist, except in one respect: Reed's trips were well-covered by the press. In 1956 he was on the cover of *Time*, but not as the CEO of the year; he was "The Grand Pooh-Bah of Travel." Somehow, the name fit, and it is still easy to call Ralph Reed "the Pooh-Bah." He was indeed the leader of a colorful, wandering tribe: the American tourists.

The issue of a charge card didn't go away. In the 1950s, living "on the cuff"—as using credit cards was called—became more and more commonplace. Credit cards emerged as the perfect instrument in the expanding economy, since they allowed Americans to buy expensive durable goods on installment. And the increasingly affluent U.S. population found cards especially useful for travel purposes. The American Hotel Association started a charge card that could be used at all member establishments, as did the Avis and Hertz car rental agencies. *Gourmet* and *Esquire* magazines also introduced credit cards that could be used at certain restaurants. By the time Diners Club went public in November 1955, it counted 200,000 members who charged about $20 million worth of meals a year.

As is often the case, the largest player in the field was slow to catch on to an emerging trend. The Pooh-Bah was still cautious, despite the success of Diners Club and its imitators. In fact, in 1956, Reed turned down a chance to purchase Diners Club.

After examining the full situation regarding Diners Club, though, Reed realized that its founders were undoubtedly onto something. He deputized senior vice president Howard Clark "to spell out how American Express can get into [credit cards] as an American Express activity." Clark, in turn, hired a consulting firm, Robert Heller & Associates, to conduct a feasibility study. And in the kind of move that gives consultants a black eye, Heller in October 1956 warned that the card would have "a substantial adverse effect on Travelers Cheques in the near future."

Still, there was mounting evidence from the field that other credit cards were already eating into the company's vaunted traveler's check franchise. In 1957, Harry Hill, a Paris-based Amerian Express executive, urged the home office to act quickly. "I would like to stress that I feel very strongly that something must be done for New York to get into this picture," he wrote. "There are too many people coming abroad with their Diners' cards and we are losing business."

Swayed by such pleas, Reed finally came around and decided to throw the full weight of the company's reputation and name behind a card. "We probably have to go all out as long as the cardholders are creditworthy," he said at a meeting in December 1957, when the company finally committed itself to a concept modeled on Diners Club.

Ralph Reed had no interest in building a new product from the ground up. That extended the risk, after all. Besides, the company was already lagging in a field crowded with charge cards. Rather, he sought out existing businesses to buy. The first was the American Hotel Association's credit card operation, which had 150,000 members. He also purchased the *Gourmet* card's 40,000 names. Next, the company began to exploit the two things that no other company had: its name and its experience. First, it began a marketing campaign that relied heavily on the American Express name. Long identified with the romance of travel, the company quickly realized that its card would have to have a certain cachet. The hunch proved correct, as thousands of individuals responded to newspaper advertisements to obtain the card, even in advance of its official introduction. Second, the company used its long-standing connections and its reputation to sign well-known establishments that would accept the card. Legendary Manhattan restauranteur Toots Shor, who had rejected the entreaties of other card companies, came on board, saying, "It's got a reputation for being clean and decent, and it'll probably lend some class to my place."

Americans spent $4 billion with their credit cards in 1958, and American Express was finally positioned to get a piece of the action. By the time its purple-colored cards were formally launched at an October 1, 1958, press conference, 250,000 people had already requested them. And from the first day, the Amex card had a place in the world, a lot of places, in fact. Among the 17,500 outlets accepting the card were favorite spots like London's Dorchester Hotel and Maxim's in Paris.

"The public is very much credit-minded and we have the organization to handle it," promised Ralph Reed, who was himself a dues-paying member (card number 101-000-001-6). "Ultimately, it's our hope to liberate the American wallet from its multiplicity of credit cards," he said. The American Express card could be used in hotels, restaurants, stores, and at airline, ship, and train ticket counters: More than any other card of the time, it could be used as a replacement for cash.

Reed's optimism represented the arrogance of a dominant company crashing into a new field. To his great chagrin, the early results were not auspicious. In March 1958, Michael Lively, who would eventually become the general manager of the Credit Card Division, estimated the card would lose $1 million its first year and earn $1 million in 1959. Even though American Express signed up 750,000 members who charged over $100 million in 1960, the card continued to lose money into its third and fourth years. There were, it turned out, major pitfalls to starting big, as opposed to building a business slowly from the ground up.

American Express had been unprepared for the logistics of collecting monthly payments from such a large number of customers and merchants. "For a while we weren't even getting all our bills mailed out on time," said company Vice President Clark B. Winter. As a result, American Express was forced to take write-offs. "We lost roughly $2 million last year, and we have made every mistake we could possibly have made in getting it going," said the board chairman, Ralph Owen, in 1960. In the rush to automate the process, the company had acquired the wrong technology. Apparently, the wrong people were managing the unit as well. As 1960 came to a close, American Express's credit card operations were a quagmire.

GEORGE WATERS TAKES CHARGE OF THE CHARGE CARD

Ralph Reed didn't have to clean up the mess. In 1960 the company's directors gave him one last trip to Europe and then named a successor. The new man was forty-four-year-old Howard Clark. Clark, a Harvard-trained lawyer who joined the company after leaving the Navy in 1945, turned over responsibility for the flagging card to George Waters in 1961.

Waters, at age forty-five, had most recently worked as chief operating officer of an Atlanta grocery store chain called Colonial Stores. An expert in data processing, he had grown up in a culture alien to credit. His father had often told him: "A person has no right to own anything, except a home, if he can't pay for it with cash." Despite this background, Waters was right for the job. Savvy and hard-driving, he moved decisively in the business world. He was, in short, the exact sort of person at whom the Amex card was aimed.

The first problem that Waters faced was relatively simple, but it forced him to make decisive moves early on. The Amex card just wasn't bringing in sufficient revenue and Waters reasoned that one easy way to boost revenues would be to increase the $6 annual fee; this might make it expensive, but then, under Waters, it wasn't supposed to be for everybody. Although there were concerns that such a move would scare off clients, Howard Clark agreed that a drastic step was necessary. "I'd rather die on the operating table than bleed to death," he said. "Let's raise the discount, and raise the price of the card from $6 to $8 and see what happens." Waters turned out to be right; revenues did rise.

Another major problem lay in delinquent card balances. When acquiring Gourmet's list and the operations of the American Hotel Association card, American Express had taken on a large number of clients without making adequate credit checks. And the company had been slow to crack down on delinquent payers; the hallowed American Express tradition was to coddle its customers, never to antagonize them. Waters moved quickly, though. Instead of giving people a ninety-day grace period, he mailed dunning notices after a month's delinquency. The company also sent humorous verses with a serious message: "But in the future, don't delay. . .We'll cut you off, if you don't pay." And Waters didn't hesitate to cancel delinquent accounts.

As a third means of increasing revenues, he unilaterally boosted the discount rate—the percentage of a sale that the merchant had to pay the company—from 3 percent to 7 percent. Again, this had the potential to alienate the firm's merchant partners. But Waters believed that American Express, with its long history of service and name recognition, could get away with it. "If you have the best product, sell it for a premium," he liked to say. "People will pay." These initiatives helped the drive toward profitability.

Even as policies were changing, the card itself was changing. The color was switched from purple to green, in a new design purposefully reminiscent of cool cash. In a major effort to boost the card's profile, the company retained in 1962 the services of a reigning advertising agency of the day, Ogilvy, Benson & Mather. The campaign that Ogilvy designed high-lighted American Express as "the company for people who travel."

American Express borrowed another tactic from Ogilvy's playbook, using extensive surveys to back up its marketing practices. In 1962, it commissioned a study that revealed that Americans misplaced or lost about $700 million in cash each year. The obvious lesson? Consumers should use the American Express card or traveler's checks for everyday use—instead of cash. To induce more companies to accept the card for payment, American Express armed itself with statistics. In 1964, for example, when American Express first hooked up with American Air-lines, the card division conducted a survey that showed 24 percent of the tickets sold under the airline's new "sign and fly" plan constituted new business brought in by the availability of credit. This kind of data would be used to approach other airlines about the value of working with American Express.

With or without statistics, Waters's instinct all along was to distin-guish the Amex card from the competition in the travel and entertain-ment field, that is, from cards like Diners Club and Carte Blanche. American Express began to refer to its cardholders as "members," im-plying that carrying the card conferred special privileges. Then it backed up the claim with exclusive services that only a company with its world-wide connections could offer. In 1963, for example, the firm announced it would cash personal checks up to $300 for cardholders overseas. Com-petitors like Diners Club, with no comparable international network, could not match this offer. On the strength of its advertising and its growing list of participating businesses, American Express in 1964 saw its volume of charged sales surpass Diners Club, posting $344 million in sales compared to $250 million for Diners Club.

POSITIONING THE CARD AS A PRESTIGE ITEM AMID COMPETITION

Credit cards in the travel and entertainment field were primarily pitched to well-off people—especially businesspeople who dined out or traveled frequently. Overall, though, the credit card began to acquire a middle-class image in the 1960s. This development was largely due to the efforts of the California-based Bank of America. In 1959, it introduced a credit card through mass mailings to 1.5 million people in the state. This card, one of the first "bank cards," operated on assumptions fundamentally different from those of the Amex card. Offering a low $100 credit limit, BankAmericard charged no fee. Instead, the bank earned profits by charging 1.5 percent monthly interest on unpaid balances. The Amex card, essentially just a charge card by comparison, offered no extended credit and so exacted no interest. Since the Bank of America was effectively offering to lend money to cardholders for relatively small purchases, it concentrated on signing agreements with retail establishments where its middle-class cardholders would shop.

The BankAmericard (later known as "Visa") built a strong base in California before making a strong national move by licensing other banks to use its brand name and its processes in 1966. Just when the Amex card was starting to dominate its old rivals Diners Club and Carte Blanche, it was faced with competition from BankAmericard and from another card, one with a familiar pedigree. In 1968, Master Charge cards swept into first place among bank cards, having been issued by a consortium of banks headed by none other than Wells Fargo.

American Express didn't rush into head-on competition with Bank-Americard and Master Charge. Since it made money from annual fees and commissions, not from interest on outstanding balances, it sought to put more cards into the hands of people who made large purchases, people, most notably, on expense accounts. Under Waters's direction, the company began to pitch the card to corporate customers. Starting in 1966, a company could establish an account with American Express and issue multiple cards to its employees. The company would then receive one inclusive bill, detailing purchases made by each cardholder.

Even as Wells Fargo's Master Charge showed up in tens of millions of Americans' wallets, its old cousin became, if anything, even haughtier. American Express continued to charge a comparatively high membership fee of $12, along with higher commissions on purchases. The company felt the costs were justified because of its service and its reach. "Where they have some of the airlines and some of the restaurants, we have them all," said an American Express marketing official in 1969.

By the close of the card's first decade, the American Express Company had been transformed. Net income rose from $9 million in 1960 to more than $75 million in 1969. During that period, the company's earnings grew at an annual rate of 17 percent, growth more common among young entrepreneurial companies than among 110-year-old firms.

Part of the growth can be attributed to the company's diversification. Howard Clark had generally left the card division to its own devices as he focused on pushing the company into new areas. In 1968, for example, American Express purchased the Fireman's Fund, an insurance company; Equitable Securities, a mutual fund firm; and even a magazine called *U.S. Camera*, which it renamed *Travel and Leisure*. Despite this flurry of activity, the company's two cashless projects—the American Express card and the traveler's check—still accounted for the bulk of its profits. By the end of the decade, the card had far outdistanced its chief competitors in the upscale travel and entertainment area, and American Express still held more than 60 percent of the market for traveler's checks. In 1970, American Express reported charge volume of $2.3 billion, compared with $935 million for Diners Club and $220 million for Carte Blanche. With clever advertising and marketing, the card that seemed likely to embarrass American Express at the beginning of the decade had become a status symbol, both for the people who carried it and for the company that had nurtured it successfully.

THE FLOAT

For nearly a century American Express has been the beneficiary of a unique wrinkle in its business. When the company began selling traveler's checks in the 1890s, it noticed a significant lag between the moment customers purchased checks for cash and the moment checks were redeemed. As a result, American Express found itself in custody of a large amount of cash, which came to be called "the float." A crucial asset for the company, *Forbes* once identified it as "the cash AmEx holds while the checks are burning a hole in your wallet." It amounted to a continuous, interest-free loan from the customers to the company. And if, for any reason, the purchaser neglected to redeem the checks altogether, the firm didn't have to pay back the "loan" at all.

Over the years, the company rolled the float into high-quality government and corporate bonds, and, to a lesser degree, into stocks. By the end of 1956, the American Express float was an investment fund of $503 million. And the company earned nearly as much from that investment as it did from all of its other corporate operations. "American Express is only in two businesses, credit cards and float," said Oppenheimer & Company analyst Donald Kramer in 1970, when the float ranged from $700 million to $1 billion. He was only half joking.

In 1978, the average check remained uncashed for thirty days, and *Forbes* estimated that American Express earned about $81 million annually from the float. By 1995, when the company reported that there were $6 billion worth of traveler's checks outstanding on any given day, returns on the investment of these funds represented a substantial portion of the company's $969 million in income from interest and dividends.

Although American Express's record in the 1960s was impressive, its card business represented only a small portion of the overall credit card industry. Between the end of 1967 and 1970 alone, for example, outstanding consumer credit rose from $8.2 billion to $13.8 billion. At the same time, many firms that rushed into the credit card game in the late 1960s quickly racked up losses due to lax oversight. "By the end of 1970, credit losses totaled $116 million, up more than 100 percent from 1969," *Forbes* wrote in 1971.

American Express had been just a bit more careful than others in its field—as it had been in any field it entered through the years. The firm avoided losses to bad credit by staying true to its core strategy. It didn't give credit, except as a thirty-day courtesy, and outstanding balances had to be paid every month. Amex customers were expected to be careful too.

In more recent years, however, American Express changed its stance. In the company's continuing process of redefining itself, it became an intricate conglomerate of financial services, expanding through a series of acquistions and expensive start-up ventures. A traditionally bland company became one of the boldest, with results that were often discouraging, and could have been disasterous if it hadn't been firmly anchored by its relatively new core-business: the Amex card.

New types of American Express cards have proliferated since the company established the original. The Optima—albeit the least successful product in the American Express roster—even offers revolving credit, like the bank cards. And while the company has expanded all operations, travel-related services accounted for 66 percent of its $15.8 billion in revenues for 1995. That year, holders of 38 million Amex cards charged up $162 billion worth of goods and services worldwide, while traveler's check sales topped $26 billion; together, these figures added up to nearly 3 percent of the U.S. gross national product.

Billions of dollars spent and not a penny to be seen. More than 100 years after American Express sold its first Travelers Check, and nearly forty years after the first American Express cardholder whipped out a small cardboard rectangle embossed with the company's distinctive logo, the cashless society is closer at hand than ever before. Little by little, and assuming as little risk as possible, American Express had learned how to replace cash with a measure of trust.

Mary Kay Ash, founder of Mary Kay Cosmetics.

MARY KAY ASH AND HER CORPORATE CULTURE FOR WOMEN

Keenly conscious of its symbolism, Mary Kay Ash wears a diamond lapel pin shaped like a bumblebee. "Aerodynamics have proven that the bumblebee cannot fly," she says. "The body is too heavy and the wings are too weak. But the bumblebee doesn't know that, and it goes right on flying, miraculously."

In 1963, when she was forty-five and when most American women did not hold full-time jobs, Mary Kay (as she is universally referred to) launched a direct-sales cosmetics company run by women. From modest origins in a Dallas storefront, Mary Kay Cosmetics grew into a vertically integrated corporation with annual sales of over $950 million. In 1976 it became the first company chaired by a woman to be listed on the New York Stock Exchange. Just how did this bumblebee soar so high?

Mary Kay's success is based upon sound business practices combined with tenacity and original thinking—about the marketplace, about corporate structure, and about women themselves. Mary Kay built a new corporate culture based on the education, participation, and empowerment of women. Her company's entrepreneurial structure inspired hundreds of thousands of Mary Kay saleswomen to become, in effect, small-business operators. With a home-spun management style, she boosted their self-esteem and confidence through constant positive reinforcement and material rewards. By harnessing the American woman's economic and productive power, she forged an economic liberation movement and flew through the glass ceiling two decades before that phrase even existed.

BIRTH OF A SALESWOMAN

Born in 1918 to parents who ran a hotel and restaurant in Hot Wells, Texas, Mary Kathlyn Wagner recognized at an unusually young age that women could hold a viable role in the workforce. In the 1920s, when her father became an invalid after being stricken with tuberculosis, her mother, Lulu, landed a job as a restaurant manager in Houston, twenty-five miles away. "For all those years, my mother was the sole support of our family," said Mary Kay, who took on the responsibility of caring for her father and running the family's meager household. While these roles placed a heavy burden on the young girl, they offered her an unusual degree of independence. "For instance, if I needed new clothing, I had to go by myself to downtown Houston," she recalled. "I took these Saturday trips alone, because my best friend was not allowed to travel on the streetcar without an adult. After all, we were just seven years old."

Although she earned straight A's and finished high school in three years, Mary Kay could not afford to go to college immediately. Dreams of higher education were further deferred when, at seventeen, she married Ben Rogers, a local musician and radio personality. The young couple had three children within seven years: Ben, Marylyn, and Richard. Following in her mother's footsteps, Mary Kay Rogers pitched in to support the young family, but as a mother with a high school education in Depression-era Texas, her options were severely limited. ". . . I had to have a good-paying job with flexible hours. The flexibility was essential, because I knew that I wanted to spend time with my children when they needed me," she said.

In the mid-1930s, a woman appeared on the Rogers's stoop peddling children's books. The saleswoman offered to give her a free set if she could sell ten, and Mary Kay started calling friends from the Tabernacle Baptist Church. She sold ten sets in less than two days. "I didn't have books to show them—all I had was my enthusiasm," she said. In the next nine months, Mary Kay sold $25,000 worth of books.

Having discovered a natural ability for sales, she enlisted with Stanley Home Products, a direct-sales housewares company. While Mary Kay enjoyed staging "shows" in friends' homes and relished earning commissions, direct sales mainly appealed to the same innate drive that led her to complete high school a year early. ". . . Nothing excited me quite as much as company contests. It was just that old competitive spirit of mine," she said. In 1937, Mary Kay attended Stanley's convention in Dallas, where she watched F. Stanley Beveridge, the company president, crown a Queen of Sales and present her with an alligator handbag. After the ceremony, Mary Kay worked up the temerity to introduce herself to Beveridge and announced that she would be a sales queen the next year. And so she was.

Her talent for selling proved fortunate. Upon her husband's return from service in World War II, Ben Rogers requested a divorce. Mary Kay was left as the sole financial support for her three children. "I had developed a sense of worth for my abilities as a wife and mother, and yet on that day I felt like a complete and total failure," she wrote. For the next seventeen years, she raised her children as a single mother while recruiting and managing dozens of salespeople, first, for Stanley Home Products, and, starting in 1959, for the World Gift Company.

The children pitched in, with son Richard often spending Saturdays packing orders. As they grew up, Mary Kay's children pursued their own interests. Ben, the oldest, married and moved to Houston, where he worked for a welding company. Marylyn got married and started a family. Richard sold life insurance for the Prudential Life Insurance Company. Meanwhile, Mary Kay's life took a turn in 1960, when she married George Hallenbeck, a Dallas businessman.

Mary Kay ultimately rose to the rank of director of national training at World Gift. However, in mid-1963 she returned from a business trip to find that her male assistant had been promoted to a position above her. The slight was the worst in a series she had encountered at the company. "I was constantly being told, 'Oh, Mary Kay, you're thinking female.' And inevitably, no matter how hard I tried, no matter how well I did my job, I still found myself reaching the golden door only to find it marked Men Only." She promptly quit. Forty-five, jobless, and without children to look after, Mary Kay had lost the two roles that had defined her life for nearly twenty-seven years. She slipped into deep depression. "I have never spent a more miserable time in my life," she said. "I just felt my life was over. I lived across the street from a mortuary, and I almost called them."

To fight the emotional malaise, Mary Kay started jotting down lists of things she had done well and obstacles she had overcome. As she did, she hit upon the idea of writing a book on management. In it, she would distill twenty-five years worth of direct-sales wisdom. As part of the outline, she drafted a roster of factors that would define the "dream company." And then a bigger idea sprang to mind: "Why are you theorizing about a dream company?" she asked herself. "Why don't you just start one?"

BUILDING A NEW COMPANY GEARED TOWARD WOMEN

Mary Kay decided to form her own direct-sales company—a company mindful of the lessons learned from decades of working as a single mother in male corporate cultures. Its structure would offer flexibility to part-time workers and allow women to maintain their commitments to family while earning extra cash. Although she wanted to make money, Mary Kay had a higher social goal in mind. "I wasn't interested in the dollars-and-cents part of business; my interest in 1963 was in offering women opportunities that didn't exist anywhere else," she later wrote.

Having sketched the outlines of a dream company, she still needed a product, and she found one in her own medicine cabinet. Back in the early 1950s, while running a Stanley Home Products demonstration party in suburban Dallas, Mary Kay had noticed that all the attendees had wonderful complexions. It turned out that the hostess sold jars of private label facial cream to her friends. The woman's father, a tanner, had used his expertise in tenderizing animal hides to create a balm that softened women's faces and hands. After trying the cream, Mary Kay became a loyal customer. "I knew that the products were special, so in 1963, I bought the original formulas from the tanner's heirs," she said.

However, her choice of products put Mary Kay up against Avon, a giant with seventy-seven years' experience in the direct-sales cosmetics market. Mary Kay found two kinks in the giant's armor. First, Avon's focus seemed to ignore skin-care products, a lucky break since she had a good one. Second, she concluded that Avon's trademark door-to-door approach was a dated sales method. Woman, she felt, had grown too sophisticated in their buying to respond to "Avon calling."

Mary Kay's sales force, or "consultants," would demonstrate the products at intimate parties, called "Mary Kay Beauty Shows," with no more than five or six guests per show. "I saw this situation as a wonderful opportunity to teach women about total skin care," she said. Mindful of working mothers' needs, she would permit consultants to stage as few or as many demonstrations per week as they wanted. If women knew enough about the products, she reasoned, and if the products were good, they would essentially sell themselves.

In response to her negative experiences at other direct-sales firms, Mary Kay's company would not sell franchises or grant salespeople exclusive territories. Consultants would drum up new recruits from their circle of acquaintances. When Mary Kay worked for Stanley Products, the company had transferred her from Houston to Dallas to develop a new market. But this move forced her to forego commissions on sales by the women she had already recruited in Dallas. "I thought that was patently unfair," she said. Mary Kay vowed that no employee of hers would suffer the same fate.

Mary Kay and her husband George scraped together $5,000 in savings to produce a small inventory and lease a cramped 500-square-foot storefront in Exchange Park, an office complex in Dallas. Then Mary Kay set about recruiting an initial crop of consultants, while George handled the finances. Together, they filled boxes with jars and plastered labels on them that read: "Beauty by Mary Kay."

The couple's plans tragically fell apart a month before the scheduled opening of the firm. While poring over business papers, George Hallenbeck suffered cardiac arrest and died at the breakfast table. Alone again, Mary Kay avoided despair by throwing herself into her work. "To me, work and growth were the same. And without my work, I found that I had no reason to get out of bed each morning," she said. Ignoring the advice of her attorney, who showed the widow a brochure documenting the high failure rate of cosmetics companies, Mary Kay decided to forge ahead with the venture. Her son, Ben Rogers kicked in $4,500 from his savings account, and Richard Rogers quit his job to work by his mother's side. "I worshipped the ground she walked on," Richard said.

Mary Kay didn't need much more start-up capital because she had devised a shrewd business strategy. First, she recruited nine consultants, who paid 50 percent of the retail price for packages consisting of five products: Cleansing Cream, Magic Masque, Skin Freshener, Night Cream, and Day Radiance foundation. She required that women pay for the packages up front. "This is not a lack of trust; it is simply our absolute belief in the wisdom expressed in our American system of cash-and-carry capitalism," Mary Kay said. Requiring consultants to pay in advance would let the fledgling company operate without taking on debt.

Having worked in the field for twenty-five years, Mary Kay knew bad debts from salespeople often caused direct-sales companies to fail.

Beauty by Mary Kay (later Mary Kay Cosmetics) began sales on an inauspicious day: Friday, September 13, 1963. Defying all negative omens, the products gradually caught on in the Dallas area. Mary Kay wrote a five-page consultants' guide, produced a newsletter, and encouraged consultants to spread the word about the company. Richard filled orders, dashing between the storefront and a storage area two blocks away. Ben temporarily left his job to pitch in. ". . . Richard, Ben, and I put in sixteen and eighteen-hour workdays as we struggled to do anything that had to be done," Mary Kay said. The company survived the crucial first months and began to grow and prosper.

To celebrate the close of its first year of business, in which sales totaled $198,000, the company threw a party. On September 13, 1964, the firm's 200 employees convened in the warehouse of a new facility at 1220 Majesty Drive in Dallas. Mary Kay made enough chicken and Jell-O salad to feed the crowd, and awarded wigs to top salespeople.

This celebration marked the beginning of Mary Kay's policy to provide inspiration, enthusiasm, and material rewards that would motivate women to sell ever greater quantities of skin cream. "Women generally lack confidence," she said. "When a woman joins our company, we immediately begin to instill confidence in her." The primary means for this were positive reinforcement and recognition for even the smallest achievements. "Giving praise where it is due has become a working philosophy in every aspect of our work at Mary Kay Cosmetics."

As the company grew throughout the 1960s, the annual sales meeting—or "seminar"—grew from humble homemade chicken and Jell-O beginnings into an increasingly lavish extravaganza. Each year, hundreds, and then thousands, of women convened in Dallas to attend classes and hear motivational speakers. The highlight was awards night, when the company recognized consultants who attained prescribed sales levels, thus ascending Mary Kay's "Ladder of Success." Each rung brought a new badge of honor. Women started with ribbons, and aspired to sashes, badges, lapel bars, diamond bracelets, bumblebee pins, and, the ultimate symbols of Mary Kay success, pink Cadillacs.

Although Mary Kay started her firm amid the first stirrings of the tumultuous 1960s, her views did not mirror the politics of the era. One newsweekly later noted that "Mary Kay has liberated more women than Gloria Steinem." But she shrank from such comparisons, embracing instead a distinctly nonpolitical brand of feminism. While Mary Kay conceived of her company as "a real women's liberation operation," its ethos was more Betty Crocker than Betty Friedan. "God, first; family, second; career, third," was one maxim Mary Kay regularly dispensed to her charges.

While the company never took a formal stance on political issues like the Equal Rights Amendment, Mary Kay was a feminist by almost any definition. Her life's experiences taught her that women couldn't rely on men to be the sole providers. She likewise knew that women were capable of producing in the workplace and grew frustrated by the failure of corporate America to recognize this fact. "I can't believe that God intended for a woman's work to receive only fifty cents on the dollar," she often said. Mary Kay—the company and the woman—believed women's liberation meant economic liberation, pure and simple.

Mary Kay's nurturing company gave women the emotional support many families didn't provide. Acting as a surrogate mother, Mary Kay made a practice of sending personally addressed birthday cards to thousands of consultants and calling to inquire after sick family members. She believed these gestures had a large impact, just as she believed her small products had an endless appeal to women of all classes. "When times are bad, a woman may not be able to afford a new dress, but she can still get a lift by buying a new lip color. In fact, buying new cosmetics can often do as much for your spirits as going out for a fancy lunch," she said.

This emphasis on personal support attracted more and more representatives. Women were eager to sign on as Mary Kay consultants where the financial incentives were plentiful. The 50 percent markup compared favorably with the 30 to 40 percent commissions offered by other direct-sales firms. In addition, Mary Kay consultants could earn commissions from the gross product orders of women they recruited. The company rewarded productivity. Women who signed up a sufficient number of consultants were made sales directors, and, ultimately, national sales directors. Dalene White, the first Mary Kay beauty consultant, became a national sales director and was one of the first "Mary Kay million-aires"—she earned $1 million in commissions.

THE COMPANY SPREADS ITS WINGS

The year 1966 proved to be an auspicious one for Mary Kay and her cosmetics company. Despite the chaos of getting the enterprise off the ground, Mary Kay had managed to rebuild her personal life. She married Mel Ash, a businessman whom she had met on a blind date. Having attained a critical mass with sales of $1.3 million, the company began to mature and Mary Kay undertook, with Richard Rogers, to pilot her company to national prominence.

Mary Kay Cosmetics became more defined in 1968, when it raised $2.34 million by selling 195,000 shares to the public. The proceeds of the offering were used to buy control of the manufacturing process. Mary Kay built a 275,000-square-foot facility in Dallas, which allowed the company to make virtually all its own products. It also expanded its market. Relying on word of mouth, the company had spread throughout Texas and into neighboring Louisiana, Oklahoma, Arkansas, and New Mexico. In 1970, consultants in these five states accounted for 90 percent of Mary Kay's sales. Encouraged by this success, the company embarked upon an ambitious expansion program, building distribution centers in California, Georgia, New Jersey, and Illinois, which also served as facilities where regional directors could train new recruits by the dozen.

With several thousand employees and $18 million in sales in 1972, Mary Kay Cosmetics was one of the nation's largest private employers of women. Mary Kay publicized her company by using pink trucks to ferry products from the Dallas factory across interstate highways to the regional centers, by awarding more and more pink Cadillacs, and by buying a spanking new office building. True to its tradition, the company paid cash when it bought the eight-story, $7-million glimmering glass building in Dallas in 1977. The building housed a growing central administration, which was run by Richard Rogers. He installed a sophisticated computer system to keep track of the activities of consultants operating throughout the United States.

Between 1963 and 1978 (a year in which Mary Kay's more than 46,000 consultants peddled over $50 million of product), sales grew at a 28 percent average annual rate. But the company's fundamentally sound business formula hardly changed. It still required cash up front for inventory. "There are no accounts payable and no accounts receivable," Richard Rogers said. And sixteen years after the company's founding, the five basic skin-care products still accounted for fully half of the company's sales.

Although Mary Kay slowly detached herself from the firm's day-to-day operations in the 1970s, she continued to blaze new trails. When her company switched its stock's listing to the New York Stock Exchange in 1976, it became the first NYSE-listed firm chaired by a woman. And Mary Kay remained a crucial and effective leader. Widowed when Mel Ash died in 1980, she spent much of her time meeting and training groups of consultants. She invited new consultants to her house, and, over homemade cookies, told her inspiring personal story over and over again. She eventually wrote it down, and it was published in her autobiography, *Mary Kay* (1981). She took top sales producers on trips to London and the Caribbean, and traveled around the country, making contact with as many consultants as she could. "I believe in the personal touch, because it makes every human being feel appreciated," she wrote.

In the 1980s, however, the company that had created so many opportunities for women became a victim of its own success. The percentage of women participating in the labor force rose steadily from 38.3

REGAINING CONTROL OF THE COMPANY

In 1985, when Mary Kay Ash and Richard Rogers took Mary Kay Cosmetics private in a leveraged buyout (LBO), they employed a financing technique that became increasingly popular as the decade wore on. The idea behind the LBO is relatively simple: a company's management borrows heavily to purchase its of shares back from the public, and then pays down the debt either with cash flow or with proceeds raised from selling assets.

As the company's stock languished in the low teens in 1985, Mary Kay and Rogers, in May of that year, offered to buy 70 percent of the outstanding shares they didn't already own for about $315 million. "We decided it would be in the best interest of our people and our customers if we got out of the stock market," Mary Kay said. After the company's board of directors rejected the offer, the mother-son duo raised their bid in July. In December the board finally approved the transaction.

The deal called for shareholders to receive $11 cash and a fifteen-year debenture with a face value of $8.25 for each of the 21 million common shares they held. Holders of the debenture would receive no interest for the first five years, but would reap 15 percent annual interest payments thereafter. Since analysts assigned these bonds a present value of $3.50 to $4.00, the bid was valued at between $14.50 and $15.00 a share, or between $304 million and $315 million.

The debentures raised between $73 million and $84 million. But the company needed $231 million to pay for the cash portion of the buyout. And while Mary Kay Ash loathed debt, borrowing was the only way to conduct a transaction of this size. So with the help of their financial advisers, Mary Kay and Richard Rogers came up with a financing package. It consisted of an $81-million loan from a syndicate of banks, $60 million raised by selling senior notes to institutional buyers, and $90 million from the company's existing cash balance and credit lines.

The move made Mary Kay Ash and Richard Rogers largely independent managers of their company, and it also meant the value of their holdings would no longer be affected by the whims of the moment. "Most important, we are not adversely affected as investors buy and sell in an ever-fluctuating stock market," she said.

percent in 1963, when Mary Kay Cosmetics opened its doors, to 53.6 percent in 1984. As other corporations and industries gradually opened up to females, women found positions in professions like law, journalism, and real estate. But some of those flocking into new careers continued to sell Mary Kay products. In 1984, one-third of the company's 192,000 consultants had other jobs. Even so, observers believed the demographic formula responsible for Mary Kay's success was unraveling. "Red ink was flowing in Mary Kay's kingdom," *Forbes* wrote. "Mary Kay's main problem was that many of the commission-only saleswomen Mary Kay had relied on to peddle the firm's cosmetics had entered the workforce."

This argument gained credence when sales fell from $323 million in 1983 to $260 million in 1985. As the market punished the company's shares, Mary Kay Ash and Richard Rogers saw an opportunity. Overcoming their long-standing aversion to debt, mother and son borrowed heavily to buy the 70 percent of the company's shares they didn't already own in a $315-million leveraged buyout. While some analysts believed too much was paid for total control, the faith the mother-son combination had in their brainchild was rewarded. Under Richard Rogers's direction, the company offered higher commissions and bonuses and focused greater attention on overseas expansion. Mary Kay Cosmetics quickly rebounded; by 1991 the company's 220,000 salespeople tallied $487 million in sales.

Entering its fourth decade, the company has managed to maintain a youthful enthusiasm among its sales force. And nowhere was the Mary Kay enthusiasm more evident than at the company's thirtieth annual seminar in the summer of 1994. Almost 40,000 women and a few dozen men (2,000 of Mary Kay's more than 425,000 consultants worldwide are male) convened at the Dallas Convention Center. They came to celebrate another record-breaking year, one in which sales totaled $850 million.

Consultants made the pilgrimage from Oregon, Oklahoma, and Ontario; from New York City and small towns in Nebraska; from Russia, Japan, and the other twenty-one countries where Mary Kay consultants operate. Housewives rubbed shoulders with Harvard MBAs and other professionals—about two-thirds of Mary Kay consultants hold full-time jobs. New recruits who had earned $5,000 in commissions sat next to national sales directors whose incomes topped $500,000. In between the sessions on bookkeeping and leadership, the awards ceremony and motivational speakers, the conventioneers could take a bus to the corporate headquarters and visit the new Mary Kay Museum. Presiding over the entire affair was the company's legendary chairman emeritus, now a seventy-six-year-old. As usual, Mary Kay helped dole out $6 million worth of prizes and awards and personally crowned four sales queens with rhinestone tiaras.

Even though the convention center stood just a few miles from the warehouse where Mary Kay held its first awards ceremony, the distance could hardly have been greater. Mary Kay Cosmetics is no longer a tiny dream company. It's a sophisticated, integrated firm that controls 10 percent of the U.S. facial skin-care market and 8.5 percent of the facial color cosmetics market. In 1993, a Texas magazine estimated the combined net worth of Mary Kay Ash and Richard Rogers at $320 million. Mary Kay's lengthy flight—that of the woman and the company with which she is inextricably linked—has been turbulent, with many bumps. As *Forbes* noted: "Occasionally the bumblebee goes in circles. But so far, it has always found a way to right itself."

Intel's founders, left to right: Robert Noyce, Andrew Grove, and Gordon Moore.

INTEL'S MICROPROCESSOR AND THE COMPUTER REVOLUTION

or the head of a $16.2-billion company responsible for 26,000 employees, Andrew Grove, the chief executive officer of Intel Corporation, still has the outlook of an entrepreneur. "The best thing is to make the right decision. Making a wrong decision is okay too. The worst thing to do is hedge. To hedge is to fail."

Intel has never hedged. From the beginning it has forged relentlessly into new territory. In 1968, when Gordon Moore and Robert Noyce left the security of a large, established firm to start their own company, their plan was to manufacture a product they had yet to invent: a tiny semiconductor chip with the same capacity to store computer memory as the large magnetic cores used in mainframe computers. Under the direction of Moore and Noyce, Intel's engineers set out to pack more and more computing power on ever smaller chips. In 1971 they made a chip that could be active in the operation of the computer. The microprocessor, as it was called, is a device now ranked with McCormick's reaper and Henry Ford's assembly line as a milestone in the history of invention.

By compacting the power of a 3,000-cubic-foot computer into a chip smaller than a fingernail, Intel's microprocessor made possible the personal computer (PC). As the PC revolution gained momentum in the early 1980s, Robert Noyce (who died in 1990) observed that an "Intel-induced change occurred in our society."

The invention of the microprocessor was simply the beginning. Intel, the early technological leader, has made a strenuous effort to maintain its lead. With the help of Andrew Grove, a kinetic manager and organizational mastermind, the company has managed to stay ahead of potential competitors for two decades. Even after establishing its microprocessors, which are produced in state-of-the-art factories around the world, as the industry standard, Intel continues to operate as if it were a research institution. In recent years its annual budget for research and development has topped $1 billion.

The heavy emphasis on research is explained by two widely quoted comments made by Gordon Moore and Andy Grove, respectively. The first, now known as "Moore's law," is that "the power and the complexity of the silicon chip will double every eighteen months." The second, explaining Intel's drive to be out in front every time the silicon chip does advance, could be called "Grove's corollary": "Only the paranoid survive."

INVENTING A NEW INDUSTRY

Gordon Moore grew up in a small coastal town south of San Francisco, where his father was a deputy sheriff and his mother ran a store. He left to pursue an education that was completed in 1954 with a Ph.D. in chemistry and physics from the California Institute of Technology. In 1956, after two years at the Applied Physics Lab at Johns Hopkins, Moore returned to California, where he took a job as a research chemist at Shockley Semiconductor. One of his co-workers there was Robert Noyce, a Grinnell College graduate with a Ph.D. in engineering from the Massachusetts Institute of Technology. Shockley Semiconductor should have been an exciting place to work; it was a well-funded research group operated by William Shockley, who won the Nobel prize in 1956 for his role in inventing the transistor. Conducting impulses through a silicon "semiconductor" pressed between two wafers, the transistor replaced vacuum tubes in electronics, paving the way for smaller radios. The breakthrough would ultimately pave the way for the personal computer.

In 1956–57, the scientists at Shockley Semiconductor were experimenting with the possibilities that lay beyond the transistor, investigating the efficacy of using it in the construction of other small electronic machines and appliances. But they were chafing under Shockley's tyrannical rule. When Noyce, Moore, and a half dozen others became hopelessly disenchanted with Shockley's administration, they sought the help of Arthur Rock, a San Francisco-based investment banker. He put them in touch with the Fairchild Camera and Instrument Corporation, a large New York company, that agreed to start a new division devoted to semiconductor research. When Fairchild Semiconductor opened in 1957, in Mountain View, California, with Noyce as division manager and Moore as the manager of engineering, it was only the second semiconductor research outfit in the area that would later be known as Silicon Valley.

Noyce was a brilliant inventor, and in 1959 he successfully tested an integrated circuit: he put an entire electrical track of multiple transistors on a single silicon chip. Before long, Fairchild Semiconductor's integrated circuitry was replacing the electromechanical switching that ran computers and other machines. Presuming that this was only the beginning of a vast reduction of scale, Gordon Moore saw endless new possibilities. If a circuit of transistors could be made to fit on a silicon chip, he reasoned, ways could be found to double the capacity of a single chip—and then redouble it. In 1965, Moore predicted that the power of the chips would double every twelve months. This prognostication—later expanded to eighteen months—became known as "Moore's law," and it justified Intel's fast-paced modus operandi in later years. (According to a 1995 article in Forbes, however, Moore's prediction was not quite accurate: "Double something every eighteen months for thirty years and it increases by a factor of over a million to one. Moore was close: Today's 4-megabit chip is 4 *million* times more powerful than its predecessor, the transistor.")

In 1963, while Gordon Moore was still assessing the possibilities of the silicon chip, he met the man who would do as much as anyone to turn those possibilities into reality at Intel: Andrew Grove, né Andras Grof. Grove had fled his native Hungary when he was twenty after the failed 1956 revolution and studied engineering at the City College of New York, completing his undergraduate degree in only three years, while working as a waiter. After receiving a Ph.D. in chemical engineering from the University of California at Berkeley, Grove joined Fairchild as an assistant to Moore in 1963, quickly establishing a reputation as a solid organizational manager.

By 1967, Fairchild Semiconductor had grown into a division with $130 million in sales and 15,000 employees. But it represented only a small portion of Fairchild's overall business, which was concentrated in aviation. Consequently, when Noyce and Moore advocated moving into new areas of research and technology, they were frustrated with the response from corporate management in New York. "Fairchild was steeped in an East Coast, old-fashioned, hierarchical business structure,"

Noyce said in a 1988 interview. "I never wanted to be part of a company like that."

Noyce and Moore wanted funds and support from Fairchild to investigate the possibilities of semiconductor memory. At the time, computer memory was stored in magnetic cores. Noyce and Moore believed they could replace the large cores with small chips. But Fairchild's lack of commitment frustrated them. One weekend in 1968, Moore visited Noyce at his home. The moment which would make them both billionaires is well-remembered: Noyce was mowing the lawn, but he stopped to talk. They griped about Fairchild's bureaucracy, and discussed setting up their own company to manufacture a semiconductor that could store memory. "We were young and arrogant," said Noyce, who was forty-one at the time. "We wanted the independence to do things our way."

Again they turned to Arthur Rock. Noyce and Moore each kicked in $250,000 of their own money and Rock raised an additional $2.5 million; Grinnell College, where Noyce was an active alumnus, invested $300,000.

Intel was incorporated on July 18, 1968, as NM Electronics (for "Noyce" and "Moore"). Rock was Chairman of the Board; Noyce was president and CEO, and Moore was executive vice president. They set up shop in Mountain View, California, just down the road from both Fairchild Semiconductor and Stanford University. Recruiting about a dozen employees from Fairchild, including Andrew Grove, they set out to fill a niche but ultimately created a new industry. "The semiconductor memory business did not exist," said Noyce. "That's key to the survival of a young company. You try to go into a business that is either underpopulated or not populated."

Even if semiconductors could be made viable for memory storage, others in the industry predicted that they would cost about ten times as much as magnetic cores. As a result, few firms saw any commercial possibilities in developing them. Intel (the company was renamed soon after the founding) intended to change this state of affairs by continually cutting production costs while cramming ever more transistors on a single chip. Within a few years, if Moore's law held true, memory chips would become cheaper and more desirable than magnetic cores. That would constitute a scientific achievement, but Intel was a business and had to establish itself in a nascent market. "We figured we had about five years to get established before the big semiconductor companies would follow in this market and become direct competitors," Moore recalled. One of the first decisions that the management team had to make was what they called the "degree of difficulty." If they produced a very simple product, others could easily copy it. If they tried for an overly complex one, the company's resources might give out before the research was complete. In the end they chose a middle path, and predicted that within five years their new firm could have annual revenues of $25 million.

Intel had a long way to go. In its first year of business it reported negligible revenues of just $2,672. After a few false starts, Intel's scientists began to focus on producing the silicon gate metal-oxide semiconductor (MOS) in 1969. "We chose a technology that was tractable enough so that, by concentrating all our energies, we could get past unforeseen difficulties," said Moore. In 1970, Intel brought out its first successful product, the 1103 chip, which contained 1K, or a thousand bytes, of dynamic random access memory (DRAM).

DRAM, despite its name, was largely passive. Information could only be stored on it. Intel's next step was to make chips that were more than simple receptacles. The company achieved this goal, in part, with a second memory product that was developed simultaneously. One researcher, Dov Frohman, devised a chip that, like the DRAM, could store data permanently. It could also be erased, and therefore could be reprogrammed. The EPROM (erasable programmable read-only memory) chip was a quick, cheap, and easy way to store not just data but the programs that could give instructions to DRAM chips. Frohman recalled, with enormous understatement "We weren't geniuses. Invention is just a process of dreaming a lot and then asking, 'Why not?' " The EPROMs helped boost the market for Intel DRAMs, and the company's sales rose to $9.43 million in 1971. The same year, Intel further bolstered its financial standing through an initial public offering that brought in $6.8 million.

PERFECTING THE PROCESS

Although the first products were major accomplishments, Intel's managers realized the company was far from realizing its goal of $25 million in annual revenues. "A lot of things are technologically possible, but only economically feasible products will become a reality," said Noyce.

From the start, the manufacture of silicon chips was complicated. In the early seventies the factory would reduce a design through photography, and then imprint it on a tiny sliver of silicon. The process was repeated time and again to pack thousands of transistors on a single chip. Production of the chips was enormously expensive, and technological breakthroughs would have languished if Intel didn't devise ways, at every stage, to produce chips at affordable rates. Andrew Grove stepped up to do just that. "Noyce and Moore were the inspiration. Grove created the organization that executed," recalled Dun Hutcheson, an executive at the computer firm VLSI Research.

Grove, who had a mind for industrial organization, was put in charge of production and helped to direct the company's initial experimentation with assembly lines. "The [fabrication] area looked like Willy Wonka's factory, with hoses and wires and contraptions chugging along," Grove recalled. "It was state-of-the-art manufacturing at the time, but by today's standards it was unbelievably crude." It worked well enough to make the chips en masse, substantially reducing unit costs. And since Intel had so little competition, it was able to charge a premium price. The company's profit margins soared.

THE DEBUT OF THE MICROPROCESSOR

Intel's first years were a mere prelude to the breakthrough that would propel the company's growth—and the proliferation of the personal computer—in the 1970s. The invention was the microprocessor, which Gordon Moore called "one of the most revolutionary products in the history of mankind." The discovery was not a calculated event, but simply a logical step in Intel's continuing effort to make its chips more intelligent and to reduce the size of the devices that provide computing power.

In 1969 a Japanese company had asked Intel to produce a set of chips that would allow handheld calculators to perform the kind of complex calculations workable only on adding machines or larger computers. Rather than array several chips side by side, the Intel engineer Ted Hoff happened upon the idea of using four chips in conjunction, with a single powerful one in the middle. In the process, Hoff devised a method to place an entire central processing unit (CPU) on a single chip. And that single chip—an inadvertent solution to meet a request from a customer—became the Intel 4004 microprocessor.

In a graphic illustration of Moore's law, the 4004—which was no bigger than a flat caterpillar with metal legs—was packed with 2,300 transistors and held as much computing power as the 1946 ENIAC, the first electronic computer, which had occupied 3,000 cubic feet. The $200 chip, introduced in 1971, could complete an astonishing 60,000 operations in one second.

The market for the 4004 took off; it powered a fad for digital watches (Intel even went into the watch business for a little while) and a new dependence on handheld calculators. In 1972, Intel made good on its promise to deliver more powerful products and brought out the 8008, a much faster and more flexible microprocessor that came to be known as the eight-bit processor. Intel's eight-bit microprocessors were the basis for most of the personal computers launched in the seventies.

The company was growing exponentially. Intel's sales soared from $9.4 million in 1971 to $23.4 million in 1972, and nearly trebled in

1973 to $66.17 million. That year, its stock price rose to $88 a share, nearly four times the initial offering price of $23.50. Noyce and Moore each held 27 percent of the stock, which was worth about $200 million between them. Intel's founders could have sold out and retired. But they were just getting started. Rather than pay out dividends or build lavish corporate headquarters, the men—engineers at heart—plowed their earnings into laboratories and production facilities. In 1973 the company spent three times the previous year's profits on research and development.

Intel's leaders didn't believe they were simply making plastic chips. Amid all the ferment of the Vietnam War protests, this group of buttoned-down engineers and chemists knew they were changing the course of history by reducing computing power into ever smaller packages. "We are really the revolutionaries in the world today—not the kids with the long hair and beards who were wrecking the schools a few years ago," Moore said in 1973.

Noyce concluded that memory chips could work in everything from office equipment to home appliances. Large computers and small calculators were just the beginning. Any electronic devices—microwave ovens, stereos—that could benefit from memory could theoretically use a chip. To prepare for what it hoped was an era of expansion, Intel reorganized. In an April 1975 executive shift, Noyce became chairman, Gordon Moore became chief executive officer, and Andrew Grove was named executive vice president. Arthur Rock remained on the board of directors as vice chairman. "The entrepreneurial phase is not entirely over at Intel," Noyce said, "but the emphasis is shifting to control." Grove's elevation signaled a greater emphasis on the management of production and systems, which was vital given the tenuous nature of a high-tech company's existence. "This business lies on the brink of disaster," Moore said. "As soon as you can make a device with high yield, you calculate that you can decrease costs by trying to make something four times as complex, which brings our yield down again."

Prices would start falling almost as soon as Intel put a product on the market, as clones found ways to sweep past copyright protection into the market and customers began to anticipate the next, faster model. "Essentially the thing that makes our industry unique is that the cost of everything goes down," said Moore. Sure enough, the 8008 was replaced in 1974 by the 8080, which could perform 290,000 operations per second. The appetite for the faster, more powerful memory seemed to be insatiable. Consumer electronic products like the Altair and TRS-80 became instantly popular, and each used an Intel chip. By 1978, when it introduced the 8086 chip, Intel's revenues were nearly $400 million.

MARKETING PRODUCTS AMID THE PERSONAL COMPUTER REVOLUTION

The 1970s turned Intel into a giant. Revenues rose from $4.2 million in 1970 to $661 million in 1979, a year in which it held 40 percent of the $820-million microprocessor market. By 1980 its stock had appreciated 10,000 percent from the original offering price of $23.50 per share. With no long-term debt and a dominant position in the market it had helped create, Intel felt its place in the industry was secure. Yet the company's leaders felt that they had just begun to understand the possibilities of the technology. By packing increasingly greater computing capability into silicon wafers, they believed that a single chip could hold the power of mainframes, those large workhorse computers, produced mainly by IBM, that drove most large-scale business enterprises.

Yet Intel's bold pioneers would face unexpected challenges. Neither size nor tradition guaranteed a company a future in the rapidly shifting computer market. As Howard Rudnitsky wrote in *Forbes* of the semiconductor industry in 1980: "Still ruthlessly competitive but increasingly capital-intensive and complex, it is no longer a business where you can start in a garage with $100,000 or play everywhere in the big time— even if you are an Intel, with $66 million a year in R & D and $150 million in capital expenditures."

By 1980, Intel no longer had the field to itself. Companies like Zilog and Motorola had invested substantial sums to improve their capabilities. And with these worthy competitors seeking to gain market share, Intel could never be sure that its chips would be chosen as standard components when computer manufacturers designed their products. If Intel didn't gain a sufficient number of these so-called "design wins," the groundbreaking work of the prior decade would have been for naught. "In the semiconductor business, the only market share you really care about is the one you maintain when the market is mature," Intel executive William Davidow wrote in his book, *Marketing High Technology*.

The newly minted 8086/8088 chips, introduced in 1978, were fast approaching maturity when Intel embarked upon a campaign to make its microprocessor chip the industry standard. In December 1979 a group of Intel executives convened to discuss strategy. Silicon chips were becoming a commodity, with many different companies producing them. The Intel executives recognized that their company had strengths, especially in the development of microprocessors. Intel had the reputation of being ahead of its time, and its chips were viewed as high-performance products. To exploit these advantages, the company embarked upon Operation Crush, a campaign of public relations and trade advertising that stressed Intel's role in creating the microprocessor. The objective was to achieve 2,000 "design wins" over competition from other technology firms. They ended up with 2,500. "By the time Crush was over [at the end of 1980], our victory was almost complete. Intel all but owned the business application segment of the 16-bit microprocessor market," wrote Davidow. Among all the design wins, one, in particular, was crucial. "The one large client we had to win over was IBM," he said. In 1980, IBM chose the Intel 8088 microprocessor as the power plant for its upcoming personal computer, which also used Microsoft's MS-DOS operating system.

The introduction of the IBM-PC changed the computing world. With the backing of a powerhouse like "Big Blue," personal computers—

machines with both a "brain" and a memory—quickly became hot products for individuals and businesses alike. The IBM-PCs immediately established Intel's 8086 as the industry standard. Since IBM didn't develop much proprietary technology relating to the PC, companies could replicate the PC without too much difficulty. So when makers of clones, like Compaq Computers Corporation, sought to copy IBM's architecture, they naturally turned to Intel, which was one of the main beneficiaries of the IBM-PC and the clone boom of the early 1980s. The company's sales rose rapidly from $789 million in 1981 to $1.6 billion in 1984. One segment of its business was under tremendous pressure, however, as competition from Japanese manufacturers brought the price of DRAM down below the cost of production for a company like Intel. The company abruptly withdrew from the market and concentrated on areas in which it could control prices with advancements in technology.

HIGH OUTPUT MANAGEMENT

Although Moore and Noyce remained at the top of Intel's corporate ladder, Andrew Grove was the driving force behind the company's powerful expansion, having been named president and chief operating officer in 1979. Extraordinarily direct and hard-driving, Grove was nicknamed the "Prussian General." He was known to keep a list of workers who arrived after 8 a.m., and in 1981, when the company was experiencing difficulties during the recession, he came up with the "125 percent solution." All professional employees were forced to clock in for fifty-hour weeks with no increase in pay.

But Grove was no mere taskmaster. He was an effective manager, who thought a great deal about the optimal methods of organizing an industrial and technological company. He developed an "output-oriented approach to management," which he described in his popular 1983 book, *High Output Management*. (For many years he also wrote a syndicated column on management called "One-on-One with Andy Grove.") In his view, output wasn't limited to engineers and factory workers; it reflected on every clerk and administrator as well. At Intel, employees were responsible not only to their boss but also to their colleagues. ". . . [Here] everybody writes down what they are going to do and reviews how they did it, how they did against those objectives, not to management, but to a peer group *and* management," Robert Noyce once explained.

Intel also tried to instill a team-based approach. Even the most senior employees worked in open cubicles, rather than in offices. The office design emphasized another one of Grove's main goals: breaking down barriers and developing personal relationships between managers and employees. Similarly, Grove advocated that managers meet employees one-on-one, to gain and impart information, and create a sense of a shared corporate culture. "[The] main purpose is mutual teaching and exchange of information," he wrote.

Though Intel had remained true to its founders' determination not to stymie creativity under layers of typical corporate bureaucracy, not everybody chose to remain with the company. Just as Grove, Moore, and Noyce had left a larger firm to seek their own fortunes, various senior members of Intel's research staff left Intel in the early 1980s to start companies such as Convergent Technologies and Seeq Technology.

MARKETING HIGH TECHNOLOGY IN AN ERA OF COMPETITION

Intel had difficulty maintaining dominance in the 1980s. Since the barrier to enter the microprocessor industry was remarkably high, the firms that did encroach on Intel's wildly profitable niche were major firms with deep pockets: Texas Instruments, Motorola, and, increasingly, Japanese firms. Due to the competition, the price of the chips kept falling, so that by 1985 Intel charged just $20 for the 8086 chip. This cut into the company's famously high profit margins. In fact, revenues declined in both 1985 and 1986, falling from $1.6 billion in 1984 to

$1.2 billion in 1986. Grove responded with typical precision and speed. To save money, Intel announced in October 1985 that it would slash pay 10 percent and close operations for six days in late December. The company ultimately laid off 2,600 workers (or 30 percent of the workforce).

Intel's salvation came—as it always had—through the invention of a new product that made its own previous standards, and those of rivals, seem logy. In October 1985 Intel introduced the 386 microprocessor, the development of which had cost more than $100 million. "A miracle of miniaturization, the microprocessor is 1/4-inch square, yet performs with the power and speed of many full-size computers," *Forbes* reported in June 1986.

By the mid-1980s, Intel had come to realize that marketing was an integral part of the business process. And so it set out to create a distinctive image for its new generation of products. The way that each new microprocessor rendered the previous one obsolete was highlighted in an advertising campaign for the 386 SX. The so-called Red X campaign featured two-page ads. One page showed the earlier "286" with a large red "X" through it. The other page had "386" with a large "SX" under it. "We were speaking directly to PC consumers for the first time, rather than marketing only to OEMs [manufacturers]," said Dennis Carter, an Intel marketing executive. Even though the company had been in business for fifteen years, it had never made a strong effort to introduce itself to the people who ultimately used its products; no semiconductor company had. As late as 1987, Grove told *Barron's*, "I really have no feel for end-use sales in the PC industry. We supply to the manufacturers. . . ." But when Intel noticed that sales of machines using the 386 began to pick up after the Red X campaign, the company changed its view. "What we learned from the Red X campaign was that we *could* communicate arcane technical ideas that, in fact, people wanted to hear them," said Dennis Carter.

The use of marketing represented a new phase in Intel's maturity. And the company grew up in other ways as well. The founders began to take a less active role in its management. Robert Noyce devoted more and more time to outside interests, including serving as a trustee at Grinnell College. In 1988 he left Intel altogether to head Sematech, a government-backed consortium of twelve semiconductor firms that banded together to conduct research. In 1990 he died of a heart attack.

Moore assumed the role of vice chairman, and later chairman, but still worked forty-five to fifty hours a week in his cubicle. One of the most respected executives in the country, he is known as a quiet man, whose words carry weight in the entire industry. "Gordon knows where to spend the money and allocate assets," Arthur Rock said of him. "He's the guy who said in a downturn we've got to build plants and mothball them and be ready when the business starts to turn up again. He's had that vision. . . . He's been willing to bet the company over and over."

In 1987, Andy Grove assumed the title of chief executive officer. As such, he had the opportunity to implement high output management from top to bottom at Intel. "We can get more output out of our existing organization," he said.

More output wasn't enough, however. Double the output was essential. In order to make an impact with a new product, Intel had to prove it was actually replacing the previous generation, not merely improving upon it. The case of the 386 chip neatly illustrates this shift in strategy. In 1988, when the company's revenues soared to $2.9 billion, about $1.1 billion came from the 386. Rather than continuing to milk the cash cow, however, Intel was already planning to put it out to pasture. In 1988 the company introduced a successor, the 486 microprocessor, developed at a cost of $300 million. The transistors themselves were only about one micron thick, or one percent of the width of a human hair; one million of them fit on one 386 chip.

INTEL KEEPS RUNNING

The 386 and 486 (known officially as the 80386 and 80346) were standard in IBM-compatible personal computers. It was estimated that in 1990 about 14 million of the 22 million PCs made worldwide included an Intel microprocessor. With each chip costing an estimated $50 to produce, and carrying a $200 retail price, Intel was raking in money. "As the sole supplier of the computer industry's most important single part, the 80386 microprocessor, Intel enjoys profit margins far greater than those of its competitors," wrote Richard Shaffer in *Forbes*.

Under Grove, Intel found it necessary to introduce a substantially improved microprocessor as often as every year or so, in order to insure its place in the market. Every time a rival like Advanced Micro Devices began shipping a chip that approached Intel's standard, the pioneering company's profit margins began to fall. "It cannot achieve supremacy in a product and sit back and count the money rolling in forever," *Forbes* wrote of Intel in 1990. "It must keep pushing back the frontiers of innovation and technology."

And that is precisely what Intel continued to do, in production as well as in design. No sooner did a new plant open than Intel's design and engineering staff began to plot the construction of a larger, cleaner, more efficient plant. "In this business you have to build your own capacity," Grove remarked.

In 1992, when Intel's IBM-PC market share remained at a solid 75 percent, Motorola, its biggest competitor, was a distant second, with 14 percent of the market. Yet that year Intel spent $1.2 billion of its $5 billion in sales on plants and equipment and another $800 million on research and development.

In June 1989, Intel began to develop the Pentium Processor. With 3.1 million transistors operating in a single chip, it was faster, smaller, and more powerful than any previous Intel processor or any other on the market. The company faced a debacle when, after a well-orchestrated launch, the new microprocessor was found to have

MAXIMIZING MINIATURIZATION TECHNOLOGY

For each new generation of chips, Intel has had to develop the parallel technologies of the chip itself and the means to produce it commercially. That's where all the research and development money goes.

The power of the microprocessor increased exponentially over its first two decades because engineers found ways to make the main components, the transistors, smaller and smaller and smaller. Transistors were no longer bits of metal and plastic, as they had been when most people first saw them inside a pocket radio. They were specks of chemicals, and it would take hundreds of them to make a ring around a human hair. Arranging millions of them in effective circuitry telescoped the capacity of a much larger machine onto a chip the size of a postage stamp. But even as specks, transistors had to be precisely drawn.

On an old-fashioned transistor, an impurity the size of, say, a cookie crumb, could interfere with performance. Next to a transistor measuring less than one micron, a germ—a single bacterium—looks like a boulder and renders the whole chip worthless. Intel had to design production rooms in which all the air was filtered every few seconds, leaving less than one such particle per cubic foot. Humans, those roving dust storms of dandruff, viruses, spit, and lint, had to be sealed inside special suits in order to work in "clean rooms."

Inside the clean rooms, the photographic process of imprinting arrays of transistors was extremely sensitive as the detail shrank. Site selection for production facilities became a matter of geology: the slightest tremor, imperceptible to humans, would distort the circuitry being exposed. Most places on earth shake almost continually at extremely low levels. A crucial factor in Intel's expansion to places such as Ireland and Israel is that the ground itself is stable in those places.

According to Gordon Moore, Intel has to produce a new generation of processor technology every three years in order to maintain its advantage in chip engineering. "We just continue to push narrower and narrower line widths and more and more complex processes, so we can increase the density of electronics on the wafer," he said in 1993. "Get more and more stuff on a chip, essentially."

a bug. At first Andy Grove dismissed it as a remote, statistical problem: "If you know where a meteor will land, you can go there and get hit," he responded, when asked if even a rare problem was still a problem. Eventually, Intel offered to replace Pentium Processors at no charge. Grove later admitted that he had a lot to learn about dealing with the public.

Even as Intel began to ship the $995 Pentium, in March 1993, the pace at Intel continued to quicken. In December 1993 Intel said it would double the capacity of its chips in the next year, slashing the product development interval of eighteen to twenty-four months down to one year. "The operative word is focus," Grove said in 1993. "You have to put all your effort behind the thing that you do better than the other people in the business, and then not hedge your bets. . . . If you focus and you're wrong, you lose—but if you're right, you win big time."

In the first week of April 1994, Intel announced that it planned to spend $150 million to market the Pentium—a stunning amount of money for a piece of silicon. Pentium, though dominant, was competing with a growing array of products made by companies like Advanced Micro Devices, Cyrix, and IBM, along with the new Power PC chip made by Apple and Motorola. The purpose of Intel's latest marketing campaign, with the tag line "Intel Inside," was to make the chip's brand name a household word, as familiar to the American consumer as McDonald's or Coca-Cola. As an inducement, the company offered to pick up half the tab for advertisements its computer-producing partners ran that used Intel logos in the ads.

In 1995, when Intel had $16.2 billion in sales and $4.9 billion in profits, Noyce and Moore's bold prediction of a quarter century earlier seemed, if anything, a major underestimation. Gordon Moore's net worth, measured largely in Intel stock, was pegged at over $2 billion by *Forbes*.

Under Grove's leadership, Intel was still paranoid in a healthy way.

After all, staying at the vanguard of the computer revolution requires a sort of perpetual motion. Like a jogger running on an accelerating tread-mill, Intel has had to run faster just to maintain its position—and even faster just to stay ahead of everybody else.

Sam Walton, founder of Wal-Mart and Sam's Club.

SAM WALTON, WAL-MART, AND THE DISCOUNTING OF AMERICA

amuel Moore Walton was a small-town kind of guy. He lived in the same neighborhood in Bentonville, Arkansas, for forty years. He rose early every day, had breakfast with the usual crowd at the local hotel, and then, except on Sunday, he went to the office. Only one thing tempted him to play hooky, and that was a chance to do some quail hunting. Walton was the sort to borrow a newspaper rather than spring a quarter for one. But he was also the sort to invite a struggling young family out to lunch with him and his wife every Sunday—a quiet, neighborly way to be generous.

Sam Walton lived in small towns, about 1,800 of them, through his Wal-Mart discount department stores. In the era of franchise restaurants, cookie-cutter shopping malls, and formula retailing, Wal-Mart was built on respect for the individual. It was a quality that emanated directly from the founder.

Controlling about 20 percent of Wal-Mart's stock, Sam Walton appeared at the top of the *Forbes 400*, with a net worth of $2.8 billion in 1985 (the holdings are now worth almost ten times that amount). Of all the innovations that helped make him a billionaire, his greatest innovation as a CEO may have been that he himself did not change. Ignoring the usual trappings of power, he was able to manage his empire as though he were looking each of his 400,000 employees square in the eye. "Associates," he called them, and the term was more than just a matter of semantics. "Only his family meant more to Sam Walton than his beloved associates," said David Glass, the man who succeeded Walton as CEO. "Literally, his second home was a Wal-Mart store somewhere in America."

Under Sam Walton, Wal-Mart imbued its store managers with icy cold attention to the bottom line, as it treated hundreds of thousands of employees and tens of millions of customers with an extra degree of respect. There was nothing half-hearted about either aspect of Wal-Mart: it was the same combination found in Walton himself, a highly successful businessman, but a small-town businessman just the same.

"HUSTLER" WALTON

"The secret is work, work, work. I taught the boys how to do it," said Thomas Walton of his two boys, Sam and James ("Bud"). Walton was a farm-loan appraiser, a dismal occupation to hold during the twenties in Oklahoma, where Sam was born in 1918. Thomas worked long, hard hours, but he and his wife, Nan, eventually moved the family to a string of little towns in Missouri. The father shifted his career toward selling real estate and insurance, the mother started a tiny dairy business, and the boys helped to make ends meet, by selling magazine subscriptions, milking cows, and delivering newspapers.

Sam Walton attended the University of Missouri in Columbia, and received a business degree in 1940. He thought about going to graduate school in the East, but he accepted a position as a management trainee at a J.C. Penney store in Des Moines Iowa. Known as "Hustler" Walton during college, he wasn't anxious to go into retailing at first. But he was impressed by the Penney store, especially by its philosophy of customer service. As a calling, work in retail suited this earnest, ambitious young man. Before long, Walton knew where his future lay.

"I didn't start as a banker or as an investor or doing anything else than waiting on customers," Walton later wrote in his company's employee magazine, *Wal-Mart World*. "Many people who run big companies never ring cash registers, nor do they wait on customers, and so I've always appreciated what it meant to be a salesclerk and how much a salesperson can influence a customer in a business relationship."

Walton interrupted his career to join the service a few months after the United States entered World War II. He was assigned to the Military Police, inspecting various facilities stateside, throughout the duration of the war. In 1943, he married Helen Robson, a recent college graduate he'd met in Oklahoma while waiting to be called up. After the war, Walton, like many other veterans, was brimming with confidence and in a hurry to make up for lost time. He didn't return to Penney's; he borrowed $25,000 from his father-in-law to buy his own business: a Ben Franklin Store in Newport, Arkansas. Ben Franklin was a well-known name in the variety-store business, competing against stores like Woolworth's and McCrory's.

In Newport, the Ben Franklin Store was on the best corner downtown, across the street from the Sterling Variety Store. One of those who worked there was Bud Hewitt, who would be Sam Walton's lifelong friend. In 1947, Hewitt later recalled, his store had a sensational new item, rayon panties for women. Even at the premium price of thirty cents a pair, they sold out at the Sterling Store, and so Hewitt did just what he was supposed to do: he placed another order from the distributor in Little Rock. But Sam Walton, a goal-oriented businessman, was obsessed with beating Sterling in annual sales. He made it a habit to know as much about all of his competitors as he did about his own store. When he heard about the run on rayon panties, he saw an opportunity. He dropped everything, and drove to Little Rock to buy the distributor out. Not only did his store have plenty, but Sterling had none.

Hewitt never held it against Walton; just the opposite was true. "The way he lived his life reminded me that I had rather see a sermon than hear one anytime," he later told *Arkansas Business* magazine.

By 1950, Walton had developed the Ben Franklin Store in Newport into the most successful location in his region. That year, however, he lost his lease. Forced to sell out, he moved to Bentonville, where he purchased another Ben Franklin store, opening it as Walton's Five & Dime. Throughout the fifties, Sam Walton continued to add "Walton's Ben Franklin Stores" to his little chain within a chain. As he did, he learned the first lesson of his empire-building days to come: large stores, at about 25,000 square feet, could succeed in towns of fewer than 5,000 people, if they offered some inducement to rural folk to make a drive of ten or twenty miles.

Bud Walton, Sam's younger brother, had been a bomber pilot during the war, and so flying was a familiar activity to the family. In 1953, Sam earned his pilot's license and bought a prewar airplane—a contraption that Bud deemed unsafe. Nonetheless, Sam used it, to hopscotch from town to town and visiting his stores. He loved to fly and splurged on some interesting planes through the years, but flying was no mere hobby. As a hands-on manager, Walton used the airplane as a vital tool. It allowed him to make regular visits to locations spread over a whole region, dropping in as easily as if they were all in the same county.

He even used the plane to scout new locations from the air, assessing factors like traffic flow and population concentration, from above.

Further afield, Walton studied other chain stores around the nation. When he heard about a pair of Ben Franklin "self-service" stores in Minnesota, he took a bus up to see them firsthand. Most stores of the day were organized around counters, at which clerks would show merchandise on request. The new self-service stores put items out on shelves, where customers could compare them. The stores' lower overhead allowed the operation to offer lower prices. Walton returned home from Minnesota to open a self-service store of his own, Walton's Five & Dime.

"One of Sam's greatest contributions to Wal-Mart . . ." said a manufacturer who worked with him for decades, "was his attitude toward experimentation. He constantly encouraged us to experiment on a small basis and if the idea worked, roll it out. If it failed, try something else. It was his attitude of keep trying, and don't be afraid of failure."

In 1948, E. J. Korvette's opened in New York City; in 1953, Ann & Hope started business in Rhode Island. They were among the first in a bold generation of discount stores, operated generally on the motto of one Southern discount retailer: "Buy it low, stack it high, sell it cheap." Walton went out of his way to visit the nation's new discount stores and to speak to the managers about what worked and what didn't.

In the late fifties, Sam Walton tried a different format, offering a wider variety of items than ever before in a few "Walton's Family Centers." Early in 1962, he was ready to try the discount-store concept, in conjunction with Ben Franklin, but the corporate executives there declined his offer to develop it. They just didn't see how they could sell merchandise to him at the low prices he needed. They did, however, suggest that Walton might as well take a look at the S.S. Kresge dime-store chain's new entry in the discount niche. It was called "Kmart," and one had just opened near the Ben Franklin headquarters in Chicago. Walton went over and took a hard look at a Kmart. Other discount stores had a flimsy, fly-by-night air, but Kmart was well-planned and well-stocked. Unlike the others, it looked like it was going to last.

No sooner did Walton return home than he chose a site for his own version of a discount mart, copied from Kmart. In naming the store "Wal-Mart," he even copied the syntax of its name. Kmart didn't suffer from the early competition: its first stores were located in the suburbs of major cities like Detroit and Chicago. The first Wal-Mart Discount City was located in Rogers, Arkansas, population 4,500. The opening day was July 2, 1962.

The store was rudimentary, consisting of items neatly piled on the floor and on tables. Shelving didn't arrive until later. Taken altogether, it bore little relation to the clean lines and streamlined layout of the modern Wal-Mart. More important, the store's relationships with suppliers were just as rudimentary, compared to the sophisticated procedures that were painstakingly developed in later years. Walton didn't have a wide choice in merchandise at the pricing he required. Among other things, manufacturers of higher-quality items simply wouldn't sell at a deep discount; some wouldn't deal with a store like Wal-Mart under any circumstances. They just didn't want to be connected with a "mass merchandiser."

As Sam Walton tinkered with the formula for Wal-Mart, he continued to earn a living with his string of Ben Franklin Stores. He made only a small profit with Wal-Mart, but he carefully honed his new store, adjusting the display, improving the product mix, and constantly trying to establish better sourcing. He was on the premises as often as he could be, even after hours. When he couldn't sleep, he often brought a sack of donuts down to the crew on the receiving dock and chatted with them when they were on break. Sam Walton didn't find inspiration on retreats or by staring into reports. He showed up wherever the work was being done.

In 1964, the second Wal-Mart opened in another small Arkansas town called Harrison. The day was hot even for the South, with a temperature soaring over 110 degrees. Watermelons stacked in front of the store cracked open. A donkey that was on hand to give free rides to children left its mark in the parking lot. The store in Harrison clicked, despite the opening-day debacle, and Walton used it as his flagship site, training managers there for other locations.

It is part of the lore of Wal-Mart that one visitor, a local business-man named David Glass, surveyed the opening and said, "it was the worst retail store I've ever seen." Twenty-five years later, as president of the Wal-Mart Corporation, Glass publicly recanted. "The dumbest thing I ever did was make that statement about the Harrison store," he said. "What I didn't count on was the quality of the people."

A discount department store operates on a small profit margin; the idea is to make it up in volume sales, of course. But the profits from a handful of new stores didn't underwrite other locations very quickly, and the Wal-Mart chain grew slowly at first. Walton borrowed money from banks, individuals, and insurance companies, but could not spur enough growth to take advantage of the gaps that he felt the big chains were missing in small towns all over his region, and perhaps the country. Sam and Bud, who was vice president of Wal-Mart, knew that they had a successful formula, but they needed stronger financing.

THE BARGAIN STORE'S BEST CUSTOMER

Three years before the first Wal-Mart opened, Sam and Helen Walton bought a tract of twenty acres outside of Bentonville and commissioned a respected architect to build a modern house that straddled a brook. The house cost $100,000 in 1959—a hefty sum, but then, it was the last house the couple would ever buy. The Walton family simply didn't spend money conspicuously.

It probably behooves a discount retailer to be something of a cheap-skate. At the height of his immense wealth, S. S. Kresge used to stuff cardboard in his shoes to cover the holes. He even gave up golf during his very first round after losing a ball in the rough. Sam Walton wasn't quite that parsimonious, but he did leave a record of home-spun frugality, for a rich man. He flew first class only once in life (on a long flight from South America to Africa); on business trips with other employees, he readily followed the company policy of doubling up in hotels. His company car wasn't exactly a limousine. Bernard Marcus, chairman and co-founder of Home Depot, recalled going out to lunch with Walton after a meeting in Bentonville: "I hopped into Sam's red pickup truck. No air-conditioning. Seats stained by coffee. And by the time I got to the restaurant, my shirt was soaked through and through. And that was Sam Walton—no airs, no pomposity."

"My shoes cost more than everything Sam Walton is wearing today," another friend commented, after meeting him at a business function. Walton took such teasing well. At a meeting in Little Rock, he stood up to show everyone the label in his business jacket. "Wal-Mart," he announced, "fifty dollars. The pants? Wal-Mart, sixteen dollars."

Personally and through the company, the Waltons gave large amounts of money to medical research, scholarship funds, Christian religious causes, and charities serving the arts. At home, the family lived comfortably on Sam's salary as an executive; at different times, both of them said that the only reason they didn't spend more money was that they couldn't really think of anything they wanted.

RAISING SPIRITS

In 1970, Wal-Mart made a public stock offering. It raised about $5 million to build six more stores and to complete the company's first distribution center. With that and subsequent stock offerings, momentum finally picked up and matched Walton's plans: After building thirty-nine stores in the first decade, Wal-Mart built 452 in the seventies and 1,237 in the eighties. From 1970 to 1990, the stock not only outperformed the rest of the market, but outperformed the wildest dreams of those who bought it. One hundred shares, purchased in 1970 for $1,650, were worth $2.6 million in 1992.

With the stock offering, managers began to participate in a formal profit-sharing plan. The next year, Walton extended the plan to include all his associates, with some regret that he hadn't remembered them from the start. Workers who had been with the company for at least a year, and who worked more than about twenty hours per week, earned bonuses of, on average, 5 percent of their annual wages. The profit sharing was held on account until the worker left the company, and, since it was paid in high-flying Wal-Mart stock, many managers retired as millionaires. So did many hourly employees.

The profit-sharing plan was a remarkable incentive for longtime workers. Even so, a major part of Walton's job, day in and day out, was in keeping hundreds of thousands of associates interested in their jobs. Though Wal-Mart tended to be a little less expensive than Kmart or Target stores, it was up to the salesclerks to make Wal-Mart truly *different*. The other stores offered a low level of service. In counterpoint, Wal-Mart's staff had to be friendly, helpful, enthusiastic; Walton depended on it.

Even as the chain expanded, Walton continued to visit a handful of stores every week, flying from site to site his private plane. Sometimes he spent his day riding in a rig with a company driver, making deliveries to stores. Normally he would simply enter a Wal-Mart store unannounced and look around a bit, before going to the public-address system to introduce himself to associates and customers. Not all of his visits were pleasant. If he found a store that was dirty or disorganized, he closed it on the spot for improvements. More often, though, a Walton visit was like a campaign swing from a political candidate, as the founder walked through the aisles, hearing out complaints and trading kind words. For all of his easy-going charm, he was a sharp-eyed storekeeper when gathering data.

As a motivator, Walton established three lines of communication. First, he attended as many store openings as he could. Using his wry sense of humor, and considerable charisma, he turned store openings and company meetings into pep rallies. He might congratulate the associates on their fine performance, but he would always follow praise with a challenge to do even better in the future. He often ended—or began—by jumping on a table and leading everyone in a cheer for Wal-Mart. Store cheerleaders even invented and practiced store cheers, such as, "Wal-Mart! Wal-Mart! That's our name!/The retailing business is our game/We've got what it takes to be number one/So watch out Kmart! Here we come!" What Sam Walton discovered was that the employees liked to belong to a company that wanted them to belong to it. And so they did belong: Cheering for Wal-Mart was just like cheering for themselves.

As a second policy, Walton wrote a column every month in the company newspaper, *Wal-Mart World*—and he wrote it himself. In 1983, he used his column to dare the associates to help the company bring in a pre-tax profit of 8 percent for that year. If they did, Walton wrote, he would do a hula dance down Wall Street. They did. Walton was widely photographed with a grass skirt (over a suit), dancing down Wall Street; while it may have wounded his dignity, it paid the bet and, moreover, it insured that everyone on Wall Street knew just how hot Wal-Mart was getting in the retail world.

Third, Sam Walton maintained an open invitation for any associate to contact him personally with a store problem, a comment, or an idea. Any of them who wrote a letter received a personal reply from Walton; any who made the trip to Bentonville received an appointment with Mr. Sam, as many employees called him.

LOWERING PRICES

In 1973, the Arab oil embargo caused energy prices to soar. For Wal-Mart, it was an ill-timed setback. Like most people in the business of distribution, Walton felt as if he were a hostage to the irrational price inflation. This event changed the way he conducted business. After the oil crisis, Wal-Mart stores were built only within a twelve-hour drive from the nearest distribution center. Situated in clusters, the stores could be efficiently supplied, reducing the overall effect of rising gas prices.

"Other retailers built warehouses to serve existing outlets," *Forbes* reported later, in 1982, "but Walton went at it the other way around. He started with a giant warehouse, and then sprouted stores around it." And so, Wal-Mart did not "go national" all at once; the plan was to make a steady march, one distribution center at a time, into new territory.

In 1974, after building Wal-Mart into a strong company, set to grow, Walton abruptly retired. He still controlled the company, as the head of the family partnership that owned about 38 percent of the stock, but at the age of fifty-six he wanted to relax. He also thought that another executive might bring fresh vigor to the company's next phase of expansion. The man chosen was the financial vice president, an ambitious forty-year-old named Ron Mayer. About a year and half later, though, Walton tired of being retired and grew anxious to return to command of his company. Sam Walton made an appointment with Ron Mayer and asked for his old job back. Mayer stepped aside—in fact, he quit Wal-Mart—and in 1976, Sam Walton was back in place as CEO.

As a CEO, Walton set a frenetic pace. The atmosphere was humble to a fault, with the unchanging goals of better service and lower prices for the customer. To those ends, he forced Wal-Mart executives to rethink every process in retailing, from purchasing through to the cash register. Weldon Wyatt, a businessman who had worked with the corporation for many years, told trade magazine *Chain Store Age Executive*, "I observed three characteristics in Mr. Walton that fascinated me. The first was his willingness to listen to anyone's ideas at any time. The second was his ability to sort through those ideas to find ideas that made sense. The third was his willingness to apply the energy and effort necessary to implement the ideas he chose to use."

"Try anyone's idea," Walton advised. "It might not work. But it won't break the company when it doesn't."

Lower prices for the customer started with the company's buyers who were notoriously cold in an industry used to glad-handing. Over the years, Wal-Mart's insistence that it would not meet with manufacturers' representatives infuriated the industry. Manufacturers were angry because under this plan they would have to send their own ranking executives to Bentonville to make sales. And reps everywhere were indignant at the implication that they were expendable. From Walton's point of view, they were. The tactic was supposed to lower prices by obviating the reps' commission, but as a matter of fact most manufacturers were obligated to pay it regardless of who actually made the sale. When Wal-Mart could enforce the ban, it claimed a savings of about 6 percent. Some manufacturers, like Procter & Gamble, did eventually work with Wal-Mart to remove excess layers from the sales process. In fact, the overall key to selling to Wal-Mart was *working with* the company. Walton wanted to work with any sources that would work with him, in any way, to lower prices for the customer.

Some considered the company unreasonable, but most accepted Wal-Mart's attitude for what it was: insurmountable. "[Sam Walton] understood, perhaps better than anyone else, how manufacturers and retailers can better serve the consumer by working closely together," conceded a spokesman for Procter & Gamble, which, after some difficult negotiation, became Wal-Mart's number one vendor.

Wal-Mart's favored method was to involve itself throughout the manufacturing process. In 1984, Bill Clinton, who was then the governor of Arkansas, called Wal-Mart looking for help for a clothing factory in the state that was about to lose its biggest customer to foreign competition. "We're going to see if we can do something that's never been done before," Walton told Clinton, after discussing the matter with his executives. Wal-Mart prepared to hand the local factory the bulk of its requirement for flannel shirts, an order previously purchased from the Far East. The retailer itself arranged to buy the fabric overseas, because no American company made quite the right pattern. But it received good publicity for bringing the piecework back to Arkansas. Meanwhile, Wal-Mart was able to work closely with the local factory to eke out efficiencies.

Looking back on the shirt deal, Walton felt that he had identified

a certain type of American company, slightly displaced by foreign competition, hungry for work, and willing to involve a company like Wal-
Mart in its future. In March 1985, Walton took out full-page ads in
major newspapers to announce the store's new "Buy American" program.
It was, on the surface, a patriotic gesture, especially fitting for a company
with a predominantly blue-collar clientele. It was also an example of
Walton looking for opportunities to squeeze out better prices. He wanted
to insure that he was buying from companies that were efficient. And
he didn't keep his ulterior motive a secret: "Our American suppliers must
commit to improving their facilities and machinery, remain financially
conservative and work to fill our requirements, and most importantly,
serve to improve employee productivity," Walton wrote in his open
letter. The store documented $1.2 billion in new domestic contracts
over the next three years, according to *Nation's Business*, though some
observers in union watchdog groups maintained that Wal-Mart remained
just as dependent overall on foreign sources as any other big store.

In 1987, Walton announced a similar invitation for suppliers to
participate in an environmental program. Wal-Mart promised to work
closely with manufacturers selling products "guaranteed not to last," as
Walton wrote in the open letter that introduced the program.

The Wal-Mart distribution centers became another distinctive factor in the Wal-Mart system. A warehouse, by itself, is the dull backstage
of retailing. But a Wal-Mart distribution center was engineered to do
more than feed products into stores; it was designed to lower their costs.
Early on, Wal-Mart found that it could truck goods at a lower cost than
most manufacturers could, and so it insisted on making most purchases
without exorbitant delivery charges included. Walton's fleet would instead pick up the products at the factory door. Three-quarters of the
stock in a store was delivered directly from a distribution center; in
1992, there were fourteen distribution centers, with the largest covering
1.5 million square feet. Fully automated, the distribution centers were
to be "smart" warehouses, receiving inventory reports directly from store
registers, as part of the Wal-Mart computer system. At the bottom of

the technology tree, Wal-Mart's trucks were routed to each of the 200 stores attached to a distribution center in such a way that they would not travel empty. Even as the Wal-Mart chain expanded into all four continental time zones, its distribution costs remained the lowest of any retailer.

When the corporation zipped past its thousandth store in 1987, no one, not even a man of the prodigious energies of Sam Walton, could hope to monitor all the Wal-Marts personally. The airplane had expanded Walton's reach once; now satellite technology greatly expanded his ability to control the Wal-Mart empire.

In 1985, Wal-Mart became one massive store with the inauguration of its own Hughes Network Systems six-channel satellite. Walton could easily address all his associates at once, via videotape, but the new technology had an even more serious purpose than that. The satellite wiped out the distances along the Wal-Mart line of command, from store to headquarters to distribution center, and even, in the case of major suppliers, to the factory. All were connected to and controlled from Bentonville. Every efficiency could be a chainwide savings; for example, the temperature in every Wal-Mart store was monitored and adjusted by the computers back in Bentonville. In 1981, the company had begun installing an electronic monitoring system in its stores. Called VideoCart, it not only flashed messages to customers roaming through the store but also watched the way people shopped and collected information on their pauses, patterns, and purchases to beam back to Bentonville. The company's computer center, built in 1984, was bigger than a football field.

Wal-Mart was the first discount retailer to test UPC scanning in 1980; after this innovation helped cashier productivity increase by 50 percent, it was installed throughout the chain. In the thirty years of Walton's leadership, Wal-Mart didn't authorize a penny for the decoration of executive offices, but it became the most technologically advanced company in retailing.

In 1981 Wal-Mart's operating costs stood at sixteen cents for every dollar in sales. Kmart's costs were twenty-two cents per dollar. Just as

"UP AGAINST WAL-MART"

Wal-Mart built a national reputation for bringing its low prices to the residents of small towns. And yet, in a backlash that began in the late eighties, it came under attack in hundreds of communities for doing just that.

Given the label "Sprawl-mart" in the early nineties, Wal-Mart stores were blamed for destabilizing the central business districts of small towns and for bringing blight to farm country. Some of the towns that fought Wal-Mart did indeed have a lot to lose: In spots like Lake Placid, New York, and Fredericksburg, Virginia, a downtown full of healthy, old-fashioned stores was an important facet of the tourist industry. Other towns, however, tried to prevent Wal-Mart from locating on commercial stretches that already contained similar stores, like Kmart or Target. "Stop the WAL" clubs formed in hundreds of towns, and in 1994 *The Nation* printed "Eight Ways to Stop the Store," a tipsheet for people who felt "Up Against Wal-Mart." By the middle of 1996, forty-five towns across the country had created enough of a fuss to keep the store out.

In many towns where a Wal-Mart opened, business actually was drawn away from small shops on the main street. That's just what happened in Taylor, Texas; but the real problem may not have been with the newcomer. As one customer put it: "Before Wal-Mart came here, those stores downtown never heard of a sale." For his part, Sam Walton had little sympathy for the shops that were losing out to Wal-Marts. "The truth is that a lot of those folks just weren't doing a very good job of taking care of their customers before we, or somebody else, came in and offered something new," he wrote, in his best-selling autobiography, *Made in America*. "The small stores were just destined to disappear, at least in the numbers they once existed," he continued, "because the whole thing is driven by the customers, who are free to choose where to shop."

Where it met opposition, Wal-Mart used legal and public-relations campaigns to defend its right to open stores in any community with a potential customer base and it had some success. But not all store owners complain when they see a Wal-Mart moving in. Some prosper by moving closer to take advantage of the increased traffic or by recasting their business into niches not served by Wal-Mart.

(*continued*)

(*continued*)

One hardware store owner in Iowa saw his sales increase by 300 percent over the first three years that he had Wal-Mart as a neighbor. He had to work harder to buy smarter and sell lower, but it kept him out of the ranks of victims; that is, merchants "whose customers know what the competition and he doesn't cause he never leaves the store." That store owner's formula for success against Wal-Mart sounded a lot like Sam Walton's formula for success in creating Wal-Mart.

Ford's moving assembly line was an amalgamation of daily improvements, Wal-Mart's system took years to develop, idea by idea.

Sam Walton was diagnosed with a rare form of cancer known as hairy cell leukemia in 1982. After treatment at a Texas hospital, the disease went into remission. When he returned, he worked almost as hard as ever, and in 1983 he was active in launching Sam's Club, a deep-discount warehouse shopping club similar in concept to the Price Club originated by Sol Price in California. The new subsidiary was a success. Next, Wal-Mart tried yet another type of store: the Hypermart, or the "mall without walls" as Sam Walton liked to call it. Standard Wal-Marts were built in five sizes, depending on the community; the biggest was 60,000 square feet. A Hypermart, which sold everything from groceries to haircuts to fishing poles, measured 222,000 square feet. As the company made plans to open its first fifty Hypermarts, grocery stores around the country found themselves in the same position as most of the rest of the retailing world: nervously drawing up defenses against the Wal-Mart juggernaut.

In 1991, Wal-Mart handed Walton a gift, an achievement unthinkable until it happened: Wal-Mart surpassed Sears as the nation's biggest retailer. Ten years earlier, Wal-Mart had racked up paltry sales of $2.6 billion, compared to Sears' $20 billion. In 1991, though, Wal-Mart had sales of $32.6 billion, vaulting past Sears' $32 billion.

Unfortunately, as Wal-Mart business speeded up, Walton's health deteriorated, and he was finally forced to slow down. Sam Walton was in a wheelchair in 1992, debilitated by a return of his cancer, when President George Bush paid a visit to Bentonville to give him the Medal of Freedom. The president concluded his citation by calling Walton a "captain of commerce, as successful in life as in business." Wal-Mart President David Glass went out to the house later in the day and Walton told him it had been the greatest day of his life.

Walton reconsidered his comment, though. "A few days later," as Glass recalled, "he told me that the greatest days of his life were when he was out in the stores visiting our wonderful associates and loyal customers."

That same year, Sam Walton succumbed to cancer. The news was sent via satellite directly to the company's 1,960 stores; when the announcement played on the public address system at some stores, clerks started crying. The obituary in the *New York Times* referred to the fortune at the time of his death, estimated at $28 billion. But that probably wouldn't have meant as much to Walton as the mention made a few paragraphs below of a Wal-Mart cashier who had $262,000 in her retirement account, after working for the company for twenty-four years.

Bill McGowan, president of MCI, in 1987.

WILLIAM McGOWAN AND MCI: A NEW WORLD OF TELECOMMUNICATIONS

n the 1960s, Microwave Communications Inc. (now known as MCI), a tiny company with a handful of employees and no revenue, decided to engage AT&T in hand-to-hand combat. What ensued was a decades-long duel that pitted the meager resources of the upstart MCI against AT&T's arsenal of industrial, financial, and legal firepower; by comparison, David and Goliath were evenly matched.

In the 1960s, competition in telecommunications was not only nonexistent, it was illegal. AT&T, which literally had invented the industry, had held a government-regulated monopoly on long-distance phone services since 1910. By 1967 its budget was larger than that of a small European country; its assets exceeded those of Standard Oil, General Motors, Ford, and IBM combined. AT&T was the paragon of American industry, the largest private-sector employer in the nation, and the issuer of its most widely held stock. Ma Bell possessed 100 percent universal brand recognition, extraordinarily deep pockets, and, in Bell Labs, one of the world's greatest research and design facilities.

But the underdog MCI had one thing that AT&T lacked: the visionary CEO Bill McGowan. He meant to make telecommunications history by breaking up AT&T's monopoly on long-distance service, and establishing competition in an industry that had none. He did just that.

THE ORIGINS OF AN UPSTART COMPANY

The story of Microwave Communications Inc. begins in 1963, when John Goeken, a former General Electric two-way radio salesman and inveterate tinkerer from Joliet, Illinois, asked the Federal Communications Commission (FCC) for permission to set up private phone lines connecting St. Louis and Chicago. Goeken hit upon the revolutionary idea of allowing many customers to tap into a private microwave system—a fairly standard technology in which conversations were carried by a form of radio wave. These waves were transmitted via antennae mounted atop microwave relay stations, each within a direct line of sight to the next. Under Goeken's proposal, companies with operations in both cities could pay a flat monthly fee, tap the line, and connect directly to their colleagues. This differed from AT&T's system, which consisted of copper-wire strung between every city and town in the United States.

But Goeken couldn't proceed without FCC approval. And while he waited for it, his fledgling Microwave Communications ran dangerously low on funds. Goeken traveled the country tirelessly, trying to raise funds through insurance companies, banks, and wealthy individuals. Eventually, a lawyer told Goeken about a prospective source of venture capital: William McGowan, a forty-year-old corporate turnaround artist and self-made millionaire whose background was more blue collar than blue chip.

William McGowan grew up in Ashley, Pennsylvania, near Wilkes-Barre, the son of a railroad engineer. He worked nights as a freight dispatcher for the New Jersey Central Railroad to pay the tuition at a local college where he studied chemistry. In 1954 young McGowan graduated in the top 5 percent of his class at Harvard Business School. A natural entrepreneur, McGowan set up shop as a consultant in New York and started a small venture capital company whose specialty was helping troubled companies get back on their feet. He became a sort of patron saint for seemingly lost corporate causes. But after turning around the fortunes of a handful of failing companies, McGowan grew bored doing the "same things over and over again." He spent the next year touring around the globe with his brother, who was a Catholic priest, and consulting for UNESCO on ways of bringing venture capital to third-world small businesses.

A VISION FOR THE FUTURE OF MCI

Upon his return, McGowan was approached by John Goeken and found a new challenge in MCI's push for an FCC license. Viewing the license as a beginning, not an end, McGowan foresaw a future for the company far greater than its founder Goeken had envisioned. McGowan wanted nothing less than a nationwide network connecting major hubs through which MCI could offer low-cost, long-distance service to the business market. After three months of discussions with Goeken and other MCI executives, McGowan took control of MCI in 1968 by injecting a much needed $35,000 into the poorly capitalized company.

After holding several rounds of hearings, commissioning various professional studies, and entertaining objections and counter-objections from MCI and AT&T, the FCC finally granted the license in August 1969. In a 4 to 3 split decision, the commissioners ruled that by offering semiprivate lines to mid-sized and small businesses, MCI met "unfulfilled communications needs." The government believed that this first serious challenge to AT&T's monopoly would have the salutary effect of shaking up Ma Bell, which, it felt, had grown slack and inattentive to customers' needs. "MCI," the Commissioner Nicholas Johnson wrote, "would add a little salt and pepper of competition to the rather tasteless stew of regulatory protection that this commission and Bell have cooked up." Over the next twenty years, McGowan would add a great deal more than spice to the telecommunications stew.

McGowan lived vigorously in all respects: he was a relentlessly aggressive and successful salesman, a heavy smoker, unabashed bachelor, and an energetic proselytizer who would devote most of his life to MCI. He was described by the press as "a paunchy, chain-smoking workaholic with a chronic disregard for rules," a friendly presence "with a bit of Mephistopheles thrown in."

McGowan's sales campaign began on the inside, with endless pep talks to staffers and investors, in which he sold them on the easy money that lay just beyond the legal and regulatory tangle. In reality, for most of its early years, MCI was more a fund-raising firm than a communications company. In 1973, MCI had 4,500 miles of routes, but was operating only the St. Louis-Chicago connection. Worse, MCI couldn't offer its services without the cooperation of AT&T. After all, any call from Chicago to St. Louis would have to originate on an AT&T local line in Chicago, switch to the MCI long-distance line, and then switch back to an AT&T line to an office in St. Louis.

In 1972, as the Chicago-St. Louis link became operational, McGowan started negotiating with AT&T for access to its local lines. Although McGowan's operation barely existed, Ma Bell saw MCI—indeed, any competition—as a mortal threat. To complicate the situation, AT&T was suffering a quiet crisis of confidence due to agitation from consumer advocates and constant customer complaints about declining quality of service. Despite its own problems AT&T's 1972 Presidents' Conference in Key Largo, Florida, focused on MCI. As MCI expanded from its Chicago-St. Louis base and sought business customers all over the country,

AT&T's regional executives had thus far refrained from confronting MCI head on. But now they wanted to fight. "I would meet 'em or beat 'em," said Northwestern Bell's President, T. S. Nurnberger, who recommended that AT&T match MCI's low rates: "[Those] bastards are not going to take away my business." John Dulany deButts, a company veteran installed as chairman just six weeks prior to the meeting, was still finding his footing, however, and decided against precipitate action.

McGowan, in contrast, knew exactly what he wanted to do. On January 9, 1973, he laid out a long-range course of action to his executives in Washington, D.C. His plan included preparing an antitrust lawsuit against both AT&T and its local operating companies, sending briefs to the Federal Communications Commission, and goading the Justice Department into taking similar antitrust action. But the boldest of his new tactics was to undertake blunt face-to-face confrontation with AT&T's head office: "The first thing we should pursue is high-pressure negotiations with 195 Broadway."

To McGowan, deButts and company offered an object lesson on how not to run an organization. While working for the New Jersey Central Railroad, young McGowan had first seen the pitfalls of the multilayered corporate structure. He described such an organization as having "bureaucratic procedures. Procedure upon procedure, with no apparent rationale." This was the AT&T weakness that McGowan's nimble firm planned to exploit. As *The Wall Street Journal* noted in 1985: "Mr. McGowan has said, only half facetiously, that he runs the company by observing what AT&T does and then bolting in the opposite direction."

WAR IS DECLARED

On March 2, 1973, McGowan stood toe to toe with AT&T Chairman John deButts, the courtly scion of a Southern railway family. The contrast in the styles and personalities between them made open conflict inevitable. DeButts, perfectly suited to his plush twenty-sixth-floor office, complete with gold carpets and antiques, represented a way of corporate life McGowan had rejected. The conversation between the two chairmen quickly degenerated into threats. McGowan attacked AT&T's new "Hi/Lo" pricing systems, introduced in February 1973 to counter MCI's bid for a piece of the action. Hi/Lo offered lower rates on so-called high-density lines (i.e., the same routes between large cities in which MCI operated). McGowan declared war: "We're going to fight Hi/Lo at the FCC, and we have better relations with the FCC than you do. We also have a number of friends in Congress." When deButts apparently dismissed McGowan's threats, McGowan insolently turned up the heat. "I have plenty of money. I can spend it on litigation, or I can spend it on construction. I would prefer to spend it on construction."

This meeting marked a turning point in AT&T's view of its junior competitor. After McGowan left in frustration, deButts turned to another AT&T executive and remarked: "Nothing about MCI can be treated as business as usual."

McGowan's bravado would prove difficult to back with action. Indeed, in the early 1970s, MCI—though it was later dubbed Money Coming In—lost money hand over fist. Between 1968 and March 31, 1974, MCI brought in just $728,000 in revenues. From 1968 through December 31, 1975, MCI had cumulative losses of $96.2 million. As a result, in April 1973, McGowan scaled back plans for the network from thirty-four cities to nineteen cities.

Despite the disappointment, he didn't give up. Having plowed through the $100 million in seed money raised a few years earlier, he raised $30 million in a 1972 initial public offering. Then McGowan rounded up $64 million in bank loans and another $17 million in equity from private investors, adding a total of $111 million to the company's war chest.

For the bankers and money managers, subscription to MCI's equity and loan offerings was tantamount to enrolling in Bill McGowan's audacious struggle for freedom from Ma Bell's monopoly. "It is obvious that Wall Street is prepared to use its resources to put some flesh on the bare bones of this daring challenge to the communications establishment," one trade publication noted. McGowan's investment bankers, who handled the selling pitches, weren't just selling stock certificates, they were selling a new era.

McGowan, of course, reveled in the role. He gleefully tweaked AT&T with such comments as "Ma Bell is a lying Mother." And at the 1988 MCI shareholder meeting he compared AT&T to Stalin's regime. He delighted in showing visitors to his mansion in Georgetown a unique feature that happened to be in the house's cornerstone: an ancient AT&T logo with a crack running through it.

FRIENDS IN THE RIGHT PLACES

McGowan's Georgetown address subtly highlights one key to MCI's success. Few CEOs of major companies chose to live in Washington, D.C., the province of regulators, bureaucrats, and politicians. But McGowan set up shop there precisely because he understood the complex relationship between government and regulated businesses such as telecommunications. As he said in 1986: "If we did not succeed in changing the regulatory situation, then all the rest was just show biz."

McGowan realized that he could create a working venture with government: "Look, government is a reality of life," he said. "Denying it—getting emotional about it—is just letting your own personal, political biases influence your business judgment." From MCI's base in a twelve-story building near DuPont Circle, McGowan regularly entertained congressional and federal staffers, and hired Washington lawyers (like former FCC Commissioner Kenneth Cox) who knew the federal bureaucracy intimately.

McGowan's high-priced lawyers and engineers went to work, looking for ways to get around the restrictions that protected mighty AT&T. In late 1973 MCI had introduced a service called Execunet, which would allow MCI customers to use their AT&T phones to dial a local access code, then punch in an authorization, area code, and number for long-distance service. The call would then bullet over an MCI line to another city, where the signal would switch to local phones through AT&T lines. Execunet cost 10 percent to 30 percent less than Bell's competing WATS line. But the empire quickly struck back. AT&T announced that it would simply refuse to allow any additional MCI's Execunet customers to use its switches. When a court ordered AT&T to provide all interconnections to MCI's Execunet lines, Ma Bell appealed. For his part, McGowan responded with a gesture that could have been viewed as either a brilliant stroke of intuition or a foolishly suicidal gesture. On March 6, 1974, MCI filed a far-reaching lawsuit against AT&T, charging that AT&T violated federal antitrust laws by refusing intracity connections. With this stroke, McGowan engaged AT&T's massive legal apparatus in what seemed to be a one-sided contest. Throughout the 1970s, MCI and its six lawyers and twenty-four paralegals spent about $2 million on legal costs. A substantial sum, but a pittance compared to the millions that fueled AT&T's dozens of in-house lawyers and outside counsel.

Fortunately for McGowan, MCI wasn't the only party fighting AT&T in the courts. The Justice Department's antitrust division had long been looking into AT&T's business practices, and on November 20, 1974, the Ford Administration filed an antitrust suit against AT&T, alleging monopolization of the long-distance and equipment markets. The government sought structural remedies and the break up of local telephone companies from the Bell system.

The final disposition of these two lawsuits in the early 1980s would insure MCI's success and change the face of American telecommunications forever. McGowan's triumph proved the virtue of patience. Victory came in 1982, but only after a decade's worth of legal struggle, during which MCI flirted with bankruptcy (the stock, which went public at 10 in 1972, fell to 7/8 in 1974; in 1975 alone the company lost $39.3 million). As McGowan later said: "We were not really in the communications business . . . we were really in the surviving business."

Execunet, which AT&T had tried to kill, was MCI's first profitable service. In the quarter ending June 30, 1976, MCI posted earnings from operations for the first time, though the company showed a loss due to interest expenses. As the litigation dragged on, MCI's salespeople continued to market its services. By 1978, when a U.S. Appeals Court forced AT&T to connect the Execunet lines once and for all, there were 41,000 Execunet customers. After the monumental decision, which essentially legitimized the idea of long-distance competition, MCI and AT&T hammered out agreements through which MCI rented access to local exchanges for $235 per line per month—a bargain that paved the way for MCI's future profits. MCI turned its first profit in the fiscal year ending March 1979, earning $7 million on revenues of $95.2 million.

McGowan's company began in 1980 to pitch its services aggressively to residential customers. As with Execunet, MCI residential customers had to dial up a local number, punch in an access code, and then the number. While the rates were 20 percent to 60 percent lower than AT&T's, McGowan conceded that the process was "a pain." So he continued to press for equal access—a system in which his customers could simply dial "1" and use MCI's long-distance network. MCI proved the technology could work in the summer of 1981, when Northwest Iowa Telephone Company, a 2,100-customer independent company, let MCI install equipment that provided direct access.

In June 1980 a federal jury ruled in MCI's favor in the six-year-old antitrust suit and awarded damages of $1.8 billion. Still, McGowan was unsatisfied and sought further damages. "Let's see how deep their pockets are," he said. But his ploy didn't work: the Supreme Court reversed the award after AT&T appealed; in the separate damages-only retrial that opened in 1985 MCI received just $300 million after seeking $15 billion.

THE FALLOUT

The U.S. Justice Department dealt AT&T a more powerful blow. In January 1981 *U.S. vs. AT&T* finally went to trial before Judge Harold Greene in Washington, D.C. As one of the government's star witnesses,

McGowan spent four full days on the stand detailing Ma Bell's alleged predations. The newly installed antitrust chief William Baxter, a conservative Stanford law professor, pursued the seven-year-old case with zeal and drove a hard settlement bargain. On January 8, 1982, the two parties ironed out a settlement under which AT&T would divest itself of its twenty-two local operating companies, which would be transformed into seven regional Bell operating companies and continue to offer long-distance services. In addition, the newly independent local operating companies would grant equal access to competing long-distance providers.

MCI, the best-positioned and most established alternative carrier, took off in the wake of the breakup. Its revenues topped $1 billion for the first time in 1982 when the company earned $86 million. MCI's stock, in the tank for much of the 1970s, soared from a split-adjusted twenty-five cents a share in 1977 to $28 in June 1983. In January 1983, with a million customers on board, MCI was enrolling 50,000 new subscribers a month. The future seemed boundless, as the $40-billion long-distance market was growing at a 10 percent annual clip. "The only limit on our growth is our ability to build the network," McGowan said in January 1983.

Relying more on technology than staff—"We use computers, not people," McGowan liked to say—MCI's chairman regarded investment in its 15,000-mile network as the key to continued success. To truly compete with AT&T, McGowan realized that MCI needed a nationwide, state-of-the-art digital circulation system and the software to make it run efficiently. Unlike AT&T, however, MCI never made its own equipment, preferring to rely on outside suppliers. Furthermore, MCI spent little in the way of research and development. "So what if we don't get a lot of patents," McGowan would say. As a result, MCI had a lower cost structure than AT&T: in 1985, MCI's total costs per minute were estimated at twenty-five cents, compared with thirty-two cents for AT&T.

The low costs were partly a result of McGowan's no-frills ethos.

HOW McGOWAN RAISED CAPITAL

The estimated cost of McGowan's mythic network was $100 million. A difficult amount for any company to raise, it was a seemingly impossible sum for an unknown company—one with neither products nor clients—that sought government permission to compete against the biggest company in the world.

McGowan pulled off the impossible by adopting an unusual approach. Reasoning it would be easier to raise the funds in small bites rather than one huge gulp, in 1968 he shrewdly set up seventeen shell companies based in distinct geographical territories, giving the illusion that MCI was a nationwide operator. Over the next three years, each would apply for FCC permission to build a chunk of the network. McGowan then set about capitalizing each company at about $5 million, drawing upon his own bank account, MCI executives, and venture capital sources. In 1972, the initial fundraising complete, McGowan reorganized the company by merging the seventeen companies into one.

When an employee innocently asked whether a new MCI office complex would have a gym, McGowan snapped: "You want exercise, go climb a microwave tower." When it came to investment in technology, however, McGowan routinely approved massive expenditures to expand MCI's network. His vision in the 1980s remained as ambitious as it had been back in the sixties. McGowan turned to Michael Milken and the high-yield bond group of Drexel Burnham Lambert in July 1983. In one of the largest corporate bond sales in history, MCI sold $1 billion in 9.5 percent subordinated notes. In 1984, with $1.96 billion in annual revenues, MCI committed $1 billion to upgrading and building its network.

The dissolution of the Bell System on January 1, 1984, brought to fruition McGowan's long-standing dream of equal access. In this new era, customers could access their choice of long-distance carriers simply by dialing "1." But by 1986 the rebel found his company in a free-for-all when MCI and dozens of new companies scrambled to sign up the 86 million U.S. telephone customers who had received ballots permitting them to choose a long-distance provider. MCI won about 13 percent of those customers.

After the breakup, the FCC ordered AT&T to cut its rates. Never to be undersold, McGowan's MCI had slashed its tariffs up to one-third. And because the FCC phased out the discount on access fees paid to local phone companies as part of the settlement, the rate MCI paid for access to local exchanges rose from $235 per line per month to $330. The combination of higher costs, heightened competition, and lower rates left MCI in a terrible position. In 1986 the company lost $498 million. As if to emphasize the intense personal connection between McGowan and the state of his business, his own health declined at this time as well. The fifty-nine-year-old McGowan suffered a heart attack and received a heart transplant in April 1987. But the hard-driving executive didn't even think of retiring. "I am ready to shake things up," McGowan said.

Reverting to his old role of turnaround artist, McGowan recovered quickly and set about healing MCI. He slashed spending on MCI's largely completed network and cut the workforce by 15 percent. MCI had grown fat by investing heavily in the residential market, but McGowan refocused attention on the company's original market: businesses. "Spurred on by McGowan, MCI management improved quality and service, and pushed for more corporate customers as well," *Forbes* noted. In rapid succession, MCI landed major contracts from United Airlines and the Pentagon. By 1988 the company was back in the black, earning $356 million on revenues of $5.1 billion.

With MCI's financial health restored, McGowan had achieved his longtime goal: MCI was a profitable company offering nationwide long-distance service. Though married to his work well into his middle age, McGowan cut back after the heart transplant. In 1991 he reluctantly ceded the CEO's chair to MCI President Bert Roberts, a company veteran who had overseen product development dating back to Execunet.

When William McGowan suffered a fatal heart attack at the age of sixty-four in June 1992, MCI had 31,000 employees, $10.5 billion in sales, and earnings of $609 million. The company he had nurtured for nearly a quarter century was no longer "in the surviving business." It could now deal on equal terms with giants like British Telecom, which paid $4.3 billion for a 20 percent stake in MCI in 1993. With about 20 percent of the nation's long-distance market, the firm McGowan built is a thriving example of the rich possibilities of competition in telecommunications.

William Davidson (standing), Charles Thompson, and Vaughn Beals (seated) of Harley-Davidson after the buyout in 1981.

THE TURNAROUND AT HARLEY-DAVIDSON

By the early 1980s the Harley-Davidson Motor Company had rolled within inches of the precipice over which many American manufacturers had plummeted in the latter third of the twentieth century. Significant market forces—including Japanese competition and a recession—and a long-term decline in quality, were pushing America's last motorcycle maker into bankruptcy.

In 1981, however, a group of executives who loved the company and its product closed ranks to rescue Harley-Davidson from decline. After taking ownership of the company from an indifferent corporate parent in a leveraged buyout, they persuaded Washington to impose a temporary tariff increase on Japanese-made motorcycles. The law gave the bikers-cum-owners the time they needed to completely remake their company from within. By adapting the successful quality control and production methods used by Japanese competitors, they reinvented their manufacturing process and improved their product. The executives gave middle managers and line workers greater decision-making power. Harley-Davidson then supported its revamped bikes with an ingenious marketing strategy that appealed to the extraordinary loyalty of its die-hard customers and enticed new converts as well.

By 1987 Harley-Davidson had regained from off-shore competitors the preeminent position in its market, proving that a traditional American manufacturer can compete, survive, and prosper in a global marketplace.

AN EARLY START

William S. Harley and Arthur Davidson—both in their twenties—built their first motorcycle in 1903, the year Henry Ford formed his motor company. Like Ford, they built a prototype in a crude wooden shed; unlike Ford, they sold only one machine that first year—their entire output. By 1910 the Harley-Davidson Motor Company was up and running, selling 3,200 bikes. Ten years later, having expanded into overseas markets, the duo sold 28,000 motorcycles.

As automobiles became easily affordable and popular, the motorcycle's market share diminished. By 1913 only two of the several dozen motorcycle manufacturers born at the turn of the century survived: Harley-Davidson and the Indian Motorcycle Manufacturing Company.

In an effort to raise funds during the Depression, Harley-Davidson sold the rights to manufacture its bikes in Japan to a pharmaceutical firm. The deal kick-started the Japanese motorcycle market and unwittingly laid the groundwork for competition that would nearly kill the Harley-Davidson Motor Company forty years later. The company survived the Depression in the 1930s and rebounded during World War II, when it supplied about 88,000 motorcycles to the army. Along with many other leaders in American industry, Harley-Davidson prospered after the war, due in part to the destruction of Japanese and European manufacturing capability. And in 1953, when Indian closed, Harley became the last remaining U.S. motorcycle maker.

By that time Harley-Davidson Motor Company had become an American institution. With appearances in cult movies such as *The Wild One* and *Easy Rider*, Harleys would become cultural icons. The ungainly "Hogs," as they were commonly known, had a macho, rumbling voice and distinctive roar: "A Harley sounds like nothing else on the road," as one enthusiast put it. Rakish, powerful, crude, loud, and tough, the bike attracted leather-clad rebels who loved its bad-boy mystique. "The bike conveys a mechanical forcefulness—it's not totally tamed," rhapsodized the longtime design chief Willie G. Davidson. Over the years, pop culture figures ranging from Elvis Presley to actor Steve McQueen and the baseball slugger Reggie Jackson proudly rode Hogs.

THE MARKET LEADER FALLS PREY TO FOREIGN COMPETITION

In the 1960s, reconstructed Japanese manufacturing firms seized a chunk of the international automobile and motorcycle markets. One of the most successful Japanese motorcycle exporters was Honda, whose lighterweight bikes were backed by aggressive commercials that portrayed riders as "nice" people—for a change. Kawasaki and Yamaha soon took their share of the lightweight market.

In 1969 Harley-Davidson was acquired by the American Machine & Foundry Company (AMF) and the former family-owned company (which had only gone public in 1965) was soon caught up in the dynamics of a huge conglomerate. At first that seemed a boon, since AMF pumped $60 million into its Harley division and boosted production to compete with the growing Japanese onslaught. Although volume exploded from 27,000 in 1969 to 60,000 in 1972, AFM's Harley-Davidson struck a curiously cavalier attitude toward the burgeoning market for cheaper, less-powerful bikes, which was dominated by the Japanese imports. In fact, in 1978, instead of increasing their production of light motorcycles, Harley-Davidson stopped making them altogether.

AMF appeared willing to cede this turf because the imports really didn't challenge Harley-Davidson's main business: heavyweight motorcycles with engine capacities of over 750 cc. As late as 1974 Harley-Davidson had no competitors in the super-heavyweight market (bikes powered by larger engines with 850 cc capacities). Having had the heavyweight market to itself for so long, Harley-Davidson had grown complacent, and the bikes reflected the inattention. Responsibility for quality control seemed to have been lost in AMF's bureaucratic maze. Consequently, Hogs in the 1970s began to acquire a deserved reputation for poor quality. As *Forbes* noted in 1983: "AMF had run unit sales up but also threatened to run the company into the ground by not investing enough in new tooling." Things became so bad that the company had to set up "hospitals," way stations where bikes that had come off the assembly line incomplete were patched up and shipped off to dealers. Despite the quality problems, Harley-Davidson continued to rack up impressive sales figures. As the popularity of mopeds and lighter-weight machines pushed the overall market for two-wheel motorized bikes to new heights, the company sold a record 50,000 bikes in 1979. But these numbers were deceiving.

By 1981 Harley's quality problems began having an impact on sales as Japanese competitors set their sites on the heavyweight market. The company's sales fell a precipitous 18 percent to 41,000, and even Harley's share of the U.S. super-heavyweight class fell below Honda's 33.9 percent to 29.6 percent. Harley-Davidson's domestic market share plunged to 5 percent. Even Hog cultists were buying Japanese bikes.

Convinced it could do little to reverse the company's declining fortunes, AMF began looking for a buyer. It found scant interest. But back at the Harley-Davidson division, senior manager Vaughn Beals still believed in his product. He and his colleagues realized that the company could only survive in the hands of loyal managers who truly grasped the nuances of the motorcycle business. They foresaw that a sale to an outside buyer would be disastrous. "An experienced, closely knit management team would have been replaced by people who didn't know the motorcycle business at all—and the long-term values of the company would have gone down the drain," he said.

Enlisting the aid of Citibank, Beals and his team of twelve Harley-Davidson executives, including Richard Teerlink, the blunt, jovial chief financial officer, began negotiations to acquire the company. In June 1981, they reclaimed the firm's ownership. In a classic leveraged buyout (LBO), they pooled $1 million in equity and borrowed the rest of the $81.5 million purchase price from a consortium of banks led by Citibank. One of the most important members of the team was the design chief William G. Davidson. Willie G., as he is known both inside and outside the company, was the heart and soul of the operation. A grandson of company founder Arthur Davidson, Willie G. largely created Harley-Davidson's retro look, which became very popular. He was a graduate of The Art Center College of Design in Pasadena, California, and had joined the company in 1963. Willie G. let his hair and gray beard grow long and wore leathers, jeans, a beret, and a skull-and-crossbones lapel pin. His presence not only lent an air of authenticity to the firm, it also provided a connection between a faceless corporation and masses of customers. "Harley riders are kind of folk artists," Willie G. said. "A lot of them are untrained designers who'd rather talk about their motorcycle than almost anything. And I'm happy to listen because I'm of the same breed."

In June 1981, Harley-Davidson's new band of proprietors rode from the factory in York, Pennsylvania, to the company's headquarters in Milwaukee, Wisconsin, to publicize the company's new vigor. But the joyride came to a screeching halt soon after they returned to corporate headquarters. The LBO had come at exactly the wrong time. As the proud owners motored across Ohio, Indiana, and Illinois, a bitter and protracted recession was hitting Harley-Davidson's traditional customers particularly hard. Blue-collar workers were laid off in large numbers, and sky-high interest rates quelled their ardor and ability to borrow the $8,000 purchase price. In 1982, estimated sales of all motorcycles in the United States fell 18 percent to 935,000, the first downturn since 1975. With Japanese-made bikes in corresponding weight classes costing 25 percent to 50 percent less than Harley-Davidson bikes, the company's condition quickly slipped from stable to critical. In 1980 Harley-Davidson had posted its first operating loss in fifty years. But the slow bloodletting quickly turned into a hemorrhage; in 1982 Harley-Davidson spilled $25 million in red ink.

To complicate the situation, the LBO had left the company without the financial resources to weather the economic slide. On May 26, 1982, less than a year after the LBO, Harley-Davidson announced a drastic austerity program. In a stroke, it laid off 426 workers, cut officers' salaries up to 12 percent, froze workers' salaries, suspended contributions to employees' savings plans, and slashed production. By the end of 1982 the company had winnowed its workforce a staggering 40 percent, to 2,200.

IMPROVING QUALITY BY MIMICKING JAPANESE MANUFACTURERS

There was no guarantee that a rising economic tide would carry the firm back to fiscal health. To further exacerbate their financial woes, lack of quality had been a persistent problem. Throughout the years, the company's factory managers and line workers had been given responsibility for producing quantity, not for monitoring quality. As a result, by 1980, more than half of the Hogs rolling off the assembly line failed inspection and required repairs. By contrast, only 5 percent of Japanese bikes failed inspection. As Cycle World magazine noted: "Some of the hardware found on Harley Davidsons looked as if it were hammered out of iron ore by rock-wielding natives along the shores of the Milwaukee River." Dealers had to place cardboard and padding under bikes in the showroom to absorb the oil leaking from various tubes and parts. And some longtime Harley vendors became so disillusioned with their products that they began selling Japanese bikes. "At first, we found it hard to believe we could be that bad—but we were," said Vaughn Beals in 1982.

Beals and his colleagues quickly realized they had to conduct major surgery to save the patient. "We were trying to work within a production system that was basically flawed," he said. Ironically, the managers found their cure-all in Japanese factories. When the company's top executives and union leaders representing Harley-Davidson employees toured the Honda motorcycle plant in Marysville, Ohio, in 1982, they were shocked and amazed by what they saw: a neat assembly line, good labor relations, and a lean management staff (the plant had only thirty supervisors among the 500 employees). Most surprisingly the factory managed to achieve high productivity despite the near complete absence of computers. (Harley-Davidson had recently invested in expensive computer technology in an attempt to improve factory management.) Beals had an immediate insight into what separated Harley-Davidson from its Japanese competitors. "It wasn't robotics or culture or morning calisthenics and company songs; it was professional managers who understood their business and paid attention to detail," he told Peter Reid, the author of *Well Made in America*.

Tom Gelb, Harley's senior vice president of operations, had conducted research on Japanese manufacturing practices and reached a stark conclusion. "We have to play the game the way the Japanese play it—or we're dead." Paradoxically, the Japanese had learned their game from an American: Dr. Edwards Deming, the father of the total quality management movement. Demings and Joseph Juran developed the programs and introduced them to Japan in the 1940s to help rebuild the country's industrial infrastructure after World War II.

Deming's strategy rested on the so-called productivity triad. The triad's three components were Just in Time (JIT) Inventory, Employee Involvement (EI), and Statistical Operator Control (SOC). With JIT Inventory, manufacturers keep just as many parts on hand as needed for immediate use instead of keeping large pools of components and tools lying around the facility. Under JIT, factories could turn over inventory twenty to thirty times a year; by contrast, Harley-Davidson only did so four times a year. In 1981, before the executives toured a Japanese plant, the company had started a pilot JIT program based on the Japanese concepts. Almost immediately Harley-Davidson realized savings on storage and inventory costs, thus leaving the company with more cash available to meet debt payments. The reduction of inventory cleared space on the factory floor, thereby eliminating assembly-line bottlenecks. Under Harley-Davidson's brand of JIT, which they called Materials as Needed (MAN), defective parts could be spotted before they were widely used. Since inventory came in smaller batches, adjustments could be made before the next supply of components arrived. The adoption of MAN let Harley cut its inventory by 75 percent and allowed its two assembly plants to operate without stockrooms.

The second major initiative borrowed from Deming—via the Japanese competitors—was greater employee involvement. In an early example of what would now be called "empowerment," Harley-Davidson sought to dissolve the distinction between blue-collar and white-collar workers. Top managers and line workers joined together to redesign the assembly lines and factory floors. "No changes were implemented until the people involved understood and accepted that change," said Tom Gelb. Given a stake in the crucial decisions that would affect the company's future, employees became problem solvers on the line.

Workers were also trained in a third Deming technique: Statistical Operator Control (SOC). In 1983 and 1984 Harley-Davidson managers were instructed by a group of University of Tennessee professors turned consultants in methods of SOC, which prescribes that assembly-line workers not simply perform tasks robotically; it recognizes that the company's employees had the greatest familiarity and intimacy with production. Aside from monitoring the process, employees were encouraged to discover kinks and problems in the process, question its efficacy, and propose solutions. Workers began to use control charts to analyze data and monitor quality. As Richard Teerlink said: "Top management must recognize that it has the responsibility and obligation to provide an environment in which an employee feels free to challenge the system to achieve success."

Harley-Davidson had recognized the need for change and had quickly implemented it. By the end of 1982 costs had dropped to such low levels that the company only needed to sell 35,000 bikes to break even, rather than 53,000 just two years before. However, Harley-Davidson sold a disappointing 27,000 bikes in 1982. Meanwhile, the company found itself confronted with another problem. In the early 1980s Yamaha and Honda, engaged in a furious war for the U.S. market share, began cutting their prices rapidly and flooding the market with their products, bringing in many more bikes than they could sell.

Frustrated, Harley-Davidson in September 1982 asked the International Trade Commission (ITC) for relief from these allegedly predatory trade practices. Harley wasn't asking for a permanent injunction against foreign competition. "All we're asking for is a little breathing room," Beals said at the time. The very survival of the only U.S. motorcycle maker hung in the balance. Politicians representing districts with Harley-Davidson operations rallied behind the company, and Senator Robert Kasten of Wisconsin became the first U.S. Senator to testify before the ITC on behalf of an industry. "What has occurred here is a truly massive buildup of Japanese inventory that bears no relationship to U.S. market needs," Kasten said.

The ITC found the arguments compelling and recommended slapping punitive tariffs on Japanese bikes. On April 1, 1983, Ronald Reagan signed off on the ITC's recommendations. The existing 4.4 percent import duty on Japanese motorcycles with engine capacity at or greater than 700 cc was immediately boosted to a whopping 49.4 percent in 1983. The measure called for tariffs to return slowly to the original level: falling to 39.4 percent in 1984, 24.4 percent in 1985, 19.4 percent in 1986, 14.4 percent in 1987, and back to the original 4.4 percent in 1988. Some Japanese manufacturers found a way around the surcharge by assembling their bikes in American plants instead of shipping them whole. But the tariff hit hard in the beginner's bike category, which was supplied exclusively by Japanese producers, and some blamed it for an industry-wide slump that took hold in the mid-1980s.

REHABILITATING THE IMAGE OF AN IMPROVED PRODUCT

Even if the tariff made certain Japanese bikes more expensive, it didn't directly solve Harley-Davidson's problems. The company still had to convince the public of its renewed credibility—they needed some intense marketing. The company launched a nationwide promotion campaign in 1983 called the SuperRide program, in which, among other things, some six hundred dealerships invited people to see—and test—the new products for themselves. Over three weekends, 40,000 potential new customers accepted the invitation.

"Our relationship with cyclists is one of the differences between us and our Japanese competitors," said Vaughn Beals. Many Harley customers, he said, weren't just buying a motorcycle; they were buying "the Harley experience." Legions of these Hog owners delighted in wearing Harley-Davidson T-shirts and leather goods; some smaller percentage of them went to the length of having the company's name and logo permanently tattooed onto their skin. Perhaps in the absence of that special relationship, Harley could not have saved itself. About 75 percent of Harley riders made repeat purchases. Given that loyalty, Harley concentrated much of its new marketing efforts on customers who already owned its bikes.

In 1983 Harley-Davidson started the innovative Harley Owners' Groups—or HOGs. Each new buyer received a free one-year membership in a local riding group, a subscription to a bimonthly publication, *Hog Tales*, and a six-month subscription to *American Iron*, a magazine for motorcycle enthusiasts. Other privileges included admission to open houses and private receptions at motorcycle events, insurance, emergency roadside service, rental arrangements on vacation, even support groups for female riders. As the Harley-Davidson marketing vice president Kathleen Lawler-Demitros said: "It humanized the company and not only gives customers direct access to the Harley family, but also it allows them to feel like one of the family." The HOGs proved immensely popular. As sales rose from 27,000 in 1983 to 43,300 in 1987, HOGs registered 73,000 members.

REPAIRING A BROKEN-DOWN FINANCIAL VEHICLE

By the mid-1980s the quality programs and marketing efforts began to show up on the bottom line. After eking out a small gain of $973,000 in 1983, the firm reported profits of $2.6 million in 1984. The company was making and selling fewer bikes than before—in 1985 the 23,000 cycles produced represented just 3.86 percent of the total market—but it was making them better and faster. Customers noticed the difference. As Michael O'Farrell, president of the Oakland (California) Hell's Angels chapter, said in 1985: "It's amazing the difference. They don't beat you to death anymore, and your kidneys are still intact."

While it had made believers out of hard-core bikers, Harley-Davidson hadn't won over hard-core bankers. Since the buyout, the company had routinely drawn above and beyond the initial credit line from Citibank. Despite the company's apparent turnaround, the financiers didn't share the executives' sunny view of the future. In late 1984 Citibank let it be known that it would no longer grant advances above the agreed upon credit limit. On the eve of a great comeback, the company was suddenly on the brink of bankruptcy. In a series of browbeating meetings, Harley-Davidson coaxed Citibank to write off $10 million of the loan. Citibank correctly reasoned that such a move would make its client a more attractive risk to other bankers. With a reduced debt load, Harley-Davidson was then able to round up new lenders, led by Chicago-based Heller Financial, Inc., which replaced Citibank's loan on December 31, 1985.

Just months after Citibank threatened to send Harley-Davidson packing into Chapter XI, Harley-Davidson made the ultimate statement about its state of health. The rejuvenated firm turned to the public debt and equity markets in June 1986, raising $90 million by selling $20 million in common stock and $70 million in subordinated notes. The following year, when Harley-Davidson switched its listing from the American Stock Exchange to the New York Stock Exchange, the company's executives thundered down the canyons of lower Manhattan astride a gaggle of Hogs.

In 1987 *Forbes* noted, "Today Harley's prospects look much brighter. . . . It finished the year with sales of $295 million and profits of $4.3 million, almost double the year before." The company had indeed come a long way in six years. Between 1981 and 1987 annual revenues per employee doubled, productivity rose 50 percent, and the percentage of bikes that were ready-to-ride as they came off the assembly line rose to 99 percent. It wasn't just a matter of numbers. Newly confident in the changed company, the Harley-Davidson executives made good on their prior promise that government aid should be a temporary crutch, not a permanent prosthetic. On March 17, 1987, the company, acting on its own volition, formally asked the U.S. government to rescind the tariffs on Japanese motorcycles about a year before they were supposed to expire. The *New York Times* celebrated the move as "a masterful stroke of public relations."

To celebrate its renaissance, the company on June 18, 1988, threw itself a huge eighty-fifth birthday party in Milwaukee, complete with a concert by the Charlie Daniels Band. In the week before the bash, more than 40,000 Harley lovers rode to the Brew City on ten different routes from across the United States. Each rumbling phalanx was led by Harley-Davidson executive: Vaughn Beals, Richard Teerlink, and Willie G. rode at the head of massive biker gangs.

Harley-Davidson once again led the pack. As the economy improved, sales continued to rebound. By 1989 Harley-Davidson had regained its preeminence, cornering 59 percent of the market for heavy-

THE HARLEY-DAVIDSON OWNER

Over the course of the 1980s the profile of the Harley rider changed dramatically. While the bikes had always had their share of celebrity riders, the company traditionally drew its customers from the working and middle classes. But as prices continued to rise and the company staked out its position at the high end of the market in the 1970s and 1980s, its energetic marketing began to attract a different class of buyers. That year, 40 percent of Harley-Davidson owners were white-collar workers compared with 31 percent of all motorcycle owners. In 1985 the average Harley-Davidson rider had an annual income of $35,700, compared with the industry average of $22,500.

In the late 1980s this trend continued. Harley's revamped high-quality image and higher prices turned the bikes into yuppie status symbols. Groups of brokers, lawyers, and accountants got together on the weekend to burn rubber, creating the phenomenon known as Rolex Riders, or Rich Urban Bikers (RUBs). In 1989 the company held a promotional fashion night at Bloomingdale's. The typical buyer in 1990—a thirty-five-year-old male—had a household income of $45,000, far above the national average. By 1990, one-third of new Harley buyers were professionals or managers, and 60 percent were college graduates.

weight motorcycles, easily outracing second-place Honda, which held 15 percent. Sales of the expensive bikes—a fully loaded Hog runs well over $15,000—grew to 41,000 in 1989. Investors who had expressed faith in the company by purchasing its stock were rewarded handsomely. As earnings grew at a 57 percent annual clip between 1986 and 1990, the stock, which was first traded at $11 a share, split and doubled several times over. By June 1990 the stock rose tenfold from its initial offering price.

Even so, Harley-Davidson wasn't content with its comeback. For its executives regarded it as a work in progress, a living and evolving example of the importance of maintaining quality. In the early 1990s management teams from dozens of other firms flocked to Milwaukee, Wisconsin, and York, Pennsylvania, to examine first-hand the healthy vital signs of what ten years before had been a basket case. And the firm continued to employ the productivity triad to great effect. "We didn't realize it right away, but we found out through experience that all three of these practices are interdependent, so you must do all of them to achieve the best quality and productivity," said Vaughn Beals. In 1990 the company was turning over inventory twenty times a year and had cut inventory levels by 75 percent and space requirements by 25 percent since 1981.

Harley's new paradigm—continuous quality improvement—requires a great amount of time and attention early in the manufacturing process. It was devised to nip problems in the bud before they developed into crises. It recognized that the rapid pace of change in technology, economies, and lifestyles requires executives to maintain a constant state of vigilance. "Change is here to stay. It's never going to go away," said Richard Teerlink. "Get used to it."

George Roberts and Henry Kravis of KKR in 1988.

KOHLBERG KRAVIS ROBERTS & CO. AND THE LEVERAGED BUYOUT

For much of the twentieth century, corporate managers regarded debt warily. It was a necessary part of the balance sheet of nearly any healthy company. But the conventional wisdom was that too much debt was dangerous. In the late 1970s and 1980s, however, senior executives began to see debt in a different way. A company could be awash in debt and still prosper; senior executives could prosper, too.

Debt became "leverage"—a means to move or control a larger object, in this case a company. In the financial strategy popularized by the founding partners of Kohlberg Kravis Roberts & Co., whom the journalist George Anders aptly dubbed "Merchants of Debt," leverage made it possible to acquire large and successful companies with little money down.

KKR, as the firm is known, based its business on a high-stakes transaction called a "leveraged buyout." In a typical LBO, a group of upper level managers, investors, and financial specialists buys back stock from a corporation's shareholders, usually at a price substantially above market value. To raise the cash for this transaction, the buyers borrow from institutions or sell high-yield bonds against future revenue streams from the acquired company.

Jerome Kohlberg, Henry Kravis and George Roberts, three specialists in corporate finance, formed KKR in 1976 with $120,000. At first, KKR focused on small companies. Later, the partners made cold calls on likely take-over targets and hoped to entice senior executives into cooperating on a leveraged buyout (LBO). In its third year, the firm acquired three corporations and spent over $407 million. KKR became known for working their deals in cooperation with management. Eventually, KKR's success gave it the strength to choose its own targets and execute buy-outs independent of a target company's wishes. As the three financiers completed increasingly impressive deals, others followed the KKR formula and used LBOs to build empires overnight. The founding partners of KKR had introduced a significant innovation to corporate finance, a sort of mortgage mentality that allowed businesses to live with massive debt as easily as homeowners did. As the field became crowded and access to cash became more crucial, KKR found a powerful new partner in Michael R. Milken, of Drexel Burnham Lambert Inc. Milken's prowess in raising huge sums through the sale of high-yield "junk" bonds gave KKR an extraordinary instrument of debt to work with, one that offered immense financial power under the right circumstances.

The 1980s were very good to KKR. By 1989, it was the general partner in the ownership groups holding such well-known American companies as RJR Nabisco Inc., Safeway Stores Inc., Owens-Illinois Inc., and Duracell International Inc. Yet KKR ran its huge portfolio with a staff of only a few dozen people. While the firm, with various investors, owned controlling interests in these companies, it was not interested in running day-to-day operations. KKR was content to let those on the scene mind the store. It used an inclusive management-style, usually allowing (even insisting) that the top managers of its acquisitions participate in ownership. As a result, to use one of Jerome Kohlberg's favorite expressions, they were "all on the same side of the table."

KKR's partners became near-billionaires by applying their initial insight: that debt enforces a unique kind of discipline on managers and owners. The KKR philosophy of using high-level debt to enhance value has since been adopted by the managers of hundreds of publicly held firms.

WALL STREET ENGINEERS

Jerome Kohlberg arrived on Wall Street in 1955 after graduating from Harvard Law School. He joined the firm of Bear Stearns, then known as a trading powerhouse. With a contemplative manner more typical of a university professor than a Wall Street dealmaker, Kohlberg stayed away from the frenetic trading pits, instead choosing to work in the corporate finance department. He advised clients and arranged financing for corporations that were merging, expanding, refinancing, or selling stock.

Business was steady in the corporate finance department. In the 1960s, impelled by the riches of a long-running bull market, many companies sold shares to the public. Still others were acquired by larger firms that were developing into conglomerates. In either case, company managers were losing autonomy in the firms they worked so hard to manage. In response to this problem, Kohlberg began to sell owners of companies on a strategy whereby they would cash in on the equity they had created without ceding control. He reasoned that groups of investors led by top management could obtain control of their firms with a small amount of equity and a great deal of debt. This would concentrate ownership in the hands of a few investors, including management. Over the years, the new owners could pay down the debt through earnings from operations.

Kohlberg found a willing client in H. J. Stern, the septuagenarian proprietor of a gold-refining firm called Stern Metals. Stern wanted to realize a profit from the firm he had built up, without selling control. "I suggested that he could have his cake and eat it too," Kohlberg later said.

In the summer of 1965, Kohlberg organized an investor group, which bought the firm with borrowed funds, leaving the management of Stern Metals and a considerable amount of company stock to the Sterns. The financier rounded up about $1.5 million in cash from the Stern family, from Bear Stearns, and from individual investors. Kohlberg also borrowed $8 million from banks. The beauty of the deal to the family was that it had received millions for their company without relinquishing its leadership. The beauty of the deal to Kohlberg was that the very presence of the debt compelled all those interested in the deal, both the outside investors and the Stern family, to operate the company efficiently. And the fruit of the deal for all concerned was a high rate of return: within four years, the value of the shares had gone up by eight times.

As Kohlberg continued to pursue LBOs, he was assisted by two younger men, George Roberts and Henry Kravis, who were cousins. Roberts grew up in Houston, and Kravis was raised in Oklahoma, the son of an oil man with many connections on Wall Street. The cousins spent a great deal of time together as children, and both attended Claremont College in California. Roberts went on to law school, and Kravis received an MBA from Columbia University, where he was singularly unaffected by the campus turmoil of the 1960s. "I left it to my liberal friends to get arrested. I had my mind on business," he later said. Roberts was the first to start at Bear Stearns; after working there during summers, he was hired by Kohlberg full-time in 1969. But Roberts, more reserved than his extroverted cousin, didn't like the hustle of New York. When Kohlberg agreed to let him work out of Bear Stearns' San Francisco office in 1970, Roberts recommended that his cousin, Henry, become his replacement in New York. Within a decade, these three men would both transform the way companies thought about debt and reconfigure the relationship between ownership and management.

To drum up business, Kravis and Roberts analyzed thousands of company reports, made cold calls to managers, and went on extensive trips to meet chief executives. Positioning themselves as friends to management, they looked for companies or executives that would actually benefit from the type of takeover in which they specialized. In general, the two were met with skepticism, though the rebuffs did give them a chance to polish their pitch to a high gloss.

Most managers instinctively viewed deep debt of the type described by the young dealmakers from Bear Stearns as a danger that could run a company into total bankruptcy in a downturn. Kravis and Roberts assured executives that Bear Stearns did its homework and would not recommend an LBO for a company without strong qualifications for it. In essence, Kravis and Roberts asked managers to regard themselves as if they were homeowners. After all, people didn't flinch at borrowing up to 90 percent of the purchase price paid for their homes. In fact, the tax code encouraged mortgage debt by allowing people to deduct interest paid on home mortgages from taxable income. Likewise, the government permitted corporations to deduct interest paid on debt from their taxable income. The corporate tax break was intended to encourage companies to invest in new plants, machinery, equipment, and research: the usual uses for borrowed money. Kohlberg and his colleagues saw an additional benefit from this tax break. Highly leveraged companies could deduct the interest payments on their debt, reducing their taxes substantially. Still, the company, like the family with a very big mortgage, would have to change its way of life and make some hard sacrifices in order to find the cash every month to make its payment.

Not all of Bear Stearns' LBOs succeeded. In 1971, Kohlberg and his colleagues orchestrated the approximately $20-million buyout of Cobblers Inc. Unfortunately, the shoe manufacturer was not strong enough to withstand the pressure of doing business in the shadow of a high debt load. Soon after the deal, the company's president committed suicide, and Cobblers went bust. When such a leveraged company went bankrupt, the equity investors lost their entire investment, and creditors lined up to retrieve what they could.

Undaunted by the Cobblers debacle, Kohlberg's section at Bear Stearns continued to develop its specialty in reorganizing the financial structure, and so the power structure, of small or midsized companies. They had to hustle, ever on the lookout for LBO candidates and sources of capital.

The leveraged buyout required two different types of financing. The first was the loan, or loans, that made up the bulk of the purchase price. The trio of budding LBO artists found that insurance companies were looking for the high returns featured in an LBO, and made contacts at John Hancock, Met Life, and Prudential, among others. The second type of financing necessary in the LBO was the cash up-front or down-payment. Those who supplied it became not creditors, but owners. These equity participants typically included Bear Stearns itself, private and institutional investors, and the management of the targeted company. Increasingly, the men saw opportunity in pursuing pieces of conglomerates. In 1972 Kohlberg financed a deal—$4.4 million in Bear Stearns' cash and $33.5 million in debt—to acquire Vapor Corp., a division of Singer Co. that made valves, pumps, and components for mass transit systems. The managers of the division felt that they could make more progress with Vapor if it were independent of the big company, and so they became partners with Bear Stearns and bought their freedom from Singer.

The deals offered the lure of extraordinary returns, but the equity positions came with considerable suspense. "You have to think at least six to seven times your money over a five-to-ten-year period, because the good ones have to make up for the bad ones," Kohlberg said. Investors in the Vapor deal didn't cash out fully until 1978, when Brunswick Corp. paid $33 a share for the company. Since the original investors had paid just $2.80 per share, the return was 1,178 percent!

Patience was necessary, because management needed time to improve the companies' operations. So long as the company performed well, KKR was content to watch from the sidelines. "We're not operating people. We offer management an opportunity to buy in at the same price as everyone else, and that includes us and the institutions. . . . This way we're all on the same side of the table, and we're all working towards the same things," Kohlberg said.

KOHLBERG, KRAVIS, AND ROBERTS STRIKE OUT ON THEIR OWN

By the mid-seventies, Kohlberg and his team could see that the leveraged buyout really worked, in the short and long term. Despite the success of their deals, though, conflicts arose between Kohlberg and his colleagues at Bear Stearns. Kohlberg wanted to set up an internal unit to focus exclusively on leveraged buyouts. But the firm, suffering along with much of the securities industry in the tough years of the mid-1970s, was reluctant to fund and compensate buyout specialists. Kohlberg decided to leave, and he took Kravis and Roberts with him. *Forbes* noted: "As the business boomed, the three asked themselves a logical question: Who needs Bear Stearns?"

In 1976, they formed Kohlberg Kravis Roberts & Co. Kohlberg contributed $100,000 and the others put in $10,000 each. The total was not used to fund any deals, it was spent largely on travel for Kravis and Roberts, so that they could track down deals. This $120,000 would prove the basis of billions of dollars in acquisitions over the next twenty years.

From makeshift, modest offices on Fifth Avenue, Kohlberg Kravis Roberts sought to work closely with the management of candidate companies, never forcing deals on them. In the ways by which it would make money in each deal, the new firm was both an investment bank and a merchant bank. As an investment bank, it received a fee from the company that it advised. But then, KKR also advised the investor group that purchased the company; for that, it received 20 percent of any profits accrued on behalf of the group and a management fee of 1 percent to 1½ percent on the cash invested. Finally, as a merchant bank, KKR also made a cash investment and took shares of the companies it acquired through a buyout. "We had no idea whether it was going to work or not," Kravis later told a magazine.

During their first year, many companies heard the KKR pitch, but very few considered the LBO a prudent idea. The partners continued to analyze prospects. At first, they looked almost exclusively at small conglomerates or manufacturing companies in unregulated industries, with stable cash flows and low debt-loads. Though buyouts were fundamentally bold, they had to be structured conservatively. As Kohlberg told Forbes in 1978, "We look at a company and ask ourselves in our financing, 'What happens if the earnings go flat; or if they drop back to where they were three years before we bought the company? Is the financing substantial enough to hold the company over a bad period?' If not, then the financing is wrong."

The primary measure of an attractive company became cash flow, or the amount of money the business generated above and beyond its operating expenses, since this would dictate the amount of debt the firm could realistically service.

KKR found its first deal in California, through connections made there by George Roberts. The company was A.J. Industries, a conglomerate that hovered on the edge of the defense and aeronautical industries, making metal fuel tanks and brake drums. Noting that its stock had fallen sharply in recent years, KKR approached the company's board and offered to acquire the firm for $5 a share in April 1977, or $26 million, including just $1.7 million in equity. It was a good deal: when the investor group cashed out eight years later, its capital had increased at a rate of 58 percent per year.

LBOs required intensive due diligence, foresight and patience. "When you go into a deal there's a lot of time and monitoring, a lot of work, creativity, and heartbreak," Kohlberg said. The KKR partners spent long hours courting executives, going over financial tables, and developing a network of support: friends in the right places. Kravis and Roberts would often do the preliminary legwork, while Kohlberg would preside as a sort of cool-headed elder statesman when discussions entered a more serious stage.

The funds that fueled the equity positions in early deals came largely from individual investors, and were raised as needed. By 1978, with three successful buyouts to point to, KKR raised a fund organized as a limited partnership, in which KKR was the general partner and made the investment decisions. The 1978 fund totaled $30 million.

In the same year, the partners identified a Florida conglomerate called Houdaille Industries as a potential acquisition target. It was very big fish for KKR to go after: one of the nation's five hundred largest companies and a New York Stock Exchange-listed firm. They contacted the chief executive officer, Gerald Saltarelli, a very conservative businessman who was reluctant to consider a buyout that would place so much debt on his company.

Houdaille was a perfect example of a company that was worth more apart than together. Working with senior managers at Houdaille, KKR responded to Saltarelli's conservatism by planning a way to pay the buyout debt quickly, just by divesting subsidiaries. On that basis, KKR's investor group, which included the senior managers, was able to make an attractive offer to the board of directors, and the parties agreed on a price of $355 million. "When we announced the transaction was going to be done, no one on Wall Street believed we could get the financing put together," Kravis said in 1983.

KKR raised $48.1 million in equity and $306.5 million in debt, much of it in the form of loans from Continental Illinois Bank and insurance companies like Prudential and Teachers. In exchange, KKR and its investment group received 25 percent of Houdaille's total common shares for $46 million, while management and Houdaille employees received 8 percent of them, worth $2.1 million. The size of the deal and its friendly acceptance on all sides attracted attention; KKR would never again be an obscure "boutique" firm. The Houdaille deal showed that Kohlberg's strategy could work on a large scale; even better for KKR, the truly stratospheric deals still lay ahead.

KKR ENLISTS PUBLIC PENSION PLANS TO RAISE LARGER LBO FUNDS

KKR needed a larger pool of capital, because the initial practice of raising funds from individuals was no longer adequate. The Houdaille deal, for example, required fifteen times more equity than KKR needed for A. J. Industries. Repositories of cash such as insurance companies had strict requirements on investment, which hindered KKR's growth. Fortunately, the partners found a new set of allies. In San Francisco, George Roberts had made the acquaintance of Roger Meier, chairman of the Oregon Investment Council, which supervised the Oregon Public Employees Retirement System (OPERS). OPERS, like other public pension funds, managed the money the state government had set aside for the retirement pensions of its employees. Though managed conservatively, public pension funds had been allowed to invest more and more of their funds in somewhat riskier stocks than previously.

KKR first tapped into this large pool of capital in 1981. Jerry Kohlberg, who had clerked for a judge in Portland, Oregon, learned about Fred Meyer, a chain of 120 grocery stores based in Portland. With the death of the founder, the company had lost its identity and its ownership was falling into disarray, making it ripe for a hostile takeover. Instead, Kohlberg himself led KKR's effort to buy it out.

The shares traded at $18.50, but KKR agreed to a $55 a share price, or $420 million. Of the purchase price of $420 million, OPERS came up with $178 million in a loan to the company. KKR's solid management appealed to pension-fund managers, who were more than willing to be silent partners in an investment group. After this deal, pension managers from Montana, Wisconsin, Washington, and other states also entrusted small portions of their employees' nest eggs to KKR. "The big state funds, that's really where the money in this country is," George Roberts said. "And it's certainly where the money in this country in the future is going to be."

Pension managers were lured not only by the professional charm of Kohlberg, Kravis, and Roberts, but by the promise of substantial returns. By 1983, KKR claimed an average annual return of 62.7 percent on its investments. In comparison, stock market investments at the time averaged about a 9 percent return per year, and safe government bonds returned about 12 percent. In 1982, with eager state pension funds standing in line, KKR raised a $316-million fund, some ten times the size of the 1978 fund.

By the early eighties, KKR had almost single-handedly turned the leveraged buyout from a small-time operation into a potent industry. Others sought to imitate KKR's approach—and its success. The number of leveraged buyouts rose from 75, worth $1.3 billion, in 1979 to 175, worth $16.6 billion, in 1983. The acknowledged master in the field, however, was KKR. In 1984 it completed its first $1 billion deal: the purchase of Wometco Enterprises, a broadcasting and cable company.

While the amounts of money involved grew rapidly, KKR itself grew more slowly. The firm moved its offices to a prestigious address, 9 West Fifty-Seventh Street, a graceful office building just off Fifth Avenue, around the corner from Tiffany & Co. The firm presented itself well: the offices occupied a lavishly appointed suite on a high floor with a stunning view of Central Park, and the walls were decorated with original art. Kohlberg Kravis Roberts signed a small number of partners, but, remarkably, it did not require a large staff. In the KKR formula, operating decisions were best left with the managers of the respective companies.

Those managers had meaningful incentives to do a good job for the partnership. In a typical deal, top executives would invest money with KKR's investor group and receive a substantial equity stake. LBOs represented a rare opportunity for a senior executive. CEOs at major public companies might own sizable blocks of stock, but did not generally have a controlling interest. The prevailing mentality on the issue of ownership and governance stemmed in part from the differentiation between ownership and management first pioneered by John D. Rockefeller, and the democratization of stockholding, championed by Charles Merrill. Under the KKR system, the high-ranking executive tied his or her own financial future to the success of the company by paying off debt and increasing shareholder value. The KKR buyout also represented a reconstruction of a company's ownership and governance, such that a senior executive was part of the group that actually owned the controlling interest in the company. KKR made the person occupying the executive suite his or her own landlord, responsible for making the debt payments on the mortgage and making sure the property remained valuable.

Since the investor group's equity stake stood to be wiped out entirely if the company went bust, KKR acted quickly when their highly leveraged companies faltered. In 1981, KKR used an LBO to spin Lily-Tulip Inc., a paper-cup maker, out of Owens-Illinois. When the existing management fared poorly through 1983, KKR pushed out the management and brought in Albert Dunlap, a former executive at Manville Corp. An expert at corporate turnarounds, Dunlap moved quickly to sell off the firm's real estate assets, slashed costs across the board, and boosted operating profit by 91 percent in 1983 and 31 percent in 1984.

JUNK BONDS ALLOW FOR LARGER AND FASTER DEALS

As the number and magnitude of LBOs escalated, a new financial instrument arrived on the financial scene—"junk bonds." These were low-rated or unrated bonds that offered high interest rates to entice investors. The leading underwriter of junk bonds was Drexel Burnham Lambert Inc. Their champion and mastermind was a Drexel executive, Michael Milken.

In the late seventies, when the equity markets were low, Milken showed companies how to issue debt in the public markets via junk bonds. He created an entirely new industry, as issuance of junk bonds rose from $5 billion in 1981 to $40 billion in 1986. Milken's reputation was made in 1984, when he was able to raise, almost overnight, $1.5 billion for T. Boone Pickens' attempt at a hostile takeover of Gulf.

As a means of raising enormous quantities of cash through debt, junk bonds were tailor-made for buyouts. The high interest payment could be written off against taxes, and selling them in large chunks let dealmakers operate without relying totally on banks. By the mid-eighties, KKR was targeting enormous corporations; it needed to tap that reservoir of cash for which Michael Milken seemed to control the faucet. By issuing junk bonds, in addition to borrowing from banks, KKR could do bigger deals. "Lots of firms can do smaller deals, but over $1 billion, we don't have any competition," George Roberts said in 1985, as more and more takeover specialists were entering the field.

Targeting KKR's market, major investment banks like First Boston, Prudential Bache, Merrill Lynch, Morgan Stanley, and American Express' Shearson Lehman Brothers formed leveraged buyout units. The rules of the game began to change. Financiers, sighting a target, launched hostile takeover bids. Rather than include management as a partner in the LBO, as KKR had generally done, buyers in hostile takeovers dislodged the existing management. Sometimes boards and managers interested in keeping their jobs would ask KKR to step into the negotiations as a "white knight," to forge a deal that would keep existing management in place.

KKR's acquisition of Safeway in August 1986 embodied many of the emerging principles in the LBO arena. The grocery chain had been assembled by Charles Merrill in the 1920s and 1930s and now was run by his grandson, Peter Magowan, who owned a small sliver of stock and ran the business rather loosely. KKR became involved after an investor group, the Haft family, started acquiring shares in preparation for a takeover bid. In conjunction with Safeway's management, KKR assembled a $4.2 billion bid that included about $2 billion in junk bonds and $130 million in equity. Afterward, Magowan began behaving like an entirely different CEO. With the aid of a consultant brought in by KKR, he reduced drastically the staff at the corporate headquarters. When Safeway realized that a small percentage of the outlets were accounting for large chunk of the profits, it began to sell off the less profitable units. These divestitures raised $2.4 billion, and enabled the company to pay off debt rapidly. Safeway's value had appreciated eightfold by the time it went public in April 1990.

COMPETITION FOR DEALS LEADS TO A NEAR DISASTER

By 1987, according to Bryan Burrough and John Helyar, the authors of *Barbarians at the Gate*, "If it were ranked as an industrial company, the businesses Kohlberg Kravis controlled, from Duracell batteries to Safeway supermarkets, would place it among the top ten U.S. corporations."

In the mid-eighties, the firm went through a major change. Jerry Kohlberg fell ill and, after a major operation, needed over a year to recuperate. On his return, he was dismayed to see the way that KKR was quietly abandoning the precepts on which it had been founded. For example, the firm's April, 1986 buyout of Beatrice Co. was not a friendly partnership with management; it was a forced takeover. In 1987, Kohlberg left the firm, with $300 million and options to participate in future investment groups. He later started another acquisitions firm.

As the 1980s wore on, more and more buyout funds entered the field. And the increased competition artificially boosted the cost of doing deals. "As prices rose and people became increasingly eager to do deals, standards were lowered steadily," *Forbes* noted in 1989. LBO activity rose from $1.3 billion in 1979 to $77 billion in 1988. "Today, the money is out looking for the deals, rather than the other way around," *Forbes* reported in late 1988.

This competition and escalation almost resulted in KKR's undoing. RJR Nabisco, the massive tobacco and consumer products company, with brands ranging from Camel cigarettes to Oreo cookies, was put into play in 1988, when the flamboyant CEO F. Ross Johnson started an LBO bid at $75 per share. KKR scrambled to join the bidding with a $90 per share offer. The RJR Nabisco deal assumed almost epic proportions, as a host of would-be deal-makers, including management, other veteran buyout firms, and Wall Street companies seeking to make a name for themselves, entered the fray, pushing the price to higher and higher. KKR ultimately won, offering a staggering $109 a share for a company that had been trading at a mere $60 only months before.

The $30 billion deal was the largest LBO ever done. The financing included more than $12 billion debt in bank- and short-term debt and $11 billion in junk bonds, and an amazing $1.5 billion in equity—more equity than in any of KKR's previous deals. KKR received nearly $75 million in fees for its participation in the deal. To many observers, however, the RJR Nabisco deal represented speculative hysteria.

In 1989 the junk-bond market crashed, which encouraged the flow of money into other bonds or equities, and led to a series of defaults on major junk-bond issues. In 1989, Milken pleaded guilty to six felony counts for violations of securities law. He had made in excess of $100 million per year from 1984 to 1986, and in 1987 he'd earned $700 million, dealing in "junk." Drexel Burnham Lambert went bankrupt in February 1990.

KKR was nursing RJR Nabisco, and its monumental debt, through crises within the company and without. Profits for the cigarette business were handcuffed by a tobacco price war. Meanwhile, the bubble that burst in the junk-bond market made RJR bondholders fearful of default. True to form, KKR and its investor group had at least as much to lose as anyone else, and stood to get wiped out in the case of a Chapter 11 filing on a buyout the size of RJR. In order to stave off any such default on RJR Nabisco's bonds, KKR and its investment partners ultimately agreed to inject an additional $1.7 billion in new cash into the company—even more than it had initially invested. In 1991, it brought the company public, selling shares on the New York Stock Exchange, in order to reduce its debt.

ADJUSTING TO THE NEW
ECONOMIC REALITIES OF THE 1990S

Between 1980 and 1989, attitudes in American business across the board had been changed by 2,385 leveraged buyouts worth a total of $245 billion. Kohlberg Kravis Roberts had chalked up twenty-eight LBO transactions worth over $63 billion. These deals helped revolutionize corporate finance, create new incentives for efficient management, and inspire risk-taking on a grand scale.

However, the RJR Nabisco deal with all its fiscal excess marked the end of an excessive era, for KKR at least. The company, which had started in the seventies in partnerships with the management of the

THE JUNK DEALER

Michael Milken became intrigued with the hidden strength of the so-called "junk-bond" when he was a graduate student at the Wharton School of the University of Pennsylvania in the late sixties. His MBA thesis argued that debt should be managed within a corporation not merely as a source of capital, but as a hedge against current market conditions. At the right time in a market, junk bonds outperformed higher rated securities, even though they defaulted more often, on average. After graduation, Milken aggressively put his theory into practice. As *Forbes* put it in 1992, "With penetrating insights, 15-hour workdays, and almost unbelievable powers of concentration, he built a medium-size brokerage firm—which became Drexel Burnham Lambert—into the terror of Wall Street."

He did this by developing a market for a high-yield, low-rated bonds. Others called them junk, but not Milken. "It grates me to call them that," he told *Forbes*. "They are a debt instrument that trades more on the underlying credit risk of the company or the industry than on movements in the interest rates. They have the legal characteristics of debt, but if things go bad, you're generally the first creditor to take on the rights of an equity owner." He was so successful at finding customers, that he then turned his attention to finding more bonds to sell, underwriting junk bond issues for large companies and small ones. Encroaching on the role of banks as sources of debt-financing, junk bonds became the instrument most associated with LBOs and more notoriously, with hostile take-overs.

When Milken started work in 1970, junk-bonds were a $6 billion market; by the time he left, after pleading guilty to violations of the securities laws, in 1989, they were a $210 billion market, and they had effectively restructured American finance. But according to Milken's own theory, junk-bonds made for good investments only some of the time, under certain prevailing conditions—not all of the time. In the late 1980s he advised his clients to substitute equity for debt but few paid attention.

The junk-bond market continued to overheat and was oversubscribed until 1988, when it was rocked by a handful of unsupported defaults. At the same time,

(*continued*)

(*continued*)

Drexel's credibility was breeched both by its failure to rescue a defaulting issue it had underwritten, and by charges filed by the Securities Exchange Commission. Other branches of government also closed in on the junk-bond trade. Prosecutors won convictions or guilty pleas in cases against Milken and other traders. And finally, Congress stepped in too. Many representatives had nervously disapproved of the take-over mania, financed in large part by junk-bonds, that swept through corporate America in the late eighties. In 1989, Congress passed the Financial Institutions Reform Recovery and Enforcement Act (FIRREA), forcing savings banks to divest themselves of all but a fraction of their junk-bond holdings. With that, the market collapsed. Savings & Loan institutions took the brunt, and many of them folded.

Junk-bonds didn't go away in the aftermath of the fall. They rebounded eventually and have remained both a viable investment and a respectable form of financing. As Milken said, speaking of his start in the field in the early seventies, "investing in the debt of American business was the best investment, not the worst."

companies it bought out, became more independent and more aggressive when opportunities thinned in the eighties. In the early nineties, it was more active as a stockseller, bringing its companies public, than as a buyout specialist. Even so, the climate was changing. "The problem is, there aren't that many good opportunities out there," George Roberts said in 1990.

Having seen what KKR did through the power of debt, corporate managers began to rethink financial structure, in both its offensive and defensive aspects. Financial officers began to leverage their companies before they were taken over. They increased debt loads to raise capital and tap off the cash flow that made a company attractive to a raider. Executive officers at conglomerates reevaluated themselves and their separate divisions, acting to carve out the fat before an unwelcome raider could come in and do the same thing. The financial world had internalized much of KKR's message, that well-managed debt, however large, did not compromise ownership.

Bill Gates at a Windows presentation in 1992.

WILLIAM GATES AND THE DOMINANCE OF MICROSOFT

On August 23, 1995, an unprecedented marketing and media frenzy reached its peak throughout the world. The level of publicity and excitement had rarely been seen before, but it was not for a new movie or even a new car. It was for a piece of software. By midnight, customers had already queued up outside computer stores to be among the first to purchase Windows 95, an upgraded operating system for IBM and IBM-compatible personal computers. Microsoft Corporation, the company behind Windows 95, spared no expense in exciting the demand for its new product. It hired the Rolling Stones for an advertising campaign, and distributed an entire issue of the London *Times*, which contained a special promotional insert. Over 500 reporters flocked to Microsoft's headquarters outside Seattle to cover the official launch, with the comedian Jay Leno presiding.

The introduction of Windows 95 marked an apotheosis of sorts for Bill Gates, Microsoft's cofounder and guiding spirit. His role in the personal computer revolution had given him a net worth estimated in the summer of 1996 at $18 billion, and had turned him into an icon of technoculture. Few American business-men have ever occupied such a niche in the popular imagination. Just as John D. Rockefeller created order from chaos in the most important new industry of the late nineteenth century, Gates and his company did the same in the most crucial industry of the late twentieth century: computers. And, like Rockefeller, Gates found ways to force the rest of the industry to follow his lead. "Gates reminds me of the nineteenth-century industrial barons who by force of will and business genius built monopolies," said the industry analyst Stewart Alsop.

Though an innovative and forward-thinking entrepreneur, Bill Gates didn't invent crucial technology. Rather, he shrewdly adapted and improved products first made by others. He recognized the coming of the personal computer (PC), long before others did, and deduced that operating systems and applications (software) would be at least as important to the PC business as the nuts-and-bolts equipment (hardware). Part of the reason for Microsoft's dominance in the field lies precisely in Gates's ability to anticipate developments in computer technology and to judge when the public will be ready for them. Another part of Microsoft's success lies in Gates's unwavering confidence in his own ideas. Through the force of his personality, as much as through the popularity of his products, Bill Gates has imposed his own order on the burgeoning computer industry.

MAKING AN EARLY MARK IN A YOUNG INDUSTRY

William Henry Gates III was born in 1955, the second of three children in a socially prominent family in Seattle, Washington. His father was a lawyer with a well-connected firm in the city, and his mother was a teacher, active in charity work. Bill was an intelligent boy, but he was overly energetic and prone to getting into trouble at school. When he was eleven, his parents decided to make a change and sent him to the Lakeside School, a prestigious all-boys prep school.

It was at Lakeside in 1968 that Gates was first introduced to the world of the computer, in the form of a teletype machine connected by telephone to a time-share computer. The machine, called an ASR-33, was rudimentary. Essentially it was a typewriter into which the students could plug commands that were sent to the computer; the responses came back typed onto the roll of paper on the teletype. The process was cumbersome, but it changed Gates's life. He quickly mastered BASIC, the computer programming language, and, along with a few other self-taught hackers at Lakeside, he spent countless hours writing programs, playing games, and generally learning his way around the computer. "He was a nerd before the term was invented," as one of his teachers described Gates at the time.

In the late 1960s, computers were developing so rapidly that schoolboys could quickly gain more expertise than trained engineers. Bill Gates, his classmate Paul Allen, and a group of friends soon acquired reputations as programming experts among local teachers and even some University of Washington professors. So in 1971, when Information Sciences, Inc., a Seattle-based computer company, wanted to develop a program for payroll services, it turned to the group of Lakeside students. In exchange for their work, they received free computer time.

While still in high school, Gates and Allen were recruited by TRW to work on a new computerized monitoring system at a power plant along the Oregon border. And it was here that Gates first exhibited the competitive and obsessive traits that would characterize his own style and, later, that of Microsoft. "We had contests to see who could stay in the building, like, three days straight, four days straight. . . . We were just hardcore, writing code," he said.

After graduating from Lakeside, Gates enrolled at Harvard, where he spent a lot of his free time playing poker and hacking in the Aiken Computation Laboratory than he did attending classes. Still, Gates led a typical undergraduate existence, until he received a phone call from an excited Paul Allen in December 1974. Allen, two years older than Bill Gates, had dropped out of the University of Washington to pursue his interest in computers full time. He moved to Cambridge to work for Honeywell, and he had just seen the January 1975 issue of *Popular Electronics*. The cover featured a new minicomputer called the Altair 8800, made by a New Mexico company called MITS. The $400 Altair, which was named after a fictional planet on the TV series *Star Trek*, had rows of toggle switches and flashing lights but no screen or keyboard; users had to find a way to connect it to a teletype or give it commands in code, using the toggle switches. But as a microcomputer that was readily available to the public, the Altair represented an important early effort to put the powerful Intel microprocessor into the hands of individuals, and it generated giddy excitement among computer enthusiasts.

SELLING PROMISES AND DELIVERING

Computer languages serve as a bridge connecting plain English to a computer's unwieldy set of coding. Through a computer language, processors are trained to make desired responses to commands. The first operating languages were developed by the U.S. Navy during World War II. Others that became prominent after the war were FORTRAN, which was effective in mathematical problems, COBOL (used in business), ALGOL, and BASIC. BASIC, developed at Dartmouth College, and a favorite of hobbyists, stood for Beginners' All-purpose Symbolic Instruction Code. Up to 1974 all computer languages in existence had been written for mainframes. Microcomputers, the forerunners of personal computers, were "born" without a computer language.

After reading the *Popular Electronics* article, Allen and Gates quickly reached a conclusion: The Altair couldn't be a practical success without an operating language. Since nobody had ever written one for a micro-computer, the two believed they were precisely the ones to do so. Allen and Gates were masters with BASIC and had experimented with it exten-sively. They started immediately to tailor BASIC for the Altair 8800. In an act of youthful audacity, Allen wrote Ed Roberts, the Albuquerque-based engineer who invented the Altair, and announced that he and his partner had already developed BASIC for the machine. (Technically speaking, that was untrue.) Roberts told them to put their program to-gether and bring it to New Mexico.

Gates and Allen didn't have an Altair, but they had developed a way to make another type of computer simulate the Altair. Shifting into their compulsive programming mode, they managed to devise a workable form of BASIC in eight weeks. In a marathon cram session, Gates and Allen scribbled lines of code on pads, pausing only occasionally to eat, nap, and, in Gates's case, go to class. In February 1975 a tense Paul Allen flew to New Mexico, never having tested the program on an actual Altair and not knowing for sure if it would work. Arriving at the headquarters of Roberts's company, MITS, he saw an Altair for the first time. Allen nervously entered the language program onto the machine as Roberts watched; most of it was on a paper tape, and some crucial last-minute commands were entered by hand. After absorbing the new instructions, the Altair responded: the teletype in front of Allen asked him a question about the specifications. He answered, and then it typed, "Ready." With that word, a new software industry was launched.

Roberts decided on the spot to offer the new BASIC with his com-puters. Allen stayed in Albuquerque to continue work on the language while Gates stayed at Harvard, though he would drop out the following year. In the summer of 1975 they founded Micro-Soft (the hyphen was later eliminated). Gates insisted that he have the greater share of a 60-

40 split, since he had performed a greater share of the early BASIC development work. The new-born firm quickly inked an agreement with MITS, under which MITS would pay royalties (about $30 a copy) in exchange for licensing rights to the BASIC program, an arrangement that paid $16,000 in royalties in its first year. Some of the money was spent on the company's first marketing effort, an advertisement in a technical journal that read: "Microsoft: What's a Microprocessor without It?"

Gates and Allen were not typical entrepreneurs. They had no business plan, no venture capital, no bankers or Small Business Administration loans. Not yet twenty-one years old, Gates couldn't even rent a car. But the young duo had everything necessary for entry into the porous computer industry of the time: They had a product, programming expertise, and, most importantly, a vision of greater possibilities. In January 1977, Gates moved to Albuquerque to be close to MITS. Far away from the east coast corporate centers of IBM and Xerox and from the renowned research laboratories in Berkeley or back in Cambridge, Gates and Allen lived in seedy motels and holed up in dusty offices, developing versions of FORTRAN and COBOL to run on the Altair. As Paul Allen recalled: "We would just work until we dropped."

The fast pace of work at Microsoft mirrored the rapid changes in the marketplace. The Altair was doomed to extinction, as larger companies invested heavily to produce more efficient and powerful minicomputers. Gates and Allen knew what was happening. To Gates, however, it made no difference whether a small company or a large one was manufacturing computers: Each machine would need a set of languages, or an operating system that acts as the "brain" of the computer. And after that, it would need programs to perform specialized tasks. "I thought we should do only software," Gates said in 1994. "When you have the microprocessor doubling in power every two years, in a sense you can think of computer power as almost free. So you ask, Why be in the business of making something that's almost free? What is the scarce resource? What is it that limits being able to get value out of that infinite computing power? Software."

Of course, computer power is not given away free. But, with technological innovation and growing competition, the cost of computer infrastructure fell drastically. While personal computer prices have remained
about the same for years, their power has increased exponentially. Computers with more power can do more—especially if they have more
software. From the very beginning of the PC age, Bill Gates was ready
with that software.

When Gates was growing up, computer languages, like BASIC, were
in the public domain. Hackers confiscated anything they found in the
way of software; it was part of the spirit of the scattered computer community of the sixties. Those easy going times ended, though, when Bill
Gates went into the software business. He railed in the press against
thieves who copied Microsoft's computer languages without handing over
the due royalties. He also spent a lot of time thinking about how to
squelch the practice of copying software, and it certainly influenced his
predilection to sell his software already installed in computers and thus,
as far as he was concerned, paid for.

In August 1977, the Tandy Corporation introduced the TRS-80
computer. With a video display terminal and a keyboard included, the
$599 machine resembled later PCs, and it would prove more popular
that any other machine of the late seventies. In one of its first important
deals, Microsoft licensed Tandy to install its BASIC computer language
in the TRS-80. Thanks in large part to the TRS-80, Microsoft's sales
rose to $1.36 million in 1978.

The company was on the move—literally and figuratively. With
the twenty-two-year-old Gates wanting to be closer to his parents, Microsoft moved back home. Washington State was a long way from the
centers of computer development in northern California and Massachusetts, but location didn't matter. The most important tools needed for
software development were brains and computers. Microsoft moved to a
suite of offices in the Old National Bank building in Bellevue, just
outside Seattle. Gates had yet to develop most of the management skills
that would make him one of America's most-respected CEOs by the

early nineties. As the head of the company, he worked his 130 employees hard—never harder than he drove himself—and the new offices took on the same frenzied pace as the ones back in Albuquerque.

International Business Machines Corporation ("Big Blue") had made a name for itself by producing adding machines for businesses and by creating massive mainframe computers for scientific and industrial concerns. Eager to stake its claim on the burgeoning desktop computer market, IBM in mid-1980 decided to produce its own model. IBM relied on existing components, including Intel microprocessors. But the new machine needed an operating system, the umbrella program that allows the computer to function. Uncertain how to proceed with such a small-scale computer, IBM began searching for an outside firm with experience in writing programs for personal computers. Most importantly, it needed a company that could deliver an operating system reliably and on time.

Just as TRW had once tapped high school graduates and Tandy had relied on a couple of college dropouts, IBM sought out a fledgling company operated by the same two wunderkinds. It was curious that IBM, an institution with nearly $30 billion in revenues, would seek out a $4-million company to provide the key component for the product that would help make its future. However, the difference between the two firms wasn't just a matter of size. IBM's blue-suited, middle-aged executives found themselves face to face with a group of computer jocks, led by an absurdly young hacker. Gates was not cut from the usual executive pinstripe cloth. He favored chinos and loose-collared shirts and would often show up to meetings without having showered or washed his hair.

Despite vast lifestyle differences, the strange bedfellows inked an agreement in 1980. Microsoft would develop an operating system for IBM's PC, and IBM would pay Microsoft a royalty for each unit sold, without assuming any ownership rights in the operating system. In a development that nobody would have predicted, the arrangement ultimately led to a new order in the computer world. Within a decade, Microsoft would take possession of the dominant position once occupied by IBM.

At the time, however, there was no indication of such great portent. After Gates coolly signed the agreement, he turned to his executive vice president, Steve Ballmer, and nonchalantly said: "Well, Steve, now we can get to work." Gates generally thrived under the pressure of deadlines. But this contract called for Microsoft to deliver a functioning operating system within three months. The company, which had been launched on a premature promise to MITS for the delivery of a version of BASIC for the Altair, had blithely guaranteed IBM the prompt delivery of a product that it had yet to design.

Fortunately, a company called Seattle Computer Products, located just twenty minutes away from Microsoft's headquarters, had already developed an operating system for computers running on the Intel 8086 chip. Seattle Computer considered its system an experiment: the "Quick and Dirty Operating System." Gates knew that Q-DOS, more officially called 86-DOS, could be tailored to run IBM's new machine. It would be a terrific shortcut. After approaching Seattle Computer, Paul Allen negotiated a deal under which Microsoft paid the company $25,000 to license the system to undisclosed end users. (Microsoft was not allowed to divulge to anyone that it was connected with the IBM project.) The following year, two weeks before IBM introduced the PC, Microsoft bought all intellectual and physical rights to 86-DOS from Seattle Computer for $50,000. (The bargain was too good to be true: Seattle Computer later sued Microsoft for further compensation and received almost $1 million in an out-of-court settlement.)

Although it was conceived in secret, the IBM-PC received a lavish public introduction on August 12, 1981, at New York's Waldorf-Astoria Hotel. It was an immediate commercial and technological success. In the first year, over 200,000 people ponied up $1,265 to buy the standard IBM-PC with cassette unit, or $2,235 for the version with a disk drive. And since each machine ran on the MS-DOS operating system, Microsoft had received a $200,000 payment from IBM, in lieu of royalties.

The clause of the IBM licensing agreement that left ownership of MS-DOS in Microsoft's hands proved crucial. Since IBM chose to use parts from other manufacturers rather than design its own hardware, its PC was easily replicated by upstart firms. Just as the TRS-80 superseded the Altair as the acknowledged market leader, and the IBM-PC bypassed the TRS-80, lower-priced IBM-PC clones sapped the market share from IBM. The early leader among the clone makers was Compaq Computer Corporation, which racked up $100 million in sales in 1983, the year it introduced its personal computer. While the clones hurt IBM, they proved a boon to Microsoft. The clones were supposed to be "compatible" with IBM-PCs, and MS-DOS could go a long way toward making them that way.

For once, Gates had misread the future of his business. He had always assumed that Microsoft would stay exclusively in computer languages and applications (or specialized) software, rather than operating systems. But after the launch of the IBM-PC, clone-makers from around the world called to negotiate the right to install MS-DOS in their machines. Gates responded immediately, first, by creating a worldwide sales force to help make sure that MS-DOS became the international standard. (Since the early eighties, countries outside the United States and Canada have accounted for two-thirds of Microsoft sales.) Second, he priced MS-DOS cheaply for installation as original equipment. And third, in an environment in which products became obsolete virtually the minute they were introduced, Gates didn't pause to enjoy the success of the first version of MS-DOS. By the time the IBM-PC was announced, Microsoft was already working on a second version. Consequently, Microsoft found itself with a whole market almost to itself. As the Gates program became the standard, his company consistently provided the operating systems for 80 percent of the PCs sold each year. The company's sales exploded, rising from $16 million in 1981 to $97 million in 1984.

Throughout the spectacular growth of the early 1980s, Gates and Allen micromanaged Microsoft. "In the beginning, our management style was pretty loose, and Paul and I took part in every decision," Gates recalled in 1995. When Paul Allen left the company after a diagnosis of Hodgkin's disease in 1983, Gates was forced to shoulder even more responsibility. Because he had difficulty delegating authority, he continued to set Microsoft's rigorous pace, often working at his desk from 9:30 a.m. to midnight, fueled by delivered pizza and caffeinated drinks. As Gates wrote in an early memo quoted by his biographers Stephen Manes and Paul Andrews: "Microsoft expects a level of dedication from its employees higher than most companies. Therefore, if some deadline or discussion or interesting piece of work causes you to work extra time some week it just goes with the job."

The complaint was often heard at Microsoft that Gates simply didn't hire enough people to handle the workload. It was as if he thrived on the heroic challenge of doing too much in too little time. Such commitment was required, because the software product cycles kept spinning faster. And while Microsoft was making money, there was never any guarantee that its growth would continue. Exponential growth defied standard planning techniques, and technological shifts blurred reliable forecasts.

By the mid-1980s desktop machines could perform the same functions fast as, and faster than, the computers that had occupied entire rooms decades earlier. The next generation of computers could fit on a person's lap. Gates had watched dozens of start-up companies fall by the wayside after they failed to follow up on a successful breakthrough product. And executives who couldn't maintain a company's spectacular growth were often thrown overboard. An early Gates competitor—and acquaintance—was Steve Jobs, who built Apple into a major computer company. Apple had developed its own hardware and operating systems, which were generally regarded as easier to use than Microsoft's. But since Apple didn't allow its technology to be licensed by clone-makers, it had difficulty gaining a wider audience. Jobs was forced out of his perch in 1985 after the company lost ground to IBM-compatible PCs running on Microsoft's operating system.

Bill Gates wasn't going to be deposed. He had received 53 percent of the stock in Microsoft when it incorporated in 1981, and had matured with the company. In 1986, when Microsoft turned ten, it had 1,500 employees and sales of almost $200 million. Gates, thirty years old, liked to drive fast cars, but didn't care much for the trappings of wealth otherwise, eating fast food for dinner and traveling coach class on airplanes. Touted at the time as the "world's richest bachelor," Gates spent his life at Microsoft.

"THE REVOLUTION IS HERE AND IT IS SOFT"

In the mid-eighties Microsoft continued to grow. Gates took the advice of veterans in corporate organization and broke the company into product groups. And while he hired professional managers, Gates insisted that every one of them be well-versed in the technical aspects of the product. The company was growing and had to employ thousands of people—just plain *smart* people, according to Microsoft's recruiting practice. Gates remained active in product planning and strategy and kept abreast of progress on scheduled projects. He also became more and more of a public figure, an effective speech-maker and corporate diplomat.

With his extraordinary competitiveness, he was not content merely to enjoy Microsoft's dominance in the market for PC operating systems. He still intended to stake out a hefty share of the market for applications software, packages tailored to common needs, like accounting, word processing, or inventory control. As Gates said in 1980: "The revolution is here and it is soft." In August 1984, as part of the process of reshaping Microsoft, he created separate divisions for the development of operating system software (like MS-DOS and its successors) and applications software. They were called the Platform Group and the Applications and Content Group, respectively.

In 1982, Lotus Development Corporation had introduced the first blockbuster computer spreadsheet program, which was called 1-2-3 and enabled users to perform fairly high-level accounting on the computer. An overwhelming success, it was responsible for enticing many small businesses into buying their first PCs. Soon after, Gates assembled a superb team of software developers and charged them with devising a spreadsheet package to beat Lotus Development's. In 1985, Microsoft introduced Excel 1.0, which was used at first only by Macintosh computers. The company had a chance to improve the product before launching the IBM-compatible version, 2.0, in 1988. It was called ". . . a work of art," by one reviewer. It simultaneously established itself in the spreadsheet market and bolstered Microsoft's latest operating system, Windows.

As the Applications and Content Group launched other software packages, including the word-processing program Microsoft Word, the Platform Group maintained Microsoft's core product: the IBM-PC operating system. MS-DOS was updated and improved every other year or so. Eventually it would have to be replaced by a new concept. In a divergence from the company's early practice of developing programs in a matter of months, Microsoft spent nearly seven years developing the successor to MS-DOS, dubbed "Windows." The drive to produce Windows wasn't predicated on financial need, for MS-DOS was a remarkably profitable and widely used product. But Gates wanted to create a new model for the IBM and IBM-compatible PC world. "The goal is to turn up the heat and make Windows an even stronger standard than DOS has been," Gates said.

In devising a new operating system, Microsoft tried to reinvent and improve on Apple's highly graphic, easily understood Macintosh system. First introduced in 1987, Windows didn't catch on. When the version for IBM-compatible computers was released the following year, it fared only a little better. The reasons actually meshed with Gates's long-range thinking. He typically aimed his software to be more advanced than the contemporary hardware, knowing that machines would inevitably catch up. Windows worked best with a more powerful computer behind it, but Gates found that IBM was not aggressive about introducing more powerful models. Compaq eventually led the way in popularizing the next step up in computers, the 386. The incompatibility of Microsoft's new software and IBM's hardware highlighted a deeper dilemma: For better or worse, Microsoft's fate was tied to that of IBM. Gates once commented, "It's like we're married or something."

As a matter of fact, the marriage was on the rocks. The two companies had been jointly developing a new operating system called OS/2 to succeed MS-DOS, and the first version was introduced in 1987. When increasing rivalries broke apart the cooperative partnership in 1989, IBM took custody of OS/2 and its further development. Yet, even subsequent versions of OS/2 failed to break the grip of MS-DOS, or block the way for Windows. It was Microsoft that was setting the standard for operating systems, despite IBM's efforts. Clone-makers were eager to install the improved Windows on their machines, and software developers labored to make their programs run on Windows. With the hardware up to date, the system let IBM-PC users deploy a mouse and click on icons and menus, rather than utilize memorized commands. The expanded capability of Windows 3.0 to access memory also let users keep several programs open at once. Projecting its authority, Microsoft spent $10 million to roll out the $150 software package on a promotional red carpet, including a send-off at Manhattan's City Center Theater. It was, Gates said, "The most extravagant, extensive, and expensive software introduction ever." Clone-makers were eager to install the improved Windows on their machines, and software developers labored to make their programs run on Windows. Largely on the strength of the Windows conquest, Microsoft's sales rose from $590.8 million in 1988 to $1.183 billion in 1990.

The business world hadn't seen such an influential technology company since IBM utterly dominated the market from the fifties to the seventies. After 1986, when Microsoft moved to new headquarters in a park setting in Redmond, Washington, it was often called "Big Green," a nod to its assumption of the mantle once worn by Big Blue.

ACHIEVING MARKET DOMINANCE, BUT FOR HOW LONG?

"Can anyone stop Bill Gates?" *Forbes* asked in 1991, when the company's stock market value surpassed that of General Motors. The answer,

GATES JOINS THE NETWORK

For a few years, as the Internet exploded, Microsoft remained on the sidelines. But as Americans by the millions began to use their PCs as a communication tool, Microsoft decided to get in on the action.

In early 1995, the company launched its own access service, the Microsoft Network, to rival America On-line. Windows 95, introduced in August of that year, had elements in place that made it easy for users to join interactive computer networks, especially the Microsoft Network. Even more than that, Windows 95 was designed to accommodate future versions that would allow PCs to transmit, as well as to receive, audio and video. To Gates, the interactive world was just that—a world—and no single step would advance it or successfully exploit it.

In December 1995, Microsoft and General Electric (the parent company of NBC Network) joined forces to operate a news network, called MS-NBC. The cable television network, which debuted in July 1996, would share programming with Microsoft Network for computers. The idea was that the viewing public could get their news from either the TV or the computer or from both at once.

Neither Bill Gates nor Jack Welch, the CEO of GE, looked at the partnership as anything but a first step for each in a completely new media. "Business will be done differently," Welch said. "Distribution will be done differently. Who better to hang around with than the company that has done more to change the world than any other?"

Within one year Gates moved Microsoft from the sidelines to the forefront of the interactive revolution. And suddenly he was in television, a fact that was not lost on the wit of Jay Leno, who began one of his monologues with this comment: "I'm the host of *The Tonight Show* on NBC . . . which stands for 'Now Bill Compatible.' "

it seemed, was no. "In the past several years, Gates has leveraged his control over one vital part of the desktop computer business, the operating system for IBM-compatible machines, into a commanding presence in a related field, application software." The only power great enough to stop Microsoft may have been the federal government. Just as Rockefeller's massive Standard Oil suffered the scrutiny of a series of antitrust investigations, Microsoft became the subject of a probe based on its trade practices.

Throughout the industry, Microsoft was a respected, but often controversial, company. Developers of applications software accused it of leaking news of upcoming products to the press, so as to kill off enthusiasm and sales for competing packages. They also intimated that Microsoft's applications developers benefited from knowing what was coming in operations platforms, a charge the company flatly denied. The Federal Trade Commission (FTC) investigation, launched in 1990, centered on Microsoft's policy of forcing licensers to pay royalties for every machine they produced, whether they included MS-DOS or not.

Gates was confident that Microsoft would emerge unscathed. "This thing will come to an end without any problem," he said in 1991. After a thirty-month investigation, the FTC commissioners deadlocked, two votes to two, on whether or not to prosecute. The Justice Department's antitrust unit, in an unprecedented move, took up the investigation. The department considered a range of possibilities that could have included the destruction of Gates's empire. In the end, the government stepped back from engaging Microsoft in full-fledged battle. Instead of trying to bust up the juggernaut, the antitrust division essentially left Microsoft intact, while forcing it to end the controversial licensing practice.

As Microsoft grew in size and scope, Gates changed his style. The one-time micromanager became less hands-on: "Well [at] first, I wouldn't let anybody write any code. . . . That's changed." Instead, he focused on monitoring important projects, acting as the chief strategist, and keeping tabs on the booming company's growing number of ventures. In 1995, with the introduction of Windows 95, Microsoft entered the business of providing Internet access, and in early 1996 it started a television network in conjunction with NBC, called MS-NBC. Gates also found time to write a book, entitled *The Road Ahead*, which contained his vision of technological possibilities.

As Microsoft's shares grew to become among the hottest on the stock market, the value of Gates's stake rose to $18 billion in 1996. Even so, his salary remained relatively low: just $275,000 in salary and $128,000 in bonuses for 1994.

Microsoft is fueled, in part, by its leader's enduring realism. While he may appear to be relentlessly confident, Gates has a strong sense of perspective. "We've done some good work, but all of these products become obsolete so fast. . . ." he told *Forbes ASAP*. "It will be some finite number of years, and I don't know the number—before our doom comes."

NOTES ON SOURCES

ome of the historical material used in writing this book was provided from the companies themselves. Extensive searches for primary and secondary material were made in the libraries of Columbia University, Harvard University, and at the New York Public Library. On more contemporary subjects, I drew upon articles in newspapers, principally the *New York Times* and *Wall Street Journal*, and magazines, such as *Forbes, Business Week, Fortune,* and *Financial World.* I also consulted annual reports, 10-Ks, and other Securities and Exchange Commission filings. These sources are listed in order of significance.

Robert Morris: America's First Financier

Robert Morris has been the subject of many biographies. The best of them is William Graham Sumner's two-volume *Robert Morris* (Dodd, Mead and Company, 1892). Other valuable Morris books include *Robert Morris, Patriot and Financier* (Macmillan and Co., 1903), by Ellis Oberholtzer; *Robert Morris: Revolutionary Financier* (University of Pennsylvania Press, 1954), by Clarence Ver Steeg; the eight volume *Papers of Robert Morris, 1781–1784,* E. James Ferguson, editor (University of Pittsburgh Press, 1973); and John Kennedy's *Robert Morris and the Holland Land Purchase* (J.F. Hall, 1984).

Cyrus McCormick's Reaper and the Industrialization of Farming

William T. Hutchinson's *Cyrus Hall McCormick* (The Century Co., 1930–1935) is the most comprehensive work on McCormick's life. Other sources were John F. Steward's *The Reaper* (Greenberg, 1931); Herbert Casson's flowery *Cyrus Hall McCormick: His Life and Work* (McClurg and Co., 1909); E. B. Swift's *Who Invented the Reaper?* (Chicago, 1897); Cyrus McCormick Jr.'s *The Century of the Reaper* (Riverside Press, 1931); *The McCormick Reaper Legend* (Exposition Press, 1955) by Norbert Lyons; and *One Hundred Fifty Years of International Harvester,* by C. H. Wendel (Crestline Publishing, 1981).

John D. Rockefeller and the Modern Corporation

Allan Nevins's *John D. Rockefeller: The Heroic Age of American Enterprise* (C. Scribner's Sons, 1941) and his *Study in Power: John D. Rockefeller, Industrialist and Philanthropist* (Scribner, 1953) are honest accounts of Rockefeller. Other good sources were Daniel Yergin's *The Prize: The Epic Quest for Oil, Money, and Power* (Simon and Schuster, 1991); David Freeman Hawke's *John D: The Founding Father of the Rockefellers* (Harper and Row, 1980); Ida Tarbell's *The History of the Standard Oil Company*; Henry Demarest Lloyd's *Wealth Against Commonwealth* (Harper and Brothers, 1899); and *History of Standard Oil Company (New Jersey),* (Harper, 1955–1957), by Ralph and Muriel Hidy.

J. P. Morgan Saves the Country

Aside from relying on the *New York Times* and *The Wall Street Journal* articles in the fall of 1907, I drew upon a wealth of biographies and memoirs. Among them were Vincent P. Carosso's *The Morgans: Private International Bankers, 1854–1913* (Harvard University Press, 1987); and Ron Chernow's *The House of Morgan: An American Banking Dynasty and the Rise of Modern Finance* (Atlantic Monthly Press, 1990). Other books include Frederick Lewis Allen's *The Great Pierpont Morgan* (Harper, 1949); Stanley Jackson's *J. P. Morgan: A Biography* (Stein and Day, 1983); George Wheeler's *Pierpont Morgan and Friends: The Anatomy of a Myth,* (Prentice-Hall, 1973); James Grant's *Money of the Mind: Borrowing and Lending in America from the Civil War to Michael Milken* (Farrar Straus Giroux, 1992); *Right Hand Man: The Life of George W. Perkins* by John Garraty (Harper, 1960); and *Across World Frontiers* by Thomas W. Lamont (Harcourt, Brace, 1951).

Henry Ford and the Model T

The best material on Henry Ford is by Allan Nevins: *Ford: The Times, the Man, the Company* (Scribner's, 1954). Additional sources include *The Cars That Henry Ford Built,* by Beverly Rae Kimes (Princeton Publishing, Inc., 1978); *The Fords: An American Epic* by Peter Collier and David Horowitz (Summit Books, 1987); Henry Ford's memoir, *My Life and Work* (Arno Press, 1973); *Ford: The Man and the Machine* by Robert Lacey (Little Brown, 1986); *Henry Ford: A Biography* by William Adams Simonds (M. Joseph Ltd., 1946); *The Legend of Henry Ford* by Keith Sward (Rinehart, 1948); *The Five Dollar Day: Labor Management and Social Control in the Ford Motor Company, 1908–1921* by Stephen Meyer III (SUNY Press, 1981); David Nye's *Henry Ford: Ignorant Idealist* (Kennikat Press, 1979); James Flink's *The Automobile Age* (MIT Press, 1988); and *The Triumph of an Idea: The Story of Henry Ford* by Ralph H. Graves (Doubleday, 1935).

Charles Merrill and the Democratization of Stock Ownership

There are no books devoted entirely to Charles Merrill and his company. The main sources were supplied by Merrill Lynch, namely: *A Legacy of Leadership: Merrill Lynch, 1885–1985*, which is filled with material like Charles Merrill's childhood memories and excerpts from the company's 1956 annual report. Joseph Nocera, in *A Piece of the Action: How the Middle Class Joined the Money Class* (Simon and Schuster, 1994), has a chapter on Merrill. I also relied on New York Stock Exchange annual reports, and newspaper and magazine articles, including *Forbes*: "Charles Edward Merrill" (November 1, 1947); *Business Week*: "Brokerage Supermarket" (November 8, 1947); *Fortune*: "Charlie Merrill Always Called Them Right" (May 1972); and a series of articles in the *Commercial & Financial Chronicle*.

David Sarnoff, RCA, and the Rise of Broadcasting

The most definitive source on the early history of broadcasting is Gleason Archer's two volumes *History of Radio to 1926* and *Big Business and Radio* (The American Historical Company, Inc., 1938–39). An interesting biography of Sarnoff is *The General: David Sarnoff and the Rise of the Communications Industry* by Kenneth Bilby (Harper and Row, 1986); *Sarnoff, an American Success* (New York Times Book Co., 1977) is an admiring memoir by the former RCA executive Carl Dreher. Other sources include Thomas S. W. Lewis's *Empire of the Air: The Men Who Made Radio* (Edward Burlingame Books, 1991), *RCA* (Stein and Day, 1986) by Robert Sobel. G. R. M. Garratt's *The Early History of Radio: From Faraday to Marconi* (Institution of Electrical Engineers in Association with the Science Museum, 1994), James A. Hijiya's *Lee de Forest and the Fatherhood of Radio* (Lehigh University Press, 1992), and *Looking Ahead: The Papers of David Sarnoff* (McGraw Hill, 1968).

Magazine and newspaper articles include *Forbes*: "Will Radio End War?" (December 12, 1927); *Fortune*: "The Fabulous Future" (January 1955); "R.C.A.: The General Never Got Butterflies" (October 1962); "By the End of the Twentieth Century" (May 1964); *Newsweek*: "The General's Biggest Gamble" (December 5, 1949); and a dozen *New York Times* articles between the years of 1920 and 1957.

Walt Disney and his Family-Entertainment Empire

Many volumes have been compiled on Disney and his work, including *The Art of Walt Disney: From Mickey Mouse to the Magic Kingdoms* by Christopher Finch (Abrams, 1995),*The Disney Films* by film critic Leonard Maltin (Hyperion, 1995), *The Disney Version: The Life, Times, Art, and Commerce of Walt Disney* by journalist Richard Schickel (Simon and Schuster, 1985) *Disney's World: A Biography* by Leonard Mosley (Stein and Day, 1985), Kathy Merlock Jackson's *Walt Disney, A Bio-Bibliography* (Greenwood Press, 1993) and Marc Eliot's *Walt Disney: Hollywood's Dark Prince: A Biography* (Carl Publishing Group, 1993).

Among the dozens of magazine and newspaper articles I used, the following are of particular interest: *New York Times Magazine*: "L'Affaire Mickey Mouse" (December 26, 1937); "A Fantasy That Paid Off" (June 27, 1966); "Disney Again Tries Trailblazing" (November 3, 1940); *New Republic*: "Leonardo da Disney," by David Low (January 3, 1942); *Business Week*: "He'll Double as a Top-Notch Salesman" (March 21, 1953); "Disney's Live-Action Profits" (July 24, 1965); *Forbes*: "Disney Dollars" (May 1, 1971); and articles in issues of *Newsweek* dated February 13, 1950, February 16, 1953, April 18, 1955, December 31, 1962, and July 13, 1965.

John H. Johnson: Finding the Black Consumer

Johnson's autobiography, *Succeeding Against the Odds* (Warner Books, 1989) is an inspiring and well-written account. Additional source material included an interview with Johnson in *Harvard Business Review*, (March–April 1976); *New York Times:* "Ebony Publisher Rebuilds Empire" (December 4, 1982); "Black Media Giant's Fire Still Burns" (November 19, 1990). *Ebony's* special issue of Nov. 1992; *Time:* "Ebony's Man" (Dec. 9, 1985); *Business Week:* "Uncle Tom's Magazine Removes the Kid Gloves" (March 23, 1968); *Nation's Business:* "John H. Johnson of Ebony" (April 1971); *Forbes:* "It's a Miracle" (Dec. 20, 1982); *Fortune:* "How Johnson Made It" (January 1968).

David Ogilvy and the Creation of Modern Advertising

David Ogilvy's own books include *Ogilvy on Advertising* (Crown, 1983), *Confessions of an Advertising Man* (Atheneum, 1963); and *Blood, Brains & Beer: The Autobiography of David Ogilvy* (Atheneum, 1978). *The Unpublished David Ogilvy*, edited by Joel Raphaelson (Crown, 1986), is a compilation of articles, speeches, and memos by Ogilvy.

I also used many articles in newspapers and magazines, including *Fortune:* "Is Ogilvy a Genuis?" (April 1, 1965); "Further Confessions of an Adman" (March 15, 1976); *Advertising Age:* "A Giant Bows to Jackasses" (May 22, 1989); "Living with David Ogilvy" (June 25, 1973). the *New York Times* advertising columns were also full of Ogilvy in the late 1950s and early 1960s; worthwhile articles include "Advertising: The Ogilvy of the Offbeat Ideas" (September 7, 1958); "A Peripatetic Adman Puts Down Roots" (August 23, 1981). Also, *New Republic:* "Behind the Hathaway Shirt" (November 2, 1963).

Ray Kroc, McDonald's, and the Fast-Food Industry

John F. Love's *McDonald's: Behind the Arches* (Bantam Books, 1995) is a thorough, authorized company history. Other valuable sources are Ray Kroc's autobiography entitled, *Grinding It Out* (Regery, 1977), and *Big Mac: The Unauthorized Story of McDonald's* by Maxwell Boas (New American Library, 1977).

Among hundreds of newspaper and magazine articles, the following are of most use: *Nation's Business:* "Appealing to a Mass Market" (July 1969); *Financial World:* While the Big Mac Sells Like Crazy (May 29, 1974); "Meaty Results at McDonald's" (May 2, 1973); "Those Doubts about McDonald's" (June 15, 1983); *Fortune:* "McDonald's Refuses to Plateau" (November 12, 1984); "The McDonald's Mystique" (July 4, 1988); *Barron's:* "Did McDonald's Deserve a Break?" (September 5, 1983); *Business Week:* "Horatio Hamburger and the Golden Arches" (April 12, 1976); "McDonald's: The Original Recipe Helps It Defy a Downturn" (May 4, 1981); "Meet Mike Quinlan, Big Mac's Attack CEO" (May 9, 1988); *Forbes:* "Or Was It 60?" (January 3, 1973); "If You Stop, They Might Catch You" (May 15, 1975); "Not for Export?" (October 15, 1975); "Where's the Growth?" (April 23, 1984); *Advertising Age:* "McDonald's Takes Fast Food Lead" (May 14, 1973); "McDonald's Invades U.K. Via Bow of 3,000th Unit" (October 14, 1974); "McDonald's Brings Hamburger (with Beer) to Hamburg" (May 30, 1977).

Betting the Company: Joseph Wilson and the Xerox 914

There are several published books on Xerox, but none were more valuable to me than an unpublished manuscript graciously provided by Blake McKelvey of Rochester. A Xerox veteran, McKelvey has written a wonderful biography of Joseph Wilson. Also useful are John Dessauer's memoir, *My Years at Xerox: The Billions Nobody Wanted* (Doubleday, 1971); Douglas K. Smith's and Robert C. Alexander's *Fumbling the Future: How Xerox Invented, Then Ignored, the First Personal Computer* (William Morrow, 1988); David Kearns' *Prophets in the Dark: How Xerox Reinvented Itself and Beat Back the Japanese* (Harper Business, 1992); and John Dessauer's article, "How a Large Corporation Motivates its Research and Development People" in *Management Review* (May 1971).

Among the first publications to notice Haloid-Xerox's potential was *Business Week:* "Out to Crack Copying Market" (September 19, 1959). Also useful were *Fortune:* "The Hardest Duplicating Job Xerox Ever Faced" (November 1966). "The Two Faces of Xerox" (September, 1971); "The Xerox Annual Report: A Guided Tour" (June 15,

1967); *Financial World:* "Leaders of the Glamour Parade, Xerox" (March 20, 1963); "Xerox—Stellar Performer" (February 16, 1966); *Forbes:* "Xerox Corp." (October 15, 1965). "Two Men and an Idea" (September 15, 1962); "Joseph C. Wilson: Living with a Myth" (January 1, 1968); "Xerox: The McColough Era" (July 1, 1969); *The New Yorker:* "Xerox Xerox Xerox Xerox" (April 11, 1967); the *New York Times Magazine:* "The Man from Xerox Multiplies His Roles" (April 24, 1966). Also see the 1975 *Harvard Business Review* interview with McColough, "The Corporation and Its Obligations," and in a *Nation's Business* interview, "C. Peter McColough of Xerox Corp." (September 1972).

American Express and the Charge Card

Two company-sanctioned histories were useful: Alden Hatch's *American Express: A Century of Service* (Doubleday, 1950) and *Promises to Pay* (American Express Co., 1977). Other sources include *American Express: The Unofficial History of the People Who Built the Great Financial Empire* (Crown, 1987), by Peter Z. Grossman. *House of Cards: Inside the Troubled Empire of American Express* (Putnam, 1992) by Jon Friedman and John Mechan. Joseph Nocera's *A Piece of the Action* (Simon & Schuster, 1994), and Lewis Mandell's *The Credit Card Industry: A History,* (Twayne Publishers, 1990).

A plethora of magazine articles were also useful including: *Forbes:* "Around the World in 80 Ways" (November 1, 1958); "Divided Minds" (May 15, 1960); "Disaster Can Be Good for You" (February 1, 1969); "Here Come the Bank Cards!" (February 15, 1969); "A Banker's Pipe Dream?" (June 15, 1971); "A Credit Card Is Not a Commodity" (October 16, 1989); *American Heritage:* "Credit Card America" (November 1991); *Business Week:* "Travel on the Cuff" (May 2, 1953); "Travel Giants Makes a New . . ." (July 20, 1957); "Tougher Going for Credit Cards" (September 10, 1960); "The Charge-It Plan That Really Took Off" (February 27, 1965); *Fortune:* "The Future of American Express" (April 1964); "The Credit Card's Painful Coming-of-Age" (October 1971); *Newsweek:* "Charge Everything" (January 3, 1955); "Joining of the Giants?" (January 23, 1961); *Time:* "Home Away from Home" (October 24, 1955); "Credit-Card Game" (September 22, 1958); "Riding the Float" (December 14, 1962); *New York Times Magazine:* "Life a la Carte" (September 8, 1959).

Mary Kay Ash and her Corporate Culture for Women

Mary Kay Cosmetics provided a great deal of information on the company and the woman who made it happen. There are also two books: an autobiography, *Mary Kay* (Harper, 1981), and *Mary Kay on People Management* (Warner Books, 1984).

Many magazine and newspaper articles were also of use: *Advertising Age:* "Mary Kay Still in the Pink" (January 4, 1988); "Mary Kay Shows Dramatic Growth" (August 23, 1982); "Mary Kay Putting on an Ad Show" (March 24, 1980); *Barrons:* "Mary Kay's Team" (July 9, 1979); "Up and Down Wall Street" (June 8, 1981); *Business Week:* "Mary Kay Is Singing 'I Feel Pretty'," (December 2, 1981); "Dumpster Raids?" (April 1, 1991); "Mary Kay Cosmetics" (March 28, 1983); *Forbes:* "Flight of the Bumblebee" (August 12, 1985); "Peeking inside LBOs" (June 13, 1988); *Fortune:* Mary Kay's Lessons in Leadership" (September 20, 1993); *Financial World:* "Mary Kay Goes for Parties" (December 11, 1974); *Journal of Behavioral Economics:* "Mary Kay Ash," by Richard E. Hattwick (Winter 1987). *Nation's Business:* "Lessons of Leadership: Flying High on an Idea" (August 1978).

Intel's Microprocessor the Computer Revolution

There are no books on the history of Intel, but Andrew Grove's *High Output Management* (Random House, 1983) and *One-on-One with Andy Grove* (Putnam, 1987), provide the best expressions of his management style. William H. Davidow's *Marketing High Technology: An Insider's View* (Free Press, 1986) contains Intel's marketing insights.

Useful articles included *Forbes:* "Intel—Right Again?" (March 3, 1980); "Go Tell the Spartans" (December 30, 1985); "Institutionalizing the Revolution" (June 16, 1986); "Who's on Second?" (March 7, 1988); "Intel" (August 6, 1990); "Intel Lives" (September 30, 1991); "Challenge and Response" (April 16, 1990); "Gordon Early Moore"

(October 16, 1995); *Financial World:* "Man of the Year: Intel's Andrew Grove" (December 11, 1990); "Gordon Moore of Intel Corp" (March 15, 1981); "Competition Is Healthy—Up to a Point" (July 1, 1978); *Dun's Review:* "Intel: Master of Innovation" (December 1980); *Economist:* "Fortune Seeqers" (February 6, 1982); "Intel: When the Chips Are Down," (November 14, 1983); *Business Week:* "Intel's Robert Noyce Kicks Himself Upstairs" (December 14, 1974); "The Microprocessor Champ Gambles on Another Leap Forward" (April 14, 1980); "Why They're Jumping Ship at Intel" (February 14, 1983); "Interview with Gordon E. Moore" (April 18, 1983); "Intel Wakes up to a Whole New Marketplace in Chips" (September 2, 1985); "Bob Noyce Created Silicon Valley. Can He Save It?" (August 15, 1988); "Intel: The Next Revolution" (September 26, 1988); "Can Andy Grove Practice What He Preaches?" (March 16, 1987); "Inside Intel" (June 1, 1992); "Intel: What a Tease—and What a Strategy" (Februray 22, 1993); "The Education of Andrew Grove" (January 16, 1995); "Intel Unbound" (October 9, 1995). *Fortune:* "How Intel Won Its Bet on Memory Chips" (November 1973); "A Computer-on-a-chip Miracle" (December 31, 1979); "The Secret to Intel's Success" (February 8, 1993); "If They're Gaining on You, Innovate" (November 2, 1992); "Intel's Plan for Staying on Top" (March 27, 1989); "Robert N. Noyce" (March 13, 1989); *Barrons's:* "Play by the Same Rules" (June 29, 1987); "Chipping away at Intel" (March 23, 1992); "Andy Grove: How Intel Makes Spending Pay Off" (February 22, 1993); Dozens of *Wall Street Journal* articles; *Management Review:* "Silicon Valley" (September 1985); *Harvard Business Review:* "Creativity by the Numbers" (May–June 1980); *Industry Week:* "Only the Paranoid Survive" (November 20, 1995); "The Auto of the Info Age" (March 4, 1996); *PC Week:* "Compaq Is Becoming a Worse Curse than Expected" (April 10, 1995); "Intel Forcing Buyers into Faster Migration from 486 to Pentium" (April 24, 1995).

Sam Walton, Wal-Mart, and the Discounting of America
The articles used for this chapter include: *Advertising Age:* "Adman of the Year" (December 23, 1981, p. 5); *Arkansas Business:* "So Long Sam" (April 13–19, 1992); *Discount Store News:* "Walton Remembered" (April 20, 1992); "Special Wal-Mart Issue" (June 15, 1992); *Financial World:* "Gold Winner" (April 15, 1986); "CEO of the Decade" (April 4, 1989); *Chain Store Executive:* "An American Original" (May 1992); *Hardware Age:* "Up Against Wal-Mart" (February 1988); *Life:* "A $5 Trim for a $2.8-Billion Head" (December 1985); *Nation's Business:* "Wal-Mart" (April 1988); *Restaurant News:* "How to Win Employee and Customer Friends" (January 30, 1989); *Texas Monthly:* "Wal-Marts Across Texas" (October 1983, p. 168); and *Time:* "Here Come the Malls without Walls" (February 8, 1988); "Mr. Sam Stuns Goliath" (February 25, 1991).

Two books that have been published on the subject are: *Sam Walton: Made in America; My Story* by Sam Walton and John Huey (Doubleday, 1992) and *Sam Walton: The Inside Story of the Richest Man in America* by Vincent H. Trimble (Dutton, 1990).

William McGowan and MCI: A New World of Telecommuinications
The History of MCI, 1968–1988: The Early Years (Heritage Press, 1993), is a massive (720-page) company commissioned tome. On AT&T, see Sonny Kleinfeld's *The Biggest Company on Earth: A Profile of AT&T* (Holt, Rinehart, and Winston, 1981), Steve Coll's *The Deal of the Century: The Breakup of AT&T* (Atheneum, 1986), and *Wrong Number: The Breakup of AT&T* by Alan Stone (Basic Books, 1989).

Among the many articles I relied upon were *Fortune:* "Frenzied Finale" (April 14, 1986); "More than Cheap Talk Propels MCI" (January 24, 1983); "The Man Who Beat Ma Bell" (January 14, 1980); *Business Week:* "AT&T Is Eating 'Em Alive" (February 16, 1987); "Now If MCI Can Just Keep the Party Going" (December 16, 1988); and dozens of *Wall Street Journal, Forbes,* and *New York Times* articles.

The Turnaround at Harley-Davidson
The story of Harley-Davidson's rise and fall is told in *Well Made in America: Lessons from Harley-Davidson on Being the Best* by Peter C. Reid (McGraw-Hill, 1990). A 1993 article in *Smithsonian* on Harley also deals with the company's history. Other articles

used were *New York Times:* "Harley-Davidson Roars Back" (October 3, 1985); "Harley Gears up for New Markets" (April 25, 1982); "Two Years of Losses at Harley-Davidson" (January 24, 1983); "Harley Gains in Profits but Loses on Wall St." (October 25, 1991); "Harley-Davidson Maps Growth" (March 14, 1981); *Business Week:* "That Vroom You Hear Is Harley" (August 17, 1987); "The Rumble Heard Round the World: Harleys" (May 24, 1992); *Financial World:* "Harley-Davidson Rides High" (October 18, 1988); *Wall Street Journal:* "Beals Takes Harley-Davidson on New Road" (March 20, 1987); "At Harley-Davidson, Life without AMF Is Upbeat but Full of Financial Problems" (April 13, 1982); "After Nearly Starving, Harley-Davidson Finds New Crowd of Riders" (August 31, 1990); *Fortune:* "Hogs with Wheels" (July 12, 1993); *Forbes:* "Thunder Road" (July 18, 1983); "Harley Back in Gear" (December 2, 1985); "Harley's Hogs" (December 2, 1985); "The Return of the Two-Wheeler" (May 12, 1980); "More Smoke than Fire" (January 16, 1984); *Advertising Age:* "Hard Times Paring Motorcycle Market" (November 1, 1982); "Harley-Davidson Trades Restrictions for Profits" (August 10, 1987); "Harley-Davidson Revs up to Improve Image" (August 5, 1985); Management Review: "Harley-Davidson Comes Roaring Back" (March 1986); *Industry Week:* "Reshaping 'Hog Heaven'" (February 9, 1987); "Born to Be Real" (August 2, 1993).

Kohlberg Kravis Roberts & Co. and the Leveraged Buyout

The best account of KKR is reporter George Anders's *Merchants of Debt: KKR and the Mortgaging of American Business* (Basic Books, 1992). Other sources include Sarah Bartlett's *The Money Machine: How KKR Manufactured Power and Profits* (Warner Books, 1991), *Barbarians at the Gate: The Fall of RJR Nabisco* (Harper and Row, 1990) by Bryan Burrough and John Helyar, and Robert Sobel's *Dangerous Dreamers* (New York, 1993).

Magazine and newspaper articles were useful, such as *Forbes:* "Do You Sincerely Want to be Rich" (July 23, 1978); "Releveraging King Midas" (December 10, 1979); "Off-Balance Leveraged Buyouts?" (October 11, 1982); "A Manager Rescues the Money Movers" (December 17, 1984); "On Borrowed Time" (December 16, 1985); "The Cardinal Rule" (April 7, 1986); "When the Music Stops . . ." (November 14, 1988); "The Buyout That Saved Safeway" (November 12, 1990); "My Story—Michael Milken" (March 16, 1992, p 78); *Barron's:* "High-Wire Finance" (September 24, 1979); *Fortune:* "How the Champs Do Leveraged Buyouts" (January 23, 1984); *Business Week:* "Leveraged Buyouts Aren't Just for Daredevils Anymore" (August 11, 1986); "King Henry" (November 14, 1988, p. 125); "KKR Is Doing Just Fine—Without LBOs" (July 30, 1990); "The 'Barbarians' in the Boardroom" by George Anders, (July–August 1992); *Business History Review:* "Kohlberg Kravis Roberts & Co. and the Restructuring of American Capitalism" by Allen Kaufman and Ernest J. Englander (Spring 1993).

William Gates and the Dominance of Microsoft

Two biographies are excellent: *Hard Drive: Bill Gates and the Making of the Microsoft Empire* by James Wallace and Jim Erickson (Wiley, 1992); and *Gates* by Stephen Manes and Paul Andrews (Simon and Schuster, 1993). More recent is Michael A. Cusamano and Richard W. Selby's book on *Microsoft Secrets: How the World's Most Powerful Software Company Creates Technology, Shapes Markets, and Manages People* (Free Press, 1995). Also see *The Road Ahead* (Viking, 1995), by Gates with Nathan Myhrvold.

Many magazines and newspaper articles have also been of use, including *Forbes:* "What's Good for IBM" (August 5, 1991); "The Monolith" (March 14, 1994); "Can Anyone Stop Bill Gates?" (April, 1991); *Forbes ASAP:* "ASAP Interview: Bill Gates" (December 7, 1992); *Fortune:* "Inside the Deal That Made Bill Gates $350 Million" (July 21, 1986); "Bill Gates Rising" (June 18, 1990); *Wall Street Journal:* "For Microsoft, Nothing Succeeds Like Excess" (August 23, 1995); *Business Week:* "Microsoft Moves into the Passing Lane" (May 16, 1986); "The Billion-Dollar Whiz Kid" (April 13, 1987); "Microsoft Is Like an Elephant, Rolling Around, Squashing Ants" (October 30, 1989); "Why Everyone Is Gaping at Microsoft's Windows" (May 21, 1990); "The FTC vs. Microsoft" (December 28, 1992); "Is Microsoft too Powerful?" (March 1, 1993).

INDEX